Organized Uncertainty

Organized Uncertainty

Designing a World of Risk Management

Michael Power

OXFORD
UNIVERSITY PRESS

OXFORD

UNIVERSITY PRESS

Great Clarendon Street, Oxford OX2 6DP

Oxford University Press is a department of the University of Oxford.
It furthers the University's objective of excellence in research, scholarship,
and education by publishing worldwide in

Oxford New York

Auckland Cape Town Dar es Salaam Hong Kong Karachi
Kuala Lumpur Madrid Melbourne Mexico City Nairobi
New Delhi Shanghai Taipei Toronto

With offices in

Argentina Austria Brazil Chile Czech Republic France Greece
Guatemala Hungary Italy Japan Poland Portugal Singapore
South Korea Switzerland Thailand Turkey Ukraine Vietnam

Oxford is a registered trade mark of Oxford University Press
in the UK and in certain other countries

Published in the United States
by Oxford University Press Inc., New York

British Library Cataloguing in Publication Data
Data available

Library of Congress Cataloging in Publication Data

Power, Michael.
    Organized uncertainty : designing a world of risk management / Michael Power.
        p.   cm.
    1. Uncertainty.   2. Risk management.   3. Economics.   I. Title.
    HB615.P69 2007
    338.5–dc22   2007006181

Typeset by SPI Publisher Services, Pondicherry, India
Printed in Great Britain
on acid-free paper by
Biddles Ltd., King's Lynn, Norfolk

ISBN 978–0–19–925394–4 (Hbk.)
       978–0–19–954880–4 (Pbk.)

1 3 5 7 9 10 8 6 4 2

For Caroline, Giles, Oliver, and Samuel

PREFACE

Another book on risk is a risky venture for any author. There are simply so many of them. The shelves of bookshops bulge, library racks are full and the internet provides instant access to all manner of materials on risk—from practical handbooks of how to manage it to advanced treatises on how to calculate it, from scholarly debates on the 'risk society' to standards and norms issued by governmental and non-governmental bodies, from discussions of risk motivated by democratic values to prescriptions for adding value to organizational activity. Yet this explosion of risk discourse, and its potential to relegate this book to just one more drop in the ocean, is precisely my focus. Why has it happened and is there any pattern to this phenomenon? At the time of writing, I am a member of the Risk Committee of the London School of Economics and Political Science; I also chair the Risk Committee of a large public company. Such committees did not exist ten years ago. Now they have become a mandatory feature of organizational life. Why?

At one level the explanation is simple; risk committees for universities, hospitals, and many other organizations now exist because risk has increased. Yet, while this may be true in specific instances, it is not generally convincing for the phenomenon as a whole. How and why has risk become such a pre-eminent part of organizational and managerial language? What has allowed management practices of very different kinds to be re-organized in the name of risk? The changing nature of dangers and opportunities in the world is, at best, only one part of the answer. As the title of this book suggests, risk and its management has become a lens through which a certain kind of rational organizational design can be envisioned. I argue that this process of re-envisioning organizations in terms of risk results from a number of different but related pressures for change which emerged in the mid-1990s and which continue to develop as I write this preface. These different pressures have elevated risk management from the technical, analytical roots established in the 1960s to the relatively new stage of organizational governance.

Governance in turn is being reinvented in terms of capabilities for effective risk management. Corporations, public sector bodies, governments, regulators, and non-governmental organizations have no doubt been mobilized to improve risk handling by the stimulus of scandals and catastrophic events. But the organization of these responses has an institutional form and logic which merits analysis.

Like most books, this one started life as something very different in scope and emphasis from what now follows. The original intention was to continue and extend the exploration of the changing role of internal auditors and internal control that was begun in *The Audit Society*. It quickly became evident that the internal control story could only be told against the background of a series of other related changes—and so the scope of the investigation expanded, guided by intuitions about the interconnected nature of transformations in the field of risk management since the mid-1990s. Yet, to talk of a 'field' is a little misleading, since the changes are about the coming into being of a new field, with its attendant panoply of practices and instruments composed from a number of different sources. Just as we are being told that grand narratives are dead in the post-modern age, it may be that they are alive and well, have vacated academia and now reside in conceptions of managerial practice. This book traces the recent history of the world-level grand narrative of risk management.

Philosophers tell us that nouns are misleading because they suggest that a clear object exists when this is often not the case. In the case of 'risk' and 'risk management' we would do well to heed their advice. However, this book takes as its point of departure the, surely uncontestable, fact that the noun has grown in use and significance in organizational life. Indeed, if the concept of 'risk society' means a society where the word 'risk' is used a lot, then we, meaning at least the UK, North America, and Australasia, are definitely in one. This is not as trivial an observation as it seems. This book argues that words, concepts, and categories are very important aspects of the transformation of risk management practice since the mid-1990s.

This book is a preliminary study of 'risk management' understood as a family of practices in motion, whose routines and tasks have a history, and which are animated by ideas and aspirations, by fictions and visions and rational designs. It is a study of key elements of a changing risk discourse, a study which adopts an idiom half way between philosophy and sociology. In writing this book, I have spoken to many practical people involved in risk management, often quite by chance. I have also been physically present in many organizations, although I would hesitate to elevate any of this activity to the label of 'participant observation'. I have also 'encountered', and immersed myself in, many texts of a non-academic nature, reading some and skimming others (I now have an extensive collection of risk management conference brochures—an archive I am reluctant to throw away for reasons I barely understand). Indeed, while it is traditional to distinguish between primary archival and secondary sources of literature, I did not think it meaningful to do so in the list of references. Who is really to say that this text is part of the phenomenon of the risk management explosion and that one is not? Often the dividing line between scholarly and practitioner discourses in an emerging and changing area is very indistinct. In fact, this is precisely what we might expect.

So, judged by the standards of formal method, this book is the product of a messy hermeneutical approach to hunches and intuitions, layered upon each other like strata in a (slow) process of accretion. The method is one of progressively and continuously refashioning a family of arguments in a process of self-critical writing, a constant and restless trade and exchange between theoretical precepts and bits of the empirical world, each mutually explicating the other in a 'to and fro' process as Habermas once put it (*hin- und hergerissen*). This repeated process of 'fitting' theory and matter never ends in principle, but the writing of a book must stop at some stage. Scholarly conventions have less to do with this act of closure than one might think. Exhaustion, nagging publishers (definitely not in my case), and the pressures of other claims on time are often decisive factors.

I suspect that every social scientist will recognize some of his or her own compromises in this account. There has been considerable methodological discipline of a kind, but the reader will need to trust me on that. I have yet to read something influential which was not also, measured against the various ideals one finds in methods courses, and books, flawed. So I hope, as any author does, that for all its many faults, this book will be of interest to scholars and practitioners who may be curious about our contemporary obsession with risk management.

To comparativist scholars of management and political science who painstakingly explore and explain institutional variety, I acknowledge that I owe a deep intellectual debt and have made significant gestures towards institutional variety in the 'social construction of risk objects'. However, the project in this book is framed with a bias towards the analysis of similarity. Where comparativists see and seek difference, both substantively and as a methodological commitment, I have been drawn to the significance of high level, rationalized forms of risk management which are rapidly diffused as sources of similarity and isomorphism. This taste may reflect my former training in philosophy and an unreconstructed appetite for, and belief in, the 'bird's eye view' of things. However, borrowing from the logic of transcendental arguments, it can also be maintained that similarity is a fundamental condition of possibility for meaningful comparative analysis of difference. So the explanation and exploration of similarity, even at an abstract level, is arguably the more basic and primitive project. Notwithstanding this bias, if this book stimulates further analyses of risk management variety to prove exaggeration on my part, it will have served a useful purpose.

To those who spend their lives developing rich qualitative case studies of organizational life, I owe an apology for trampling all over their field. The four cases of emergent risk management practice I discuss are probably not cases at all in the sense that management scholars understand them. There is clearly some kind of phenomenon to be explained, but it has what Foucauldian theorists might call multiple 'surfaces of emergence' and is trans-organizational in form. Single organization studies can support the analysis of the phenomenon, but are insufficient in themselves to suggest the kind of systematicity and reach represented here. No doubt these scholars will also find instances of overstatement in this book—but I hope the claims are at least interesting.

To those who work in science and technology studies, regulation studies, and organization theory, I also hope that this book, for all the obvious simplification in my representation of scholarship in these respective areas, does demonstrate that a conversation across boundaries is profitable. I hesitate to call this an interdisciplinary book, though it will no doubt be regarded as such, because I have never imagined myself as working *across* disciplines at all. Indeed, a good academic accountant is always aware of his or her inherent hybridicity and the necessity of borrowing. Once intellectually interesting translations and links are made between bodies of work, it is as if the borders separating them were imaginary anyway—the connectedness takes on an obviousness despite institutional separation. In any case, how academies divide up knowledge and validate fields is constantly being challenged by the world itself. Yet, trying to be sensitive to a large field creates its own burdens and risks, not least a very demanding reading programme spanning academic and practical work across relatively segmented literatures.

To scholars outside the United Kingdom, I intend that the ideas in this book have portability despite the obvious bias towards examples drawn from the UK. The analysis takes some leads from world society theory but I am all too conscious of the spectre of British exceptionalism, particularly in the so-called UK 'audit culture', which creates risks of extrapolation. Equally there is also a bias in the illustrations towards the financial services industry which is likely to irritate scholars of environment, health and safety, social policy, and the nuclear industry—the traditional heartland of non-financial risk analysis. This reflects my background as an accountant, but I hope it will be tolerated for the reason that the arena of financial services in the 1990s has been a powerful source of regulatory and risk management innovation and diffusion in recent years, and is therefore systemically significant in its own right as a source of ideas. In addition, it is a field in which pressures for globalization in forms of practice may be most advanced and indicative of more general processes of financialization. Naturally, this suggestion needs more defence than I can provide here. There remains, as there always does, more specific work to be done to understand the emerging institutionalization of a pervasive model of risk management through definitions, attributions of responsibility, communicative structures and accountability demands.

To those who like their theory spread 'thick', this book may be a disappointment but I hope that it can be read as a theoretical endeavour with transferable insights and suggestions. Indeed, the most profound intellectual influences hardly reveal themselves in public citation at all—they inhabit the style and sensibility of the whole. My training in the philosophy of language is not far from the surface and the theme of governmentality stalks this book and appears at various points. No doubt critics may feel that the analysis tends too much towards a celebration of neoliberalism and its managerial forms but my intention is primarily and solely to begin to understand and explain the institutional strength of these forms. The analysis is also informed by a moderate and materialist risk 'constructivism', namely the idea that dangers and opportunities may be real enough, but must be subject to representation and framing within management processes broadly defined.

Finally, to a body of thoughtful and reflective practitioner commentators on risk management, I hope this book will have some appeal as an overview of the recent history of a practical field in motion and in change, in which new categories and fictive ideas play very concrete roles in mobilizing intellectual and practical attention. I do not apologize for what may appear to be academic jargon in the belief that it is necessary to manufacture some critical distance from the ideas and categories of practice in order to analyse them properly. This requires some invention and deliberate unfamiliarity in the use of language. If I have only scratched the surface of a phenomenon, I hope it can be agreed that the phenomenon is real enough, and merits further investigation.

This book is based on a number of papers from the recent past. Chapter 2 began life as the 1998 P. D. Leake lecture 'The Audit Implosion' and, together with earlier versions of Chapters 3 and 4, formed the three P. D. Leake Trust lectures given at the Säid Business School, University of Oxford, in March 2002. I was honoured to be invited to give these lectures by Anthony Hopwood and thank the Trustees of the Institute of Chartered Accountants in England and Wales for supporting both this event and my tenure as P. D. Leake Chair of Accounting from 1997 to 2004. Chapter 3 also draws on 'Organizational Responses to Risk: The Rise of the Chief Risk Officer' in Hutter and Power (eds.) (2005) *Organizational Encounters with Risk*, published by Cambridge University Press, and on 'Enterprise Risk Management and the Organization of Uncertainty in Financial Markets' in Knorr-Cetina and Preda (eds.) (2005) *The Sociology of Financial Markets*, published by Cambridge University Press. Chapter 4 is substantially based on 'The Invention of Operational Risk' published in the *Review of International Political Economy* in 2005. The entire book is an expanded version of *The Risk Management of Everything* published by Demos in 2004.

This book is a product of the intellectual milieu at the ESRC Centre for Analysis of Risk and Regulation (CARR), which I helped to create in 1999 and co-directed with Bridget Hutter for five years. It is impossible to acknowledge fully the contribution of the CARR agenda to my recent development but there is no doubt that a very different and more ambitious book has been written, within a larger space, than might have been written prior to 1999. Arguably CARR itself is a child of its time and part of the very phenomenon I try to describe in the pages that follow. I thank colleagues at the Economic and Social Research Council for supporting the creation of CARR, particularly

Stephen Wilks. I also thank Michael Peacock who supported CARR from its early days, as have Hugo Banziger at Deutsche Bank AG and Christopher Swinson, former managing partner at BDO Stoy Hayward. I am also very fortunate to belong to the most interesting and vibrant accounting research group in the world, whose intellectual pluralism is as valuable and unique as it is vulnerable in these days of growing intellectual standardization and declining curiosity. I hope that this book is a just representation of, and testimony to, both the originating spirit of CARR and to the unusual dynamism and quality of accounting research at LSE over the last two decades.

I am, of course, grateful to a large number of people who have made comments and suggestions either directly on the chapters in this book or on various earlier manifestations of the ideas it contains. In particular, I thank: Kerstin Sahlin, Michael Barzelay, John Braithwaite, Adam Burgess, Clive Briault, Julia Black, Wai Fong Chua, Claudio Ciborra, David Cooper, Andrew Croft, Bill Durodie, Ana Fernandez Laviada, Yves Gendron, Howard Gospel, Jan-Erik Gröjer; Christopher Hood, Anthony Hopwood, Michael Huber, Christopher Humphrey, Bridget Hutter, Sheila Jasanoff, Felix Kloman, Liisa Kurunmaki, Richard Laughlin, Javier Lezaun, Martin Lodge, Andrea Mennicken, Yuval Millo, Mary Morgan, Jan Mouritsen, Peter Miller, Onora O'Neill, Fabrizio Panozzo, Christine Parker, Nick Pidgeon, Keith Robson, Colin Scott, John Thirlwell, Bill Tonks, and Brian Wynne. I am also very grateful for the research assistance of Lea Clavecilla and Pauline Khng. I hope all these people are not displeased to be associated with this outcome.

Particular thanks go to David Musson at Oxford University Press who has been a colleague and supporter for well over a decade. I can only apologize for testing his patience to its limit this time. I am also grateful, for very different reasons, to Andrew Frankel and his colleagues who, by managing my personal encounter with risk since 2002, have made this book possible and much more besides. Finally, I thank Caroline who has endured this inhuman writing process with good cheer and given me the kind of support without which it could not have been completed.

CONTENTS

Glossary   xvii

1. Organized Uncertainty: An Introduction   1

2. Turning Organizations Inside Out:
   The Rise of Internal Control   34

3. Standardizing Risk Management: Making up
   Processes and People   66

4. Putting Categories to Work: The Invention of
   Operational Risk   103

5. Governing Reputations: The Outside Comes in   128

6. Making Risk Auditable:
   Legalization and Organization   152

7. Designing a World of Risk Management   183

References   204
Index   233

GLOSSARY

ABI	Association of British Insurers
AICPA	American Institute of Certified Public Accountants
AIRMIC	The Association of Insurance and Risk Managers
ALARP	As Low As Reasonably Practicable
ARROW	Advanced Risk Response Operating Framework
AS	Australia Standards
BBA	British Bankers' Association
BIS	Bank for International Settlements
BRA	Business Risk Audit
BSI	British Standards Institute
CIPFA	Chartered Institute of Public Finance and Accountancy
COSO	Committee of Sponsoring Organizations of the Treadway Commission
CPA	Certified Public Accountant
CRO	Chief Risk Officer
CSA	Control Self-Assessment
CSA	Canadian Standards Association
CSR	Corporate Social Responsibility
DIN	Deutsches Institut für Normung eV
EIU	Economist Intelligence Unit
EMAS	Eco-Management and Audit Scheme
ERM	Enterprise Risk Management
FEI	Financial Executives International
FSA	Financial Services Authority
FSA	Food Standards Agency
GARP	Global Association of Risk Professionals

GAS	German Accounting Standard
GRI	Global Reporting Initiative
HSE	Health and Safety Executive
ICAEW	Institute of Chartered Accountants in England and Wales
IEC	International Electrotechnical Commission
IFAC	International Federation of Accountants
IIA	Institute of Internal Auditors
IPO	Initial Public Offer
IRM	Institute of Risk Management
JSA	Japanese Standards Association
NED	Non-Executive Director
NZS	New Zealand Standards
POB	Public Oversight Board
PwC	PricewaterhouseCoopers
QIS	Quantitative Impact Study
RAROC	Risk Adjusted Return on Capital
RATE	Risk Assessment, Tools of Supervision, Evaluation
RMA	Risk Management Association
RMAR	Retail Mediation Activities Return
SEADOC	Systems Evaluation Approach: Documentation of Controls
SEC	Securities and Exchange Commission
SRA	Society for Risk Analysis
TCF	Treating Customers Fairly
VaR	Value at Risk

1

Organized Uncertainty: An Introduction

What do the following activities have in common: catching the train to work, mountaineering, lending money, investing in new technology, drilling for oil, taking children on school trips, smoking, buying a personal pension? Years ago the answer would have been—very little. And yet we have come to think of these things as having something very important in common, namely the taking of risk, both by individuals and organizations. In 2006, risk 'talk' seems to be all around us and the risk-based re-description of organizational and personal life has become conspicuous. As far as formal organizations are concerned, this is much more than a 'private sector' phenomenon affecting large corporations. In a relatively short period of time, in a number of different countries, hospitals, schools, universities, and many other public organizations, including the very highest levels of central government, have all been transformed to varying degrees by discourses about risk and its possible management. In addition to financial risk, categories of clinical risk, health risk, insolvency risk, legal risk, political risk, and many more have become prominent.[1]

A growing body of scholarship in fields such as social policy, business management, law, psychiatry, sociology, political science, and international relations increasingly analyses the nature of risk and its management in different settings. In social theory and beyond the meaning of Beck's risk society thesis is debated, challenged, and applied.[2] In economics and finance, quantitative tools for risk analysis are developed. Within political science and law, newly developed understandings of the 'regulatory' state suggest that risk management is shaping conceptions of government itself. Risk has become ubiquitous (Hood *et al.*, 1992: 135) and it seems as if we must take a risk-based description of everything (Power, 2004c).

Evidence for this expansion in discourses of risk and its management is easily found in a policy, business, and regulatory literature explosion since the mid-1990s.[3] Many prescriptive textbooks and articles on risk management have been published since the late 1990s, a period which has seen the flowering of numerous practitioner magazines with the word 'risk' in their titles, and the conscious amendment of existing titles to include it.[4] Occupational associations, particularly those with strong foundations in insurance, a traditional stronghold of risk management thinking, have also taken up an expanded and more generic risk management agenda and their websites have become reference points for risk management thinking which is rapidly diffused.[5]

In the UK, slender guidance documents, such as the 'Turnbull Report', have become powerful points of reference in a reform process which has seen the emergence of standardized organizational forms, such as risk committees, appearing throughout the private and public sector (ICAEW, 1999a). A casual internet search using the term 'risk management' yields numerous professional articles in areas as diverse as housing associations, anaesthetics, and sport.[6] Risk management is one of the five 'pillars' of clinical governance[7] and even concepts of national security and ideas of 'preventative' military action are being imagined within the conceptual architecture of risk management. Security services are reaching out to more traditional risk management communities as a consequence of new challenges to their legitimacy and effectiveness.

This growth in a literature rich in aspiration and vision is indicative of the expansion of a risk industry beyond its specific sub-fields to become a source of principles for organizing and managing in general. There has been a conspicuous fusion of ideas about organizational governance and corporate responsibility, new models of regulation are in vogue, and there have been changes in attitude to the traditional mechanics of risk analysis with an evolving accent on risk communication. In addition, technological progress at the level of information systems continues to create possibilities for the expanded reach of risk management. There is no question that the underlying substance of these developments in different fields of practical and scholarly endeavour varies a great deal. Yet, this variety is also profoundly structured by a generic and abstract language of risk and its management, a language which has acquired increased organizational and social significance since the mid-1990s.

This book analyses this specific phenomenon, namely the abstraction, rationalization, and expansion of risk management ideas since the mid-1990s. These ideas have emerged from their position within specific fields (e.g., insurance, engineering) to become implicated in new visions of the way in which organizations should be governed and constituted. In a short period of time the dominant discourse of risk management has shifted from the logic of calculation to that of organization and accountability. A statistical 'empire of chance' (Gigerenzer et al., 1989) which has developed over centuries to provide our contemporary actuarial and calculative conceptions of risk has been rapidly subsumed within a new empire, namely that of the management control system.[8]

Philosophers remind us to be wary of assuming that our most treasured nouns refer to anything, and this is nowhere more true than in the case of 'risk'. The social disposition to regard and describe more and more possibilities and events in terms of 'risk' has occurred despite and probably because the concept remains elusive, contested and 'inherently controversial' (Fischoff et al., 1984). Many specialist definitions and classifications attempt to secure its meaning. In traditions focused on health and safety, risk is equated with possible hazards and dangers; within finance it is a technical matter of volatility in expected outcomes, both negative and positive. In other business and political settings, risk is closely associated with the spirit of enterprise and the creation of value. There is no attempt in this book to develop another definition of risk and none should be assumed. The project is rather to analyse a phenomenon: the rise of a 'managerial' concept of risk management and the different logics and values which underlie it. So while expert commentators may bemoan the lack of consensus about what 'risk' is, and point to the confusions of using it within diverse settings, it has become an empirical fact that the concept of risk in its raw form has acquired social, political and organizational significance as never before, and this needs explanation even if, as seems likely, risk itself is an essentially contested concept.

If we accept this fact, then the question of defining risk is not as important as analysing the nature of the social and economic institutions which shape and frame our knowledge of, and management strategies for, risk, including the definition of specific 'risk objects'. This is a project of examining 'the discursive and practical operations through which the concept becomes attached to the events it purports to describe' (Knights and Vurdubakis, 1993: 731). In this way the enquiry is directed away from the noun *per se*, and its various semantic bewitchments, towards the role of managerial and administrative *practices* organized for the explicit purpose of representing and handling risk. The underlying theoretical commitment of this book is therefore broadly constructivist in the hopefully uncontentious sense that managing risk depends critically on management *systems of representation*, and on instruments for framing objects for the purpose of action and intervention. This also seems to be the meaning of Ewald's (1991: 199) much cited claim that, 'Nothing is a risk in itself; there is no risk in reality. But on the other hand anything *can* be a risk; it all depends on how one analyses the danger, considers the event.' Or, as Garland (2003: 52) puts it, risk is not a 'first order thing existing in the world' outside of processes for its recognition. Indeed, these recognition processes have become systematically more managerial in form since 1995. It will be argued that, notwithstanding the theoretical preference of governmentality scholars to focus on the multiplicity and diversity of technologies for representing risk (e.g., Dean, 1999: chapter 9), auditable management systems for risk emerge as generic and totalizing instruments of risk governance, in rational design if not in operation. It will also be argued that the transformation of risk management ideas since the mid-1990s can be understood as an 'audit explosion' (Power, 1994; 1997a) in new clothing, a new mode of accountability and monitoring in the name of risk.

The emergence of rational designs for risk management systems reflects social, economic and cultural influences. It is as if the managerial instruments of the 'risk society' have undergone a mutation which cannot be entirely explained in Beck's (1992) terms of the increased risk reflexivity of individuals. Rather, the phenomenon is better described as a new reflexivity of organizations and organizing around risk management. Discourses of risk have become more explicitly managerial and regulatory in form, a mode of governing as such (O'Malley, 2004: chapter 1). From this perspective, the expansion of risk management ideas, an apparent risk management of everything (Power, 2004), suggests a new kind of organizing authority for the category of risk. This is not only a matter of the category being attached to more and more possible outcomes, but also its role in conceptions of good organizational governance.

A stream of apparent failures, scandals, and disasters from the 1990s onwards have challenged and threatened institutional capacities to organize in the face of uncertainty, suggesting a world which is out of control, where failure may be endemic, and in which organizational interdependencies are so intricate that no single locus of control has a grasp of them. In the face of these experiences, there is an observable functional and political need to maintain perceptions of control and manageability. As Douglas and Wildavsky (1982: 1) famously put it: 'Can we know the risks we face, now or in the future? No, we cannot: but yes, we must act as if we do.' Central to this response imperative is the production of visionary documents and designs in the form of standards and guidelines for individuals and organizations. These recipes and recommendations constitute a new normativity for risk management at a time when it is becoming a central part of the definition of organizational governance. There are extensive efforts to design risk management which allocate responsibility and which appeal to values of science and rationality. A recurrent theme in this drama of risk responsibilization in organizations is the spectre of the low probability, high impact event.

Another way of thinking about the normativity of risk management draws on Luhmann's (1988; 1992) argument that the concept of risk, unlike that of danger or uncertainty, implies a domain for decision making about the future and a corresponding allocation of responsibility for that decision. This suggests that the phenomenon of the 'risk' management of more and more aspects of social and organizational life reflects an increase in social *expectations* about the decidability and management of dangers and opportunities. More possible outcomes in the world are subject to demands for human decision and intervention, rather than being left in the hands of the gods (Bernstein, 1996a; 1996b). In this book, the distinction between uncertainty and risk does not refer to two different classes of 'object'. Nor does it quite match Knight's distinction based on the availability, or not, of probabilistic knowledge. The distinction has to do with a dynamic of organizing to produce decidability and actionability. Knightian uncertainties become risks when they enter into management systems for their identification, assessment and mitigation. The distinction between uncertainty and risk in this book is in essence an institutional and managerial distinction between those events and issues which are expected to be treated within management systems as 'risks' and those which are not. Uncertainty is therefore transformed into risk when it becomes an object of management, regardless of the extent of information about probability. Indeed, as we shall see, society can demand the construction of management for issues at the limits of knowledge, making the most recalcitrant objects into risks. When uncertainty is organized it becomes a 'risk' to be managed.

This is not a claim that all risks are 'manageable'. This would be a misunderstanding and simply false on empirical grounds. It is rather a matter of the 'as if' logic or grammar of risk. When objects of concern are described in terms of risk, they are placed in a web of expectations about management and actor responsibility. The apparent risk-based description of organizational life and personal life corresponds to widespread expectation that organizations must be seen to act *as if* the management of risk is possible.

The organization of uncertainty to be analysed in this book involves the creation of ideal frames for the management of issues under the description of risk. These visions of 'risk' manageability also constitute a new space of responsibility and actionability. It will be argued that the organization of uncertainty in the form of risk management designs and standards is related to expectations of governance and demands for defendable, auditable process. Ultimately, Beck may be right that 'no one is in charge' of a runaway world, but the focus of the analysis which follows is to understand the institutionalized frames which underwrite social accounts of the control and manageability of risks.

This introductory chapter sets the scene for the arguments that follow by drawing attention to four critical themes. The next section analyses the tension between uncertainty as a fundamental and constitutive feature of organizations, and risk management as a specific occupational sub-discipline. Having been carved out as a series of technical practices, since the mid-1990s risk management has come to assume a more generic form. This discussion leads directly to the next theme which describes a shift in the conception of risk management, a shift from a discipline with its foundations in analysis and calculation, to a more general governing framework both for risk analysis and for management in general. The third theme alludes to a recurrent tension visible within recent risk management discourses between the logic of the risk society focusing on hazard, loss, and disaster and a neoliberal 'logic' of opportunity, enterprise, and value creation. Finally, the fourth theme emphasizes the catalytic role of ideas and new descriptive categories in changing conceptions of practice in general and risk management in particular. Taken together, these four themes constitute the intellectual sensibilities which inform the analysis in subsequent chapters.

Organizations, Uncertainty, and Organized Uncertainty

A number of critical developments in the field of risk management have taken place since 1995. However, before analysing them in detail, it is necessary to remember that the discrete practices which have come to be called risk management have a complex genealogy and have emerged from more generic relationships between organizing and uncertainty handling.

Formal organization has always existed in a fundamental, even trivial, sense to manage uncertainty. Uncertainty management, understood abstractly as lowering the costs of coordinating and monitoring, is a constitutive feature of organizations according to transactions cost theory. Relatedly, principal-agent models place the analysis of uncertainty at the centre of organizational design principles. From this point of view both 'risk management' and 'governance' are fundamentally about the design of contracts with the power to bond agents to principals.[9] Risk-sharing arrangements provide incentives for the production of goods and services within a fundamentally contractarian theory of organization. This theory has demonstrated its explanatory and analytical purchase on the world, and reflexively becomes more real as the governance of organizations is designed with these neoliberal contracting principles as blueprints (Drori, 2006). Contracts, both theoretical and real, cannot embody every possible state of the future and are essentially incomplete. So the formal contract, as a risk management technology, is itself always risky. There is always 'residual risk' and an extensive corporate governance literature focuses on who is allocated any residual variation in performance (Hart, 1995). Empirically, contracts have also come to play an important role in the management of large projects which explicitly involve risk-sharing and cooperation (Froud, 2003), and scholars of contract law have always had an intellectual purchase on the idea of risk management (e.g., Baldwin and Cane, 1996).

Many approaches to understanding the relationship between organizations and uncertainty focus on the organization–environment relationship. There is considerable variation in research approach involving very different conceptions of the entity of analysis. 'Dyadic' approaches examine exchange relationships between organizations and their environments, in terms of other organizations in supply chains and customer relationships, or in terms of resources and capabilities, such as technology and labour. The management of uncertainty created by these elements in environments is fundamental to the existence of an organization and is necessarily co-extensive with strategy. It is for this reason that strategy experts may be unimpressed by the apparent risk management explosion since 1995; strategy has always fundamentally involved risk and the concept of 'strategic risk management' may be regarded as a neologism.

While these dyadic theories of organizational exchanges with environments tend to focus on the individual organization as the strategic entity, other significant strands of work focus on the organized nature of organizational environments themselves and their institutional character (Davis and Powell, 1992). Thus the sharp distinction between organization and environment is blurred, placing organization theory closer to more general theories of society. Specifically what has come to be known as the new-institutionalism examines organizational environments as a *resource* for uncertainty management by supplying the scripts, routines, ideas and forms of management knowledge which formal organizations adopt to deal with a particularly significant aspect of uncertainty, namely legitimacy (Powell and Dimaggio, 1992). Based on observed tendencies for some organizations to become more similar in their formal structure, it becomes difficult to distinguish organizations, at least in their formal character, from their institutionalized environments. This way of thinking about organizations also emphasizes mimicry and isomorphism as modes of uncertainty management with intuitive ecological appeal; copying immediate neighbours has always been a natural survival strategy.[10]

These and other theoretical accounts of how organizations process uncertainty provide a common reminder that risk management, in an abstracted sense, is constitutive of organization. Organizing and managing are fundamentally about individual and collective human efforts to process uncertainty. However, uncertainty in this very general sense is an analytical construct of the organizational theorist and is not the primary interest of this book. Rather, we are concerned with how specific uncertainties become *objects,* risk objects, for a management process and this demands an analysis of the manner in which they are represented and constructed within organizational and managerial fields. Uncertainties in the form of possibilities of financial loss, of danger and damage which may or may not be labelled risks, do not exist *sui generis* but must of necessity be organized, ordered, rendered thinkable, and made amenable to processes and practice of intervention. Risk analysis is itself part of this organizational construction of risk from uncertainty. Organizations never encounter risk as a pure given; attention must be triggered, interpreted, and coordinated (Hutter and Power, 2005a).

This focus on the managerial processing of uncertainty also necessitates a regard for the endogenous uncertainties which are a product of these very efforts to manage and organize. Such 'unintended consequences' of organizational action have been a defining subject for social scientific attention and an industry of risk regulation has grown in response to social and political demands to deal with these side-effects, though not without further side-effects of its own. The theme of organized uncertainty which motivates this book therefore captures both the sense of organizations as processors of uncertainty (by formal risk management and other means) and the sense of organizations as producers of risk, sometimes resulting from the very effort to seek reliability (Busby, 2006).

For example, it is now widely accepted that financial risk models may be a source of risk and may be self-defeating when all market participants use more or less the same one. In a crisis of liquidity they will all tend to react in the same way (selling), which collectively exacerbates the crisis. Thus the institutionalization of a risk analysis technique can generate 'endogenous risk' in the form of herd behaviour (Danielsson and Shin, 2003). In a similar way it has been argued that safety regulation may make individuals less vigilant leading to lower safety overall. The contingencies of interconnectedness may be cumulative in unforeseen ways (Kunreuther and Heal, 2005), an idea which is largely consistent with Perrow's (1984) concept of the 'normal accident'. Inherent failure is a particular kind of uncertainty produced by large scale human organization, and provides a counterweight to technocratic dreams of perfect control. The paradoxical concept of the normal accident also moves the discussion from the level of general theories about organizations and environmental uncertainty to the specific characteristics of organizational vulnerability and response.

Failures and crisis in large organizations have been diagnosed under the motif of the 'man made disaster', a concept which focuses attention on organizational and managerial processes which 'incubate' disaster or crisis (see Turner and Pidgeon, 1997).[11] Broadly speaking, empirical case analyses suggest that rigidities of core beliefs, managerial distractions, disregard for the views of outsiders, lack of regulatory compliance, and difficulties in assembling critical information tend to be systemic factors contributing to organizational failures. In most cases, a point supported by Vaughan's (1996) analysis of the Challenger space shuttle launch decision, relevant information is readily available but is not assembled and acted upon because of deep-seated organizational assumptions. Although easy to note in retrospect, many disasters exhibit this common pattern of failure to process information at appropriate levels of seniority, particularly anomalous information and gossip that does not fit habitual channels of data processing. These organizational and governance issues have been conceptualized within the field of finance as 'operational risk' (Chapter 4). Thus, financial scandals, such as Barings, Daiwa, and Sumitomo, have come to be understood as management and governance failures rather than failures of analysis and information (Tschoegl, 2000; Hogan, 1997).

Within this stream of organization research 'incubation theory' refers to the analysis of potentially deviant normalities embodied in routine patterns of activity which inhibit intelligent risk processing. Crises and catastrophes do not just happen suddenly; they are in an important sense 'organized' and have their origins in failures of management and intelligence processes (Vaughan, 1996). In some cases deviant behaviour may unfold over a long period of time (Beamish, 2002). Early warning signals, red flags, gossip, and other forms of intelligence may get overridden, ignored or reinterpreted because of a desire not to take them seriously. Analyses of corporate scandals and failures uniformly demonstrate a tendency not to act on these early warnings (Ermann and Lundman, 1996). It follows that corporate governance norms are a risk management strategy for a distinctive kind of risk—the failure of senior management to prevent risk incubation.

The list of disasters which seem to fit this analysis is long and well known: including Bhopal, Chernobyl, Piper Alpha, and many others. More recently, apparently surprise or random acts (the terrorist attacks of September 11th 2001; the Turkish earthquake) have been traced to historical organizational and intelligence failures (fragmentation in Security and Police Services; non-compliance with construction regulations). Indeed, the *9/11 Commission Report* spent nineteen weeks in the *New York Times* best seller list and has come to be regarded as an important 'business' book for its analysis of failure in organizing warning signals. Together with the report on the Columbia shuttle disaster, it has provided a platform for organizational consultants and thinkers to emphasize much of what Turner anticipated, namely the need for 'disruptive intelligence' and the elimination of 'perfect place arrogance' in risk management.[12]

Yet despite these accumulated experiences of organizational failure, they do not automatically lead to the creation of 'disruptive intelligence'. One reason for this, to be explored in this book, is that a climate of organizational defensiveness and a logic of auditability pervade the concept and practice of risk management. Organizations adopt rationalized approaches to show that they have done everything that is reasonable because of fear of institutional sanction. Burgess (2006) argues that organizations are now more active in seeking out risks. Risk 'scares' rather than silent incubation have become the norm for risk specialists who have a tendency to amplify danger. Burgess suggests that an unreflective risk culture has emerged in the UK which is the very mirror image of the organizational blindness described by Turner and others. The 'projection of worst-case scenarios' has become a new form of risk governance; there is new populism which defines the responsible organization as one which leaves 'no fear unturned'.[13] So, far from generating a climate of intelligent challenge and a capacity to abandon existing organizational hierarchies in a crisis (Weick, 1993), the imagination of ever more exotic forms of uncertainty and risk has given rise not only to new social anxieties (Wilkinson, 2001) but also to more elaborate formal representations of management practice, including risk management. It will be argued that the form of risk management today, to be described in detail in Chapters 2, 3, 4, and 5, has been shaped by experiences and discourses of organizational failure, by the availability of institutional remedies and rationalized frameworks, and by wider rhetorics of opportunity and enterprise.

The theme of organizations and uncertainty should not be mistaken for something very novel. There is a long normative, theoretical, and explanatory history in the fields of economics and organizational sociology in which risk management and organization are almost the same thing; managing and uncertainty are two sides of the same coin (Smith and Tombs, 2000: 7). This explains some of the irritation with recent academic and practitioner enthusiasm for something called risk management as a field. Some organization scholars view this enthusiasm with suspicion since risk is something they have always, implicitly or explicitly, concerned themselves with within their respective fields, particularly in the case of high reliability organizations. And yet, even if true, there is still something to analyse and explain, namely, why risk and its management has emerged at a particular time from specific sub-fields to become a visibly preferred idiom for such a wide range of practices and a model for governance itself.

From Risk Analysis to Risk Governance

The history of risk management is partly a story of the intersections between mathematical and statistical experimentation on the one hand and commercial interests on the other (Bernstein, 1996a; 1996b). Shipping had always presented challenges for commercial adventurers and Lloyds of London emerged and grew by virtue of its capacity to pool exposures to hazard. Natural insurance principles of collectivized security were also implicit in organizational forms, such as cooperatives and mutuals. Practices remained intuitive and mathematically underdeveloped until probability theory came to be applied to practical issues of quality control in fields such as agriculture and munitions. Modern risk management also emerged from new institutions for the collection and statistical analysis of data, such as the census. According to Hacking (1990: 5), an 'avalanche of numbers' in the nineteenth century supported a climate of 'political' arithmetic for the knowledge and control of the population, not least in the evolution of life assurance as a technology of government (Knights and Vurdubakis, 1993; O'Malley, 2004: chapter 6). Modern managerial ideals of 'governing by numbers' have their historical roots in these developments.

While insurance underwriters were long established as a distinctive occupational community of risk operatives, Starr's (1969) paper marks an important take-off point for the professionalization of a generic technical discipline called risk analysis (Hacking, 2003). Subsequent institutionalization followed a standard pattern via the establishment of academic and professional associations, such as the society for risk analysis (SRA). The knowledge base of risk analysis communities with strong natural hazard (fire, flood, earthquake) and health and safety interests came to be enshrined and institutionalized in textbooks. Risk analysis scholarship and practice also flourished in the area of technological failure and crisis management. Within this field, so-called high-reliability organizations in the nuclear, chemical, and transport industries became a particularly strong focus, and techniques for modelling complex processes and extreme events, such as fault trees and scenarios have come to form part of the risk analysis toolbox. So when the UK Royal Society report in 1992 defined risk as 'the chance, in quantitative terms, of a defined hazard occurring', it expressed an idea with a long institutional history which had become a matter of common-sense, even for risk analysts concerned with as diverse subjects as quality control, chemical toxicity levels, epidemiology, and accidents in the workplace.

As with all quantitative disciplines, such as accounting, abstraction and non-field specificity have been important to the rise of risk analysis (Abbott, 1988). The development of risk analysis exhibits an ever-expanding frontier of formalization in which techniques are applied to new uncertainties and new risks are measured.[14] The ambition of risk analysis to model recalcitrant or complex interacting hazard phenomena effectively transforms acts of god into possibilities for rational decision-making and policy. From this point of view, Knight's famous distinction between risk and uncertainty, which is often the starting point for definitional anxieties about risk, must be taken as historical and changing rather than invariant. The project of taming incalculable uncertainties as calculable risks is a dynamic one which reflects in part an evolving cultural trust in numbers as a basis for rational decision making (Porter, 1995).[15] For example, analytical developments in financial risk management, particularly the invention of portfolio theory and the development of options pricing models, enabled financial economics to progress as a distinctive field of theory with practical potential (Pearson, 2003; Mackenzie and Millo, 2003; Whitley, 1986).

A deeper investigation of risk analysis reveals a complex hybrid of different elements (Hood and Jones, 1996a; Miller *et al.*, 2006). Notwithstanding the manifest institutional differences between the fields of finance and non-financial hazard management, risk analysis can be understood as an over-lapping family of methods for the calculation and measurement of risk based in the statistical sciences. Yet the reach and coherence of these methods should not be overstated. For example, insurers often provide cover for 'incalculable' risks at the limits of formal knowledge (Ericson and Doyle, 2004). This suggests an entrepreneurial attitude to uncertainty rather than a rationalized and actuarial calculative approach to risk (O'Malley, 2000; Boyne, 2003: chapter 1). Even actuaries admit to using quantitative frameworks to structure their 'guesses' (Ericson *et al.*, 2003: chapter 5). More generally, work in organizational theory suggests that most decisions are actually made in the absence of calculable probabilities and under conditions of enormous contingent complexity (March and Shapira, 1987), although they may be presented as if they were mechanical.

The model of the rational actor which has been important to the development of decision science, and therefore risk analysis, has come to be questioned by views about how individuals act under conditions of uncertainty: 'risk-related decisions often are embedded in organizational and institutional self interest, messy inter- and intra-organizational relationships, economically and politically motivated rationalization, personal experience, and "rule of thumb" considerations that defy the neat, technically sophisticated, and ideologically neutral portrayal of risk analysis as solely a scientific enterprise' (Short, 1992: 8). Purely calculative, machine-like solutions to technical problems only work well in situations where there is a very high level of agreement about knowledge and a high degree of organizational and political consent about the issue (Burchell et al., 1980), so that such value judgements which inevitably enter the decision process are widely shared. It is also well known that even expert assessments can exhibit considerable variance (experts disagree), that in some areas extrapolation is highly judgemental and that there is often an impression of 'false precision' (Jasanoff, 1991: 31), which is a function of the cultural and instrumental values of expert communities rather than a window on reality (Mackenzie, 2003; Wise, 1995). So, complex risk management problems, particularly involving matters of public policy, are mistakenly conceived as machine-like problems of risk analysis. It is frequently argued that a model of risk knowledge dominated by engineers must accommodate processes of consent management involving the views of non-experts or 'stakeholders' (Flyvbjerg et al., 2003).[16] At the centre of the consent building process lie questions of risk acceptability and tolerance.

The precise relationship between risk analysis and risk management has been much debated in the United States (Silbergeld, 1991). On the one hand such a separation presumes a questionable scientific purity for risk analysis; on the other hand it appears to locate key elements of discretion about risk with administrators (Jasanoff, 1986; Pollack, 1995). More generally, questions of risk acceptability, degrees of precaution and the multiplicity of principles for determining acceptability (e.g., ALARP) have came to be understood as values lying at the boundaries of formal risk analysis, embedded in political cultures and giving rise to variations in regulatory style (Vogel, 1986). Such cultural differences necessarily disturb illusions of scientificity.

The emerging significance of public risk perceptions has also challenged the ideal of rational risk analysis. The research literature on risk perception and behaviour dates back to studies in the 1970s and Kahneman and Tversky's (1979) prospect theory demonstrates that individuals process and react to dangers in a wide variety of ways, often dependent on how risk is framed and presented (Slovic, 2000).[17] While critics, such as Douglas and Wildavsky (1992), argue that individuals' attitudes to risk should be traced to larger cultural frames, thereby making risk itself highly relativistic, others focus on the conditions under which individuals respond to evidence of risk and to the framing and communicating of risk information (Mayo and Hollander, 1991; Slovic, 1991). Notwithstanding these debates about the objectivity or otherwise of risks in the light of perception variation, the broad direction of critique is the same: risk analysis cannot progress as a mathematically isolated discipline; it needs to take some account of public risk perceptions. Dangers and harms might be real enough, but ideas of risk and safety are complex social constructions subject to processes of framing (Renn, 2008).

A parallel challenge to technical risk analysis has come from debates within science studies about the authority of scientific expertise. Wynne's (1982) pioneering study of lay knowledge of risk in the context of sheep farmers in Cumbria marked an important step in creating a field of science and public policy studies to challenge risk analysis. Jasanoff (1994) has also drawn attention to the multiplicity of narratives within which risk and the ex-post analysis of disaster are necessarily situated. From these points of view, formal risk analysis is part of a more general scientific and technical paradigm whose cultural authority is not self-evident and whose political power is often invisible.[18] In very broad terms, these and other analyses of the politics of risk analysis are based on democratizing impulses to reinstate excluded voices in the world of expert risk analysis. A rich stream of work on science and its publics, on regulatory science and on risk regulation has followed, which challenges the divide between informed experts and ignorant publics, which emphasizes the role of risk communication in public policy, which argues that risk objects are more complex and ambivalent than risk analysis admits, and which situates risk analysis and project management in a broader space of democratic aspirations (e.g. Irwin, 1995; Irwin and Wynne, 1996; Flyvbjerg et al., 2003; Renn, 2008). Widening participation in risk analysis may also be a better organizational strategy for enhanced risk identification (Smith and Tombs, 2000), particularly in the field of environmental risk management (Gouldson and Bebbington, 2007).

In the United Kingdom the 1992 Royal Society report included material on public perceptions of risk and the risk management process, indicating a prima facie receptivity to these issues from the scientific community. But the synthesis between the two 'sides', technical scientific conceptions of risk analysis and social-psychological analyses of risk perception, was evidently an uneasy and imperfect one in the UK.[19] A later report in the USA was more successful in this integration[20] and policy receptivity to risk perception issues has changed over time, usually repositioned as an increased focus on 'risk communication'. At the level of practice, efforts to enfranchise lay publics and their perceptions in the business of risk regulation have been varied and participatory and consultative processes remain debated as a basis for 'governing' expertise (Rothstein, 2004). These gestures towards the democratization of risk policy have led to a sustained focus on risk acceptance principles in risk analysis. In particular, precautionary principles of risk acceptance have been much discussed, notably in the case of GM foods (Levidow, 2001). Opponents of this principle, which tends to place the burden of proof on demonstrating safety, argue for the importance of innovation, for the damaging effect of institutionalized fear, and for the need for some kind of cost-benefit approach to risk acceptance (Starr et al., 1976; Sunstein, 2005). More generally, it is argued that debate about these principles is not the sole preserve of expert committees and individuals. Demands by pressure groups for consultation and for the elicitation of views of diverse publics has given focus groups an organizing and epistemological significance in the identification of risk and in the development of principles for acceptance or tolerance.

These cumulative pressures for varied forms of openness in risk policy, for forms of participation and risk communication, have exacerbated the usual problems of decidability and actionability in risk policy. Attitudes to risk vary across individuals, may be different at different levels of an organization and may also vary across different aspects of same risk and with new information (Hutter, 2000). Policy makers seeking to aggregate these views for risk acceptance decisions therefore face severe operational difficulties, not least being the problem of preference aggregation itself and of knowing which public understandings of risk to take seriously or not (Renn, 2004; Lezaun and Soneryd, 2006). In some cases, the public may understand risk issues very clearly, in others inherent ambiguity creates a politics of uncertainty which was previously private and invisible. In the face of the risk of consultative exhaustion and undecidability, regulators often exhibit a preference for uni-directional forms of disclosure and transparency over dialogue.

One of the most significant pressures for change in the practice of risk analysis, and also a stimulus for research, has come from scandals and disasters. Modern states have played a role describable as risk management since the production of legislation to protect workers in the nineteenth century and the rise of the welfare state in the mid-twentieth. In the post-war period states became more self-conscious about their role in regulating risks to the public and dedicated regulatory organizations were created, employing many risk analysts and inspectors.[21] In the fields of energy provision, public transport, health, financial services and large-scale infra-structure there have been major and publicly visible disturbances to these modes of risk regulation. In the UK, the handling of the BSE event had a catalytic effect on government, creating a pressure to manage risk more explicitly with more transparency and accountability of the risk analysis and management process itself.[22] The public risk perception problematic was transformed from a challenge *within* risk analysis to a challenge to the legitimacy of government. Ideas about 'risk communication' in the UK acquired a new political significance as a strategy to manage public expect-ation and its potential disappointments. As part of a general demand for greater accountability for risk handling, UK risk regulators came to be more explicit and public about their risk analysis and assessment practices (e.g., HSE, 2001). Security services have not been immune from these pressures for transparency of management process as the 'quality control' issues about intelligence on Iraq have demonstrated in both the UK and USA.

In the UK, the drive for improved public transparency of risk assessment coupled to a need for better capacity to identify and organize risk management draws explicitly on private sector designs and norms, in just the same way as public management reforms in the 1980s did. These risk management ideas started to become part of the official self-description and self-understanding of central government activities in the late 1990s. UK policy documents by the Cabinet Office built on earlier ideas developed by the National Audit Office, in turn translated from the private sector. The result was a wave of formal risk management guidelines for government departments, supported by an educational and cultural change programme headed by 'risk improvement' managers (RIMs) (Black, 2005; Rothstein *et al.*, 2006b).[23] This central government initiative in the UK drew selectively on academic ideas of risk perception. Indeed, the emphasis was more on organizational process than on democratic engagement. The perceived need was for 'organized paranoia' to enhance government capacity to identify new risks in incubation.[24] There was also a concern to manage public expectations in areas of service delivery and project management, particularly following the examinations and passport fiascos.[25] The gap between public expectations and service delivery came to be recognized as a risk for government and its regulatory agencies. The performance of UK risk regulation agencies was simply one aspect of this larger public service issue.

The UK case suggests how risk communication strategies, discussed in the 1980s in terms of making risks clearer to the public, came to be strongly influenced by discourses of *reputational* or *institutional* risk. More importantly for the purposes of this book, the emphasis of communication was increasingly on the *process* of risk management rather than on its content. Regulation is embodied in a class of organizational actors called regulators, and these organizations are concerned in part about political perceptions of effectiveness and the possibility of blame. So the peculiarities of the UK climate suggest that scholarly critiques of risk analysis, their varied forms of constructivism, and their demands for public representation in the risk regulation process,[26] filter into policy discourses, if at all, in a very uneven way.[27] For example, the idea of the public understanding of science (PUS) came into being as a policy category, but is itself highly contested (Wynne, 1995). Discourses of public perception and culture, which emphasize the importance of context, have manifestly failed to dent the continued 'objectivication' of risk inherent in traditional modes of risk analysis (Burgess, 2006). In part, the practical difficulties and cost of instrumentalizing context and culture for decision making has been a barrier to the transfer of these insights into the policy domain. But even where the significance of these matters has been championed, prevailing public management discourses exhibit a preference for rationalism and standardization in making public science accountable. The result is a conception of risk governance heavily framed by rationalized notions of a risk management process.

Organizations involved in 'governance' have grown dramatically and the word has acquired policy and scholarly momentum since the mid-1990s.

Yet governance is itself a contestable concept, a hybrid in which logics of democracy and of managerial process are variably intertwined and live uneasily together (Drori, 2006). Where the former points to greater external world responsiveness and engagement, the other is more inward-looking and focuses on technical design and coordination issues for control systems. These different logics also give rise to cultural variation in the institutional form of risk governance. In the United States processes of legalization and the role of law in adjudicating on administrative discretion are prominent forces and place risk analysis in a public space of political competition (Jasanoff, 1990). The history of risk analysis in the United States reflects heightened attention to accountability within a culture which is largely respectful of science and less trusting about administrative discretion. In the United Kingdom, auditability mechanisms play a similar functional role to legalism in the USA, but may provide a mirror image of the American case—accountants are trusted at the expense of scientists.

As Pollack (1995: 189–90) notes, a common problem with securing public trust in science and risk assessment is the problem of verifying that regulators are doing a good job. Risk assessments themselves are often 'complex counterfactuals about the distant future' which do not lend themselves to easy forms of public verification. However, while risk assessments may not be directly 'auditable' in this sense, the managerial process by which the assessments are made can be. The 'governing gaze' has increasingly shifted from the science of risk analysis itself, and its epistemological debates, to the organizational system within which it is embedded. This is the sense of risk governance to be discussed throughout this book i.e. governance of the risk assessment and management process, which is necessarily framed as an *organizational* process.

The recent history of risk regulation in the UK suggests this new emphasis on the governance of the *organizations* which analyse risk, to include regulators and private corporations. In part this may reflect relative degrees of institutional confidence in opening the 'black box' of risk analysis; US lawyers venture into science where UK lawyers may hesitate. Demands for risk regulation and greater accountability in risk handling face a choice of institutional design: make accountable and audit the science or the process within which the science is conducted. The shift from risk analysis to risk governance which is a guiding theme in the rest of this book is properly understood as a shift towards a form of risk governance which is more corporate in form and constitutes the governance of risk management. Democratic ideals of participation by relevant stakeholders are certainly not eliminated by this broad shift, but they are increasingly positioned within ideals for good governance of the risk analysis process. Risk analysis and the urge to calculate risk remain institutionally strong and varied in form, but scientists and engineers now find themselves operating within the larger logic of public management and being organized and governed by a management process which is in principle auditable and inspectable.

Whereas the rise of risk analysis in the period since 1965 represents a growth in the capacity of experts to populate the *content* of risk knowledge, the period since the mid-1990s reflects the rapid growth of models of the management *process* within which risk analysis operates. To understand this development, the scholarship discussed above which emanates from psychology, politics, and the sociology of science, and which supports studies of institutional difference in risk management, must be supplemented by critical theories of organization and auditing. Put another way, the social construction of risk must engage with the social construction of management practices to govern risk. And while many scholars have emphasized the governing logic of calculation and actuarialism, it is also necessary to understand the governance of risk as something accomplished by instruments of auditable management process, which have grown in significance as modes of organizational and regulatory control (Power, 1997b).

We have seen that pressures for greater democracy in risk analysis, particularly over questions of risk acceptance, characterize long running debates about risk governance. These debates involve demands for improved risk communication and greater transparency of the risk analysis process. Yet, in many fields risk governance is taking shape more as the corporate governance of risk analysis than as democratic engagement. The reach of this managerial modality of risk governance is much wider than the world of the state, i.e. public risk policy and its regulatory agencies discussed above. Risk analysis in private sector management thinking has also become transformed within a broader governance setting which focuses on matters of organization design, the quality of senior management, and accountability for the effectiveness of internal controls. Here it has become very clear that a logic of organization pervades the world of risk analysis, a logic which is being increasingly imported into public risk regulation via structures and values created by public management reform. Risk communication processes may in fact involve the participation of non-experts in risk regulation regimes, but they are increasingly framed as an organizational strategy to manage public expectations. Here lies the essential ambivalence of risk governance. While the UK state has wanted to get smarter about risk identification and analysis in the wake of various policy failures, the shift in many fields to managerial forms of risk governance is also potentially defensive. Public perceptions of risk are not simply a new factor in more intelligent risk analysis, they are a source of risk in themselves. So, the shift from risk analysis to risk governance is in part a strategy to govern unruly perceptions and to maintain the production of legitimacy in the face of these perceptions (Power, 2003).

From Risk Society to Opportunity Society

The third theme which runs through this book takes as its point of departure Beck's (1992) much discussed risk society thesis.[28] The point is not to take issue with Beck specifically, as many others have done, but to note that the popular success of the 'risk society' idea lies in its capacity to name nascent anxieties. Beck's ideas appeal in contexts where there is increasing consciousness of self-produced risks and also doubts about the capacity of a flourishing risk regulation industry to cope with them. The 'risk society' idea also suggests a growing degree of institutional mistrust—the 'end of tradition' in Beck's terms—and the reception of his central concept has generated interest in risk aversity at the societal level. There are publicly voiced concerns that some societies have become more systemically risk averse and more prudential in their outlook, with individuals and organizations seeking to avoid having adverse outcomes attributed to them (notwithstanding Beck's comments on the impossibility of attribution). The growth of dedicated risk regulation agencies, which seem to grow their own mandates, is held responsible by some for amplifying this risk aversion. And accusations of the choking effect of regulatory bureaucracy is never far below the surface of public commentary, leading to the creation of new institutions for 'better' regulation. For many commentators the 'institutionalized non-management of problems' (Beck, 1992: 105) is readily evident as an empirical fact.

These receptions, uses, and criticisms of Beck jointly raise the conception of risk as a hazard or undesirable outcome to a principle of social organization.

However, in the four cases to be discussed in this book, another significant logic of risk is also visible which posits a risk society of a very different kind from Beck's analysis and with a very different organizational and individual morality. In short, risk is not only to be governed in a management process for the sake of enhancing the capacity to avoid or mitigate harms. It is also to be done in the name of opportunity and enterprise as notions of enterprise risk management, to be discussed in Chapter 3, suggest.

As O'Malley (2004: chapter 3) argues, the rise of risk as an organizing category belongs not only to precautionary sensibilities but also, crucially, to a neoliberal logic of the entrepreneurial subject. He suggests that where calculative rationality belongs to the historical project of bureaucracies collecting numbers for processing, enterprise belongs to the logic of risk-taking for gain, an idea with a very long history. At the level of the individual, an entire programme for a newly responsible self is visible in the change programmes of the 1980s and 1990s. New modes of control, and the intensification of audit and accounting, were argued to be consistent with validating entrepreneurs in the pursuit of risk as opportunity—particularly in a reformed public sector. Such entrepreneurs were to be accountable for nothing more than outcomes. At the extreme, we are all exhorted to become our own risk managers in areas of lifestyle, of financial security, of emotional commitment. Risk enters into the description of the everyday in a manner coextensive with personal responsibility and innovation. Popular magazines celebrate risk-taking individuals. In the UK the risk programme in the civil service has as much to do with creating new enterprising and innovative subjects as it does with the improved handling of downside risk.

O'Malley's insights can be extended from the level of individuals to that of formal organizations—the focus of this book. In both the private and public sectors the concept of risk is being enrolled in a new focus on outcomes and performance. In the private sector this is visible in efforts to link investments in control activities to organizational objectives and value creation within frameworks for enterprise-wide risk management (ERM). The world of insurance has been similarly transformed over time as part of the selling of risk management (Baker and Simon, 2002). In the UK public sector 'risk', rather like customer responsiveness, is emerging as the basis for self-challenging management practices in the absence of direct competitive pressures. Large consultancy firms sell risk management designs as much more than a preventative technology. Rhetorics of opportunity, enterprise, and value creation pervade the new governance of risk management.

Deregulatory discourses also contribute to the momentum of this logic of opportunity. As we shall see in Chapter 2, neoliberal strategies of risk regulation in many areas involve the cooptation of regulated organizations in the regulatory process. Rational regulation is be risk-based and focuses effort and resource on the most risky entities. Yet, risk-based regulation is simultaneously a discourse of opportunity which emphasizes a domain of freedom for those who can 'prove' they are less risky. Organizations have thereby become co-responsible in regulatory processes where the state is risk manager of last resort (Moss, 2004). This alignment of organizational governance, regulation and enterprise is the conceptual and normative space within which concrete practices of organizing uncertainty now operate and which, as the following chapters show, has allowed control operatives to reinvent themselves as representatives of enterprise with a foothold in the world of strategy. This logic of opportunity is encountered in a number of guises but is most recognizable in its populist form, the often invoked slogan that 'risk management is good business'.

The logic of opportunity is also a moral logic in so far as it speaks to a new organizational self, in much the same way as O'Malley's concept of 'enterprising liberalism' speaks to a new economic citizenship (Miller and O'Leary, 1993). As Meyer (2006) and others have argued, the explosion of organizations in recent years corresponds to a new conception of organizations as actors which are complex, confident, and responsible. A mass of standards for organizational behaviour, including codes of corporate governance, supports an increasingly 'self-reflective and self-improving' organizational actor. This moral flavour to the logic of opportunity also imagines organizations as capable of facing and managing uncertainties in a rationalized way, an image which will resurface in the various cases which follow. However, the logic of opportunity being described here, its language and conceptions, is just that—a logic, a mode of discourse which is distinct from the language of avoidance and aversion. It will be suggested in Chapter 5 that there is yet another distinct logic informing risk management discourses, one which has been largely overlooked in psychology and science studies. It is a managerial logic concerned with values of auditability and accountability for due process. In both the public and private sector, risk management may seek to align itself with enterprise values, but it is also central to a distinctive style of organizational discipline and accountability.

Ideas, Risk Objects, and Boundary Objects

This book is about implementation, but not in the commonly understood sense. It is not a study of how one or more organizations adopt and adapt technologies. And it is not about the processes of negotiation between agents of change, whether managers or inspectors, consultants or workers. This would require a much more comprehensive empirical endeavour than is intended here. However, it is very much a study of implementation in another sense, namely the 'implementation' of the key *ideas* within broad management discourses. Ideas are much easier to implement and adopt than other features of practices (Brunnson, 2000) and the chapters which follow describe and analyse the rise and 'discursive acceptance' of specific ideas and their role in constituting the mission of risk management practice.

The analysis embodies an implicit theory of the significance of ideas and concepts in structuring practices. Ideas are not something apart from practice; concepts and classifications are the ideational building blocks of the practical domain. These concepts may originate in analytical form within scholarship and may come to shape practices, but they rarely exist in their pure form as Chapter 5 on reputation management will show. Equally, common popular assumptions and ideas can structure both practice *and* research, and scholarship may simply engage in the explication of concepts which originate in the practical field. More generally, powerful ideas which begin life as part of an external description of an organization come to be part of that organization's self-description and hence part of the organization (Strathern, 2000: 312).

In all these cases, the trajectory of key ideas, and the narratives and networks in which they are embodied, is central. All management practices *necessarily* embody and are constituted by ideas of what they could be. These aspirational, programmatic or *as if* elements are often linked to larger value systems (Rose and Miller, 1992). The constitutive significance of ideas is a matter of philosophical common-sense and, according to Wittgenstein (1976: §570), 'Concepts lead us to make investigation; are the expression of our interest, and direct our interest.' Hacking (1986: 231) takes this philosophy of language one step further: 'all intentional acts are acts under a description. Hence if new modes of description come into being, new possibilities for action come into being in consequence.' This contrasts with the popular and naively materialist conception of practices as *practical* in the sense of being somehow beyond ideas. Once ideational distinctions are made, new realities come into being—entities and possible action descriptions emerge hand in hand with the invention of new categories (cf. also Tribe, 1978). This 'dynamic nominalism', as Hacking describes it, is readily visible in the transformation of risk management since the mid-1990s. Certainly, practices contain many material elements, such as physical processes and technologies. Yet these elements are in themselves insufficient or blind without the animating role of ideas, and cannot be understood apart from descriptions of their purpose. Risk management is always a practice under some description or other, a description which embodies ideas about purpose and which embeds practices in larger systems of value and belief. Very similar material routines can be mobilized by actors around different ideas and descriptions, and dynamic nominalism means that they are distinct practices. Equally very different routines can be allied to the same idea, making them the same practice—at least temporarily. The ideational and the material, facts and technology, cannot be readily distinguished in socio-technical systems such as risk management (Bijker *et al.*, 1989) and a book like this which focuses primarily on changing ideas about practices is nevertheless *about* practice.

From this point of view, definitions of risk and risk management do not exist prior to practice but are themselves a part of the organization of uncertainty. Hilgartner (1992) argues that insufficient attention has been paid within risk analysis to the process through which 'risk objects' are conceptually constructed because of a hardware and technology emphasis. 'Risk objects' are essentially ideas about harm with implicit causality and may become the focus of 'sociotechnical networks' understood as 'seamless webs' of elements and actors engaged in strategies for institutionalizing or de-institutionalizing particular objects of knowledge. In terms of the list of activities at the beginning of this chapter, the corresponding risk objects might be 'defective signals', 'bad weather', 'poor credit analysis', 'dry holes', 'levels of teacher supervision', 'cigarettes', 'mis-selling'. Each of these conceptual objects inhabits a different and dynamic sociotechnical network of ideas, resources, experts, regulations, and organizations in which practice is constructed. Social attention to these objects in the form of risk control activities is dynamic and varies. Experts work hard to construct objects for attention, to make them a common-sense object for management purposes, but as Hood *et al.* (2001) show, objects such as 'dangerous dogs' and 'background radiation from radon' exist within very different institutional frameworks for standard setting, monitoring, and enforcement. In the financial sector, the 'rogue trader' has been a significant popular risk object and the origins of corporate governance guidelines in the early 1990s were animated by ideas about 'rogue directors'. The emergence of new categories of risk object like this, and their implied causality, go hand in hand with efforts at regulatory and managerial reform and design.

A focus on the sociotechnical networks which support, or destroy, risk objects requires definitions of risk to be endogenized, rather than treated abstractly (Bijker *et al.*, 1989). Much of what we today call risk management is 'uncertainty management' in Knightean terms, i.e. efforts to manage 'risk objects' for which probability and outcome data are, at a point in time, unavailable or defective. Yet, while more calibrated taxonomies of uncertainty have been developed (Stirling, 1998), the issue for the present study is not purely whether a 'better' definition of risk is possible, but a need to understand the dynamics of any particular risk object in organizing definitions and descriptions of a practice and its constituent elements: 'the process of constructing a risk object consists of defining an object and linking it to harm. The task is a rhetorical process performed in texts that are displayed in specialized organizations or in public arenas, and it usually involves building networks of risk objects' (Hilgartner, 1992: 46). This is consistent with Hacking's conception of 'dynamic nominalism'. To emphasize the importance of ideas in practice is to suggest neither that they are exogenous nor that actors are dupes (Blyth, 1997); ideas are part of a continuous dynamic in which practices get performed and contested under accepted descriptions.

Hilgartner suggests that an analysis of the production and destruction of ideational risk objects leads us away from a focus on the public, the obsession with risk perception and culture discussed above, and back to the expert communities of risk analysts working hard to make risk objects visible. However, such a methodological prescription, while important for orienting an empirical work programme, suggests an 'archipelago' of risk objects within their own distinctive sociotechnical networks or risk regulation regimes. This book analyses a much broader class of risk objects which are managerial in form, a managerial form which gives them a very wide institutional reach, wide enough to escape the contingencies of specific sociotechnical networks. In addition, Hilgartner's analysis focuses on risk objects as harms, whereas the discussion of the previous section suggests that, for a new class of managerial 'risk object', there is a rhetoric of opportunity in which causal links to benefits are also posited. So, in the case of school trips, there are both 'risk objects' of harm, such as 'insufficient supervision', and opportunity, such 'mind-broadening experiences for children'. This suggests that the idea of the risk society can be reposed as a society where there is a systemic tendency to construct, describe, and stabilize an increasing number of harm-based risk objects.

The ideas which matter most in this book are essentially design ideas about organizing and managing. As Czarniawska and Joerges (1996) suggest, formalized ideas of managing, embodying new purposes and aspirations, can travel rapidly and can change organizations in very material ways—the case of operational risk management in Chapter 4 demonstrates this. Indeed, notwithstanding Hilgartner's demand for an inventory of risk objects in all their variety, it is the very idea of risk itself which has been transformative in the last decade, both extending the number of risk objects receiving institutional attention, for example the case of school trips noted above, and also animating a distinctive managerialization and formalization of the manner in which organizations deal with uncertainty.

Not all ideas have the same status and institutional reach. The successful institutionalization of more abstract managerial ideas to be discussed lies in their role as boundary objects, that is, as a focal point for practical change with the ability to appeal across boundaries to a multiplicity of interest groups and potential allies. A boundary object is an object which can inhabit 'several communities of practice and satisfy the informational requirements of each of them. Boundary objects are both plastic enough to adapt to local needs and constraints, yet robust enough to maintain a common identity across sites' (Bowker and Star, 1999: 297). For example, the idea of internal control, and its boundary spanning capacity across different groups, such as IT security specialists and human resource teams, reshapes practice and possibilities for action for communities which might otherwise remain unconnected.

The notions of risk object and boundary object will be important to the subsequent analysis of key changes in the risk management field. We have already hinted at these changes. The shift from risk analysis to risk governance can be understood in terms of the consolidation of specific risk objects within more general managerial descriptions. For example, the risk object 'defective O-rings' has been located within another—'deviant management culture at NASA'. The former risk object mobilizes a relatively tight socio-technical network, of the kind Hilgartner and sociologists of technology take as objects of study. The latter is implicated in much a broader world of rationalized ideas and aspirations about management mobilized by general risk objects such as 'the tone at the top', 'management culture'. These ideas do not necessarily originate as the projects of technical experts; they are much more programmatic than that and have organizing potential. New ideas are performative in so far as they establish new normative climates for decision making and determine the way specific risk objects are 'conceptualized, identified, measured and managed' (Short, 1992: 4).

This book focuses on the emergence and transformation of managerial categories and classifications which provide a basis for the legitimate organizational self-description of risk management. The chapters which follow seek to analyse how ideas and categories can mobilize and animate changes in a practical field. This is a kind of ideational implementation; organizational actors engage in definitional work as part of efforts to organize concrete practices and routines to manage risk objects. They produce a world in which conceptual objects of governance, organization, risk, and management are being continuously co-defined. Specifically, they construct an idea of risk governance which demands the rational design of risk management process.

Organized Uncertainty

The four themes highlighted above constitute the driving sensibilities of the analysis which follows, namely attention to the institutional construction of a risk management process, a process expressed and materialized in standards and guidelines and mobilized in the name of good governance and opportunity. Since the mid-1990s new categories and ideas have re-shaped discourses of risk management, giving them a more central role in organizational governance, aligning them with ideals of enterprise and subsuming more traditional forms of risk analysis. This re-organization and reconceptualization of management activity in the name of risk marks a distinctive form of administrative innovation, involving the diffusion of new process frameworks, the organization of new concepts of risk and its management;

and the creation of new classes of organizational actors as authorized representatives of best risk practice. The aura of scientificity of risk analysis is being placed in a larger, rationalized, managerial, governance, and regulatory frame of meaning.

The chapters that follow deal with the details of this broad process of change. Chapters 2 and 3 deal with the genesis and design of new blueprints for risk management processes. Chapter 2 analyses an important dimension of the shift from risk analysis to risk governance, namely the 'turning inside out' of organizations as a consequence of the rise of corporate governance from the beginning of the 1990s. While the idea of corporate governance is itself complex and multifaceted, a common feature across all global and national initiatives is an emphasis on the integrity of 'internal control' systems. This chapter describes how internal control came to acquire conceptual autonomy from financial auditing and was reframed as risk management. This helped to create the necessary conditions for 'whole-of-entity' approaches to risk management with near universal applicability. In this story, the internal auditor emerges from the shadows as a significant organizational and regulatory actor, speaking for a logic of opportunity and seeking a foothold in a competitive space inhabited by risk analysts and strategists.

Chapter 3 takes up the focus on 'whole-of-enterprise' risk management by examining the different origins of this idea, one coming out of the developments described in Chapter 2 and another with a more technical foundation in the fields of finance, risk analysis, and control theory. The chapter analyses the emergence of standardized and formalized generic approaches to risk management, and their consequences for all organizations, including states adopting risk-based approaches to regulation. It is argued that a massive institutionalization of process-based risk management has taken place with important implications for the moral economy of organizations, not least the accountability of senior management for the management of risk. New actors, such as the chief risk officer, have emerged to oversee value-adding risk management empires, to supervise expert risk analysts, and to ensure the integrity of the organizational self and its responsibility for risk governance.

Taken together, Chapters 2 and 3 provide evidence of the distinctive subsumption of risk analysis within managerial and business frameworks for risk management. This in turn reflects neoliberal ambitions for the constitution of a new kind of organizational self. Chapters 4 and 5 provide two further case studies of this process, paying particular attention to new concepts and new forms of organizational risk narrative. Chapter 4 deals with the emergence of the category of operational risk in the banking sector during the late 1990s, analysing both the occupational tensions between different claimants on the field of operational risk, and the different degrees of allegiance to calculation and management in the organization of risk. The case is more generally instructive about the role of concepts and categories as catalysts for practical change, and the sense in which the creation of new risk objects is fundamentally a practical and organizational achievement. The category of operational risk is an invented and fictional one with concrete significance for the governance of diverse risk management communities and for a potential consolidation of the risk 'archipelago' (Hood and Jones, 1996a).

Chapter 5 focuses on another significant category within recent risk management thinking, namely 'reputation'. Reputation has come to be an object of governing significance for organizations as they operate in densely populated and active institutional environments. The chapter explores the many different interests which find a common opportunity in the idea of reputation and seeks to explain why reputation has become a significant object of concern for organizations and governments. Reputations can be at risk, but the management of reputation, and ethics and CSR, are also conceptualized as organizational opportunity: 'social responsibility is good business' is another much invoked slogan. Yet, despite evident management salience, reputational risk management is paradoxical not least because *external* forces are prominent in defining and calculating organizational reputation. In addition the inherently pervasive nature of reputational issues demands meta-practices of oversight by cross-functional committees rather than a new unit or department.

Having examined the contours of designs for risk management in terms of a new accent on rationalized internal processes, and new risk categories and officerships, Chapter 6 provides a more critical analysis of these developments. It is argued that the extension of risk management and the language of risk both into new domains and also upwards along the organizational hierarchy represents a new phase in the 'audit society', as states, organizations and individuals internalize the imperative to demonstrate that things are in control. In place of uncertainty as the space of entrepreneurialism, organizations of all kinds are being organized, legalized, and made auditable. Beneath the claims for strategic significance and the logic of opportunity lie fears and anxieties about accountability and blame. The production of defendable proof about the management of risk pervades the construction of risk management.

Chapter 7 draws together the arguments of the book as a whole and suggests three avenues for future analytical and empirical enquiry which may correct some of the overstatement in the current argument. First, more needs to be done to examine the social construction of risk objects and managerial processes and their entanglements with each other. Second, the world-level role of specific risk governance designs, such as enterprise risk management, in defining a self-validating set of moral norms needs to be explored further in specific organization settings. Third, more work is needed to understand the working out of the logic of auditability. If arguments for its pervasive and constitutive nature are not grossly overstated, there are some important policy implications, not least a need to rethink standard strategies for de-regulation. Individuals, corporations and governments may have little choice but to organize the uncertainties they face, but policy makers need to recognize that the organizational obsession with risk management since the mid-1990s embodies immaculate images of organizational process, and fantasies of opportunity and value, which may be self-defeating.

Notes

1. The category of tax risk, as a new basis for selling professional services, has become recently prominent on the back of this general expansion in risk management ideas. See Godman (2006a; 2006b).
2. See, for example, Franklin (1997); Denney (2005); Richter *et al.* (2006).
3. See for example, NAO (2000); HSE (2001); Cabinet Office (2002); Dibb (2003); Raban and Turner (2003). *Managing Risk* (London: European Business Forum and Marsh, 2003); *Living Dangerously*, Economist Survey, January 2004.
4. See for example, Hanley (1999); EIU (2001); Larkin (2002); Lam (2003). Journals include: *Due Diligence and Risk Management*; *Healthcare Risk Management*; *Risk Management*; *Energy and Power Risk Management*; *Australia Institute of Risk Management Journal*; *International Journal of Risk Assessment and Management*; *Opthalmic Risk Management Digest*; *Australian Risk Management*; *Operating Room Risk Management*; *Strategy and Risk Management*; *Public Sector Risk Management*; *Community Risk Management and Insurance News*; *Risk*; *Operational Risk and Compliance*.
5. The UK Treasury website has links to a number of these associations as knowledge resources, including the IIA, GARP, and the IRM.

6. See section 17 on 'risk management' from Royal College of Anaesthetists (2000). Events like the football world cup and the Olympic games are also explicitly organized with risk management principles in mind. See Jennings (2005). Football clubs which are publicly listed must also make disclosures about how they have managed risk.

7. See Day and Klein (2004).

8. See also Callon (1998) for whom 'calculative agencies' have become more important in constituting economic life than calculation itself.

9. Economic theory has become more sensitive to concepts of culture and mission which go beyond a purely contractualist model. For example, see Ghatak and Besley (2005).

10. While 'isomorphism' may be a useful analytical description of certain organizational processes of copying from the outside, it may not be adequate to the self-description of specific organizational practice, except in the loose sense that practitioners admit to explicitly copying best practice.

11. This is also called 'disaster incubation theory'. See Rijpma (2003).

12. See J. McGregor 'Gospels of Failure', Fast Company Magazine, www.fastcompany.com Issue 91, February 2005, 62.

13. In March 2005, a UK conference on risk perception and assessment addressed the topic of 'Risk Hypochondria—are we looking too hard for risk?'.

14. See Starr *et al.* (1976) for a conceptual framework for risk-benefit analysis.

15. From Knight's (1921) point of view, such a trust in numbers amounts to a distrust of forms of judgement and enterprise in the face of radical uncertainty.

16. See also Hood and Jones (1996b: chapter 4).

17. For a sociological review and critique of this work see Heimer (1988).

18. This critique is replicated within insurance studies which argues that actuarial practices of risk calculation and classification play a decisive role in modes of social control and identity formation (Simon, 1988; Ericson and Doyle, 2004).

19. See the Preface to Hood and Jones (1996b: xi).

20. See National Research Council (1996). For further discussion see also Okrent and Pidgeon (1998).

21. Among the largest in the UK are the Health and Safety Executive (HSE), The Food Standards Agency (FSA), The Financial Services Authority (FSA), The Environment Agency. Work in the field of socio-legal studies has shown how inspection, compliance and analysis are outcomes of complex organizational processes. Research has also shown the persistence of institutional heterogeneity in the manner in which risks are processed by these state agencies; the 'government of risk' is by no means uniform across problems and functions and risk analysis is embedded in very diverse frameworks. In particular, the manner in which public perceptions and moral frameworks are incorporated within risk regulation is a source of variation across these 'risk regulation regimes.' (Hood *et al.*, 2001).

22. In the UK the Phillips Report on the BSE crisis (http://www.bseinquiry.gov.uk/index.htm) was criticized for being too traditional in its conception of risk analysis.

23. The Treasury Risk Support Team absorbed the work of an earlier UK Interdepartmental Liaison Group on Risk Assessment (UK-ILGRA).

24. Phrase attributed to Geoff Mulgan speaking at a conference entitled 'Panic Attack', 9 May 2003, The Royal Institution, London.

25. Based on an allegedly leaked memorandum reported in the UK press in late April 2004.

26. See for example Stirling (1998) and Okrent and Pidgeon (1998).

27. In the USA, Vaughan is a counterexample of the influence of social science. She wrote one of the chapters in the Columbia shuttle enquiry and ideas about the 'normalization of deviance' have had some policy influence as a consequence.

28. It is highly debatable whether the world is 'more risky' or more objectively dangerous now than in the past. It has also been argued that Beck ignores serious distributive issues in favour of the 'democracy of the toxin' (Smith and Tombs, 2000: 17–19) and has an objectivist view of risk, risk analysis, and expertise.

2

Turning Organizations Inside Out: The Rise of Internal Control

On 1 December 1992, the concept of corporate governance acquired a new organizational and public policy significance. On that day, Sir Adrian Cadbury, chairman of the Committee on the Financial Aspects of Corporate Governance, a committee convened by the Institute of Chartered Accountants in England and Wales, published his report and code of principles ('The Cadbury Code'). Thirteen months earlier, Robert Maxwell had been found dead and the pension fund of his Mirror Group was discovered to have a £440 million deficit. Prior to this, the Bank of England had closed the Bank of Credit and Commerce International and other UK corporate scandals had already created a climate of unease about the financial transparency of large corporations entrusted with public assets. While the production of the Cadbury Code may be read as an attempt to head off more direct government regulation of a corporate sector which was becoming scandal-laden (Freedman, 1993), it had much wider effects than could have been imagined at the time. The theme of governance would dominate corporate regulation for the next fifteen years and beyond.[1]

Since the publication of the original code, practitioner and scholarly writing on the subject of corporate governance has grown almost exponentially across the world. The 'voluntary' principles of governance first laid down by a small committee of a UK professional body with a narrow remit have become transformed, adapted, and exported as a transnational blueprint for national regulatory systems, and further refined by a variety of supranational organizations.[2] A report intended to address the financial aspects of corporate governance of listed companies in the UK has been widely diffused and has acquired significance for organizations of all kinds, both private and public. Conformity with some version of these principles has become a badge of legitimacy for any organization, whether it be a hospital or school, a bank or a mining company. In short, ideas and principles of corporate governance have acquired a 'world-level' status; it is hard to imagine organizational design without reference to them.

This chapter focuses on, and explores the significance of, one specific aspect of the principles of corporate governance, namely the requirement that organizations maintain a sound and effective system of internal control. Although there were antecedents and ideas 'in waiting', it is difficult to exaggerate the extraordinary rise of the concept and practice of internal control since the original Cadbury Code was published. The evolution of internal control in its various manifestations provides a distinctive case study of the broad movement described in Chapter 1 by which technical risk analysis and assessment has been subsumed within mechanisms of governance, and how these mechanisms are more managerial than participatory in flavour. Internal control systems now lie at the very centre of governance thinking and practice; their design principles are now global (IFAC, 2006). From a lowly technical and bureaucratic function, of interest to relatively insulated specialists, the idea of internal control has moved into a broader public space and has undergone a profound transformation in its organizational and regulatory significance across the world. It has also come to be understood by many as co-extensive with risk management, and as a distinctive mode of organizational uncertainty handling (Power, 1999: Spira and Page, 2003).

In the next section, the emerging significance of internal control is placed in the context of regulatory philosophy and strategies. The development of principles of corporate governance reflects a broad regulatory style visible also in other regulatory fields, such as health, safety, and environment. This style is reflected in a commitment to work with the internal resources of organizations in a cooperative fashion, while subjecting these inner workings to ever greater transparency, audit, and evaluation. The discussion establishes the significance of internal control as something demanded by regulatory strategy. This is followed by an analysis of the supply-side forces for change within the external financial auditing process, changes which reinforce a managerial and supervisory focus on internal control. The argument then deals with the specific rewriting and reconceptualization of internal control as risk management within a new logic of enterprise, strategy and opportunity, and with the related difficulties and issues of reporting publicly on internal control and risk management systems. The transformation of internal control into risk management gives accountants in general and internal auditors in particular a professional potential in the world of risk management as carriers of a new kind of risk knowledge. Taken as a whole the chapter argues that internal control as risk management reflects a more general 'managerial turn' in regulation, and a new phase in the organization of uncertainty in the form of frameworks which emphasize management *process* in a field hitherto dominated by experts in risk *analysis*.

Governance and Regulation 'From the Inside'

What is the nature of regulatory processes in a post 'command and control' world? It has long been recognized in many different countries that the various agencies and departments of the state have neither the resources nor the expertise to regulate directly in a commanding and controlling style in many areas of social and economic life. Indeed, the 'command and control' model was always more aspirational than descriptive as scholarship in socio-legal studies has demonstrated (Baldwin and Cave, 1999: chapter 4). For example, against the 'legalistic illusion' which assumes that regulatory processes follow their prescribed blueprints, empirical investigations have revealed the negotiated and variable nature of compliance (Hutter, 1998; Hawkins, 2003). The necessity for regulatory strategies which work with, and draw on, the resources of regulated organizations has been transformed from the street-level pragmatism of front line inspectors into principles for regulatory design. In addition, associations like the ICAEW which sponsored the Cadbury Code, and non-governmental organizations of various kinds, have long been recognized as significant in the production of social order and norms of governance (e.g., Streeck and Schmitter, 1985). Indeed, there has been an increase in scholarly and practical interest in the range of non-state organizations which contribute to regulatory outcomes and which are involved in prescribing governance norms and rules to govern the conduct of organizations, not least insurers.[3]

Analytical concepts have been developed to represent a complex regulatory landscape. Ayres and Braithwaite's (1992) concept of 'enforced self-regulation' characterizes the potentially cooperative relationship between regulator and regulated (Baldwin and Cave, 1999: 133–6). As a normative blueprint abstracted from practice, the concept suggests that, in the first instance, a regulatory organization should prefer a cooperative style, prescribe principles, permit organizations to develop and enforce their own detailed rules, and periodically inspect. In cases of breach or dissatisfaction, the regulatory body has, or should have, options to escalate its enforcement process with ever more serious consequences for the regulated organization. The analysis lends itself easily to the tools of game theory. State regulatory agencies should work with a tit-for-tat strategy, to trust first, to distrust and sanction when trust is violated and finally, if the game is extended, to forgive and trust again. The theory is that this regulatory model generates considerable self-regulation and 'natural' compliance by the regulated organization.

Many regulatory systems are linked to licensing privileges where a license to trade or conduct an activity is conditional on compliance with formal or procedural norms (such as having 'effective' internal controls). The sanction of withdrawing a licence is usually a last resort and the outcome of extensive prior negotiation. The 'enforced-self regulation' model therefore reflects a regulatory preference for indirect action and influence by prescribing frameworks and principles and by enrolling self-regulating resources, in particular the management system of internal controls. Organizations have an incentive for compliance because the regulatory process may focus on desired outcomes rather than regulating detailed process, with regulatory intervention as a last resort. In the UK, the Financial Services Authority has recently sought to regulate in some areas via high level principles.[4]

The 'enforced self-regulation' model is not the only theoretical and normative possibility. It is part of a family of related concepts of 'mutual regulation', 'de-centered regulation', 'smart regulation', and 'soft law'. All these approaches add nuance to the basic idea: the key elements of regulation, namely the production and enforcement of norms may, and should, be dispersed across many different actors (Gunningham and Grabosky, 1998; Black, 2001). It is broadly accepted that regulatory systems can make a virtue of this necessity by combining the benefits and authority associated with the ability to enforce sanctions with the benefits of cooperation. In this manner, the more traditional deterrence model of regulation comes to be embedded within a larger strategy which relies heavily on cooperation and self-regulation (Reiss, 1984; Hutter, 1997: 238–243; Parker, 2002).[5] This reflects a broad shift in regulatory preference from *ex post* discovery of norm violation to *ex ante* anticipation, and to prevention and self-discovery via internal systems of compliance which secure organizational conformity.[6]

This accent on self-enforced compliance as a preventative strategy is the heart of what has come to be called risk-based regulation (to be discussed further in Chapter 3). In essence both regulators and regulated observe propensities for non-compliance with desired norms of behaviour. Self-discovery and reporting by the regulated entity is an ideal. This mode of regulatory control is exemplified by the growth of programmes which develop performance standards for compliance in technical terms (Parker, 2000). The ideal is that potential for first order failure and deviance, such as fraud, is signalled in the first instance by 'technical failure' or 'near miss', typically signals of control system design weakness or operational deviance. It is argued that such compliance based strategies encourage organizational learning and responsibility (Hutter, 1997; Parker, 2002), thus positioning internal control as a 'moral technology' at the heart of governance. Perhaps nowhere is this more evident than in efforts in the financial services sector to incentivize and embed self-regulation.

In the United Kingdom in the 1990s, the Securities and Investments Board (SIB), the predecessor of the Financial Services Authority, explored ways of rewarding financial firms that establish good controls and effective internal auditing procedures. In a similar vein, prior to the changes in the institutional structure of financial services regulation in 1997, the Bank of England adopted a 'quality assurance' based approach to supervision to ensure that regulations are being applied.[7] This subsequently developed into an explicitly risk-based approach to supervision, following advice from Arthur Andersen, known as RATE (Bank of England, 1997a; Black, 2003a). The Bank of England approach emphasized the common interests of management and supervisor. The intensity of external supervision and of audit could be varied depending on the control culture in the target bank (Bank of England, 1997b). The FSA inherited and developed this approach further (to be discussed in Chapter 3), making the quality of internal controls a core principle (Gray and Hamilton, 2006: chapter 3).

More generally, regulatory design increasingly embodies an aspiration for a style of regulation which operates with the incentives of organizations

(Braithwaite and Makkai, 1994; Goodhart *et al.*, 1997) and which places the operational substance of control within organizations themselves, with a corresponding 'responsibilization' of senior management (Gray and Hamilton, 2006: chapter 4). Within this cooperatively constructed baseline model for regulation, the degree of external audit in principle becomes part of the 'ladder of response', an escalatory option available to the regulator, rather than an ongoing standardized fixed-period statutory requirement.[8] The Audit Commission in the UK public sector traded intensity of inspection based on evidence of good governance (Bowerman *et al.*, 2000) and evidence of good environmental management systems, as prescribed by frameworks such as EMAS or ISO 14000, can form the basis of 'smart' deals with regulators about intensity of inspection (Aalders, 1993; Gunningham and Grabosky, 1998) and with insurers about the costs of cover.

Borrowing from Shapiro (1987) it can be argued that these changes in regulatory philosophy, and the emphasis on modes of self-regulation and control systems, has much to do with the rise of 'trust' as an organizing principle in modern societies. Despite suggestions that modern societies are often characterized as being less trusting, the growth of agency relationships, whereby agents are entrusted with custody and discretion over the management of the assets of other people, suggests the necessity of trust between strangers remote from each other in space and time who must rely on the representations of the other. Actors may work hard to personalize and re-embed economic relationships, but this is a costly activity and impersonal trust, supported by systems trust (Giddens, 1990), is a both an inevitability and a part of the logic of opportunity. The rise of these trust-based relationships in modern life drives a demand for new guardians of trust who can explicitly balance the incentives for principals to take risks with those of agents to engage in deviant behaviour. These guardians are typically, but not exclusively, regulatory and inspection organizations which focus on the conditions of trust inside organizations.[9] Accordingly, internal control systems and related public disclosures, such as financial statements, have been transformed into the material representation or proxy for trusting organizations and their leaders. Internal control systems have become central to a 'regulatory epistemology' in which demands for trust create corresponding demands for evidence.

Within regulatory scholarship there is a difference between an emphasis on internal control systems which values their technical properties in enabling more efficient coordination, and an emphasis which regards them as the basis for more substantive improvement of, for example, health, safety, environment, investor protection.[10] Internal control systems embody *both* potentials—of greater efficiency and coordination on the one hand, and of greater sensitivity to social responsibility issues on the other. This is the sense in which such systems are 'moral technologies'; in their expanded role and conception they embody and intertwine the two logics of management and democracy which Drori (2006) identifies within the concept of governance. We might be sceptical about the managerialization of CSR by such systems in *particular* cases e.g. the observed variability of the role of EMAS in contributing to environmental protection, and of firms' commitments to environmental compliance (Gunningham *et al.*, 2003). However, the general mobilization of management control as a regulatory resource has been animated by a rationalized vision of its responsibilizing and ethical potential in making the inner life of organizations observable.

Supervisory capacity in the broadest sense, including that of external auditors, to detect first order violations, such as fraud, is limited and often not timely. The more easily detectable violation is the breaking of organizational trust and this leads to a regulatory preference for preventative regulatory strategies which focus on systems designed to make key trust variables visible. In place of direct surveillance, an impossible pure transparency, the regulatory process 'observes' in the first instance the conditions under which trust is supported, that is, the norms of behaviour to which organizational agents are held to account by their own managerial commitment to self-regulation. This is meta-regulation or the regulation of self-regulation (Parker, 2002: chapter 9) and it amounts to a profound turning 'inside out' of organizational life. The distinction between internal self-governance and external regulatory process is increasingly blurred and technical features of internal control systems are bearers of trust values. As a consequence of these developments, the normative climate of organizations, variously characterized as the 'tone at the top', 'organizational culture', or 'control environment' has become a significant focus of regulatory attention via its auditable proxies—internal control routines, checks, and structures.

Internal control has become central to the rise of a 'regulatory state' which is broader than the growth of agencies and encompasses control departments and units *within* organizations, including the risk management function. Internal control has become part of a new governmentality of organization life in which traditional distinctions between mandated and voluntary regulation are blurred. For example, since its creation in 1992, principles of corporate governance in the UK have changed formal status from a so-called voluntary, private regulatory system, to a public one required by listing rules. UK companies are now required to state whether they comply with the principles and must 'explain' if they do not. Formally, non-compliance with the principles is possible provided the organization explains itself, thus being compliant in a second order sense. This 'comply or explain' principle typifies a regulatory emphasis on combining the flexibility with informative disclosures. However, the significance of the Code approach lies much less in its formal status as either a voluntary or mandatory set of norms. Indeed, this distinction, although important in law, is largely unhelpful in characterizing the sense in which the principles of corporate governance across the world have marked out the inside of organizations as a kind of regulatory and disciplinary space (Hancher and Moran, 1989). These principles are experienced as binding regardless of their source. The family of neoliberal regulatory strategies described above draw our attention to the many sources of control, discipline, and normative order beyond the state (Rose and Miller, 1992). This means that the 'regulatory state' is much more than a system of semi-autonomous agencies; it is also a distinctive mode of self-observation and self-discipline for organizations, a reflexive mode of regulation mediated in part by dedicated officerships (see Chapter 3). Internal control systems in their broadest sense play a critical role in neoliberal regulatory regimes which operate indirectly via the 'control of control'.

As the distinction between mandated and voluntary norms is blurred, so too is that between managerial and regulatory process itself. Such an elision provides a platform for a new logic of opportunity and enterprise in organizational fields by which control activities can be imagined both to be 'compliant' and to facilitate core business processes in an organization. This neoliberal compliance ideal anticipates a potential where the traditional 'problem of compliance' no longer exists because regulatory and business goals are perfectly aligned. That this ideal is not an empirical reality, and principal-agent models reminds us that it is not aligned with theory either, should not detract from its broad discursive status as an aspiration or *telos* of regulation. Internal control systems have been placed within a new web of concepts and categories and can now be envisioned as the critical interface between regulatory and business values, and hence between society and organizational operations.[11] In short, internal control systems make possible the displacement of government by *governance* as an emphasis on the internal conditions and benchmarks of organizational trustworthiness. Internal control systems are at the heart of a process by which organizations are being turned inside out and made into newly responsible actors.

In summary, the regulatory environment of organizations in many different policy areas has taken a 'managerial turn' with an increased emphasis on systems of control, senior management responsibility and 'naturally' enforced cultures of compliance. Corporate governance changes in the early 1990s catalysed the role of internal control systems as important objects of public policy. Formal regulatory bodies like the UK FSA can be conceptualized increasingly as meta-regulators observing the self-regulation of organizations, an approach which represents a radical internalization of regulatory activity and where the distinction between organizing (managing) and regulating is increasingly blurred. However, this regulatory convergence on, and demand for, effective internal control and management systems is not a sufficient condition for the rise of internal control. There must also be a supply of ideas, knowledge, and templates with a corresponding body of carriers. For this we must look, at least in part, at recent transformations in the field of financial auditing.

The Audit Implosion

It has been suggested above that the 'regulatory state' should be understood as more than a network of sectoral oversight agencies for regulation. Of equal significance in governing economic life has been the growth of audit and evaluation practices. This audit explosion (Power, 1994; 2005b) has been a conspicuous feature of the transformation of public services in the UK in the 1980s and 1990s, and has also been driven by the emergence of the corporate governance principles described above. In the UK public sector, audit came to signify not simply a new technical and operational basis for control in public services, but was part of a critique of closed, 'club government' (Moran, 2003). New forms and intensities of auditing were mobilized in the name of ideals of transparency, efficiency, and accountability, and the scope of auditing and inspection was extended in many regulated sectors. At the heart of these changes, internal control and related performance measurement systems grew in significance as the focus of audit and inspection processes, and this reflected the general shift in regulatory strategy indicated above. Such systems came to be part of a broadly based organizational reform process to make accountable organizations auditable and inspectable. These changes have been registered in the heartland of the audit, the financial auditing process, and have catalyzed practitioner interest in markets for internal controls and risk assurance.

The financial audit is simple in concept. Many organizations publish representations of their financial performance and strength known as financial statements. Such statements are checked by auditors whose work adds a level of additional assurance to these statements, thus enabling critical capital allocation decisions to be made by investors and providing signals about the integrity and legitimacy of management (Power, 2003a). Yet, beneath this apparent unity of purpose, financial auditing has been in an almost constant process of reform and critique—with the collapse of Enron in 2001 and other corporate scandals providing the backdrop to global debate in the new century. Even before this event and the eclipsing effect of the Sarbanes-Oxley legislation in the United States, concerns with the future of financial auditing had been conspicuous in the 1980s. Committees were formed, reports were published, professional structures were criticized, research was commissioned and education systems were re-designed—all with a view to meeting the perceived challenges of a symbolic millennial landmark. Auditing became a site for professional reinvention (Robson et al., 2007),[12] and two closely related but distinguishable change programmes are visible in discourses of reform.

There were demands to reinvent the technical basis of the financial audit on the one hand, and there were focused efforts by the large professional service firms to develop markets for possible assurance and advisory practices on the other hand.[13] The emergence of rival proprietorial audit products in the 1990s, for example CLASS at Coopers and Lybrand, AuditSystem/2 at Deloitte and Touche, the strategic-lens approach at KPMG, represented professional change programmes to construct a new alignment between a need for greater cost efficiency in the audit process and a need for a new marketing concept of audit as a 'value adding' advisory service. To this end, explicitly risk-based approaches to financial audit came to replace a more traditional regulatory framing of auditing and drew on more generalized discourses of risk, enterprise, and strategy (O'Malley, 2000). A universalistic logic of opportunity rationalized the reduction of costly transactions testing and a more selective focus on high-risk areas of greater 'value' to the client.

The idea of a risk-based approach was hardly new to auditing in the 1990s (Adams, 1991; Humphrey and Moizer, 1990) and was a natural development from the systems-based audit (Lemon *et al.*, 2000).[14] As internal control systems became more complex, auditors set themselves the task of focusing on where key risks exist and on how they are controlled and mitigated in these systems. Indeed, such an approach to the audit could be easily sold as an incremental change to business as usual—as a new formalization of the need to understand the auditee. For example, in 1997 the Audit Faculty of the ICAEW ran a series of educational roadshows aimed at small practitioners with the title—'The Audit of Tomorrow'. These events sought to communicate a new potential for the audit process if a business risk assessment is performed at the outset. Subject to agreed scoping with the client, it was argued that such an assessment could perform a dual function simultaneously as both a planning tool for the audit and as a client directed service. In this way, a risk-based approach was articulated both as best practice and as a business opportunity—for auditors themselves. The aspiration was to reconstruct auditors as 'added-value' business advisors (ICAEW; 1997a; 1998b; Robson *et al.*, 2007).

Although the audit risk model developed in the 1980s approached inherent risk and compensating controls as a sub-unit of the statutory financial audit process, the ICAEW programme anticipated the development of internal control as an advisory focus in its own right. The traditional management letter identifying control weaknesses was normally considered to be a by-product of the statutory financial audit process. Now it would become a primary focus for advice. To some commentators in the 1990s it appeared as if financial audit was being reinvented as a by-product of business services and that independence was being designed out of the financial auditing process (Jeppesen, 1998).[15] The audit opinion was to become a part of a larger risk assessment process as developments in the KPMG audit approach demonstrate. Bell *et al.* (1997) outline the structure of a new audit approach—a 'business measurement process' intended to access audit risk through a 'strategic systems lens'.[16] At the heart of this approach is the need to understand the auditee organization 'holistically'. The KPMG authors intended that the BRA process described above should focus explicitly on key interrelationships between the internal and external environment of the organization, which both generate risk and are sources of risk-taking. At the centre of this analytical process is a focus on understanding the client's business strategy and on understanding the risks that threaten, and the key processes to realize, these objectives.[17]

While the KPMG approach was constructed on the site of existing internal control practices, it also took the concept of the audit process into areas in which it had not hitherto been formally involved, not least the conceptual space of business strategy. This led to considerable issues in implementation because nothing less was at stake than the creation of a new kind of auditor with new skills (Eilifsen *et al.*, 2001; Knechel, 2007; Curtis and Turley, 2007; Peecher *et al.*, 2007). Indeed, while the focus on risks to business strategy objectives gave a new accent to the audit process, allowing auditors to focus on control in the widest sense, it also weakened the operational links to financial statement assertions. The business risk approach required that the auditor focus primarily on the risks that the organization will not meet its strategic objectives; the financial statements were to be understood as a derived regulatory product of this focus, that is, a specific information system for representing wider economic events.

These transformations within the external audit process in the 1990s created a focus on business risk control systems in their widest sense. The re-conceptualization of the financial audit paralleled efforts to expand advisory and consulting services. The category of 'audit' went out of fashion in the self-representations of the large firms (Robson *et al.*, 2007) creating a new action space for accountants. The risk-based reinvention of the statutory audit came to be seen as one element of a broad advisory field. The work of Robert Elliott, a leading reformer in US accountancy profession in the 1990s, exhorted practitioners to recognize the potential markets for new assurance services, locating the statutory audit as one part of this emerging field, a field in which this audit would need to compete for talent and prestige. As in the UK, the AICPA emphasized the need for CPAs to understand the changes facing financial auditing both as risk and as opportunity (AICPA, 1996). During the same period, the large firms began to develop internal audit practices to provide outsourced internal assurance services, a move which will be discussed further in the next section below.

Another important challenge to the traditional financial audit as a form of periodic regulatory inspection was the effect of technological development in information systems and the emerging need for real time continuous assurance services: 'Users will need data assurance at points in time other than just at the end of a year or a quarter. Some users may require "continuous audits" of a broad data set, others "just-in-time-audits" of key transactions or data, and still others mixes of the two. When users' real-time access to databases becomes routine, they will need continuous data assurance' (AIPCA, quoted in Miller and Young, 1997, note 11). These ideas of timely assurance posed a further radical challenge to the external audit. They pointed in the direction of an explicit shift from periodic, retrospective audit to contemporaneous, proximate auditing (Vasarhelyi and Halper, 1991) in which the audit process becomes more closely aligned with organizational operations. A new potential was constructed for practices of real-time assurance of internal control systems, an idea which matched regulatory preferences for the substitution of internal for external assurance where possible. This was also a fundamental challenge to the traditional disclosure-based certification of periodic financial statements, a challenge which codes of governance in the UK and regulatory developments elsewhere amplified.

Developments within professional discourses of external auditing during the late 1980s aligned auditing with increasingly popular ideas of risk and opened the door to a new practice focus on controls assurance (Robson et al., 2007). Pressures for change within the audit process were not simply technical; they were simultaneously pressures for expansion of advisory markets as a response to an emerging corporate governance agenda. Criticisms of the untimely nature of financial statements and, by implication, of the external audit process, found a new platform in marketing claims for new assurance services. Organizational and regulatory demands to manage uncertain futures grew hand in hand with a supply of ideas about internal control as the self-observation of organizational risks. While the audit of control systems (rather than transactions) had been important to external audit practice throughout the twentieth century, now such control systems were transformed into a stand-alone focus for professional assurance services. As a regulatory window on the integrity of management and as a signpost for the future these management systems became significant objects at the centre of a world of governance in which accountants could claim to have expertise.

The rise of internal control as an autonomous field of expertise and norm production has been described as an *audit implosion* (Power, 1999) and as an *internal control explosion* (Maijoor, 2000). In the United States the Sarbanes–Oxley legislation ('Sarbox') radicalized and continued this focus on internal control, creating new statutorily backed markets for internal control assurance. Financial auditors have been returned to their more traditional role as independent verifiers of financial statements, although standards for risk-based auditing have done much to formalize and rationalize the firm-specific innovations of the 1990s (Robson *et al.*, 2007). Under Sarbox rules, for any particular client, firms must now choose between doing an audit or providing advice on controls and risk management. It may be ironic that the principles of corporate governance developed during the 1990s, which explicitly sought to strengthen the authority and process of the *external* financial audit, in fact helped to support a new market focus on internal controls design and assurance which has created a new platform for *internal* auditors. However, the risk-based re-design of auditing in the 1990s promised a consulting platform which is now constrained by rules and regulations. The claimed knowledge-spillover effects from other services has had to confront a regulatory preference for a purer conception of the financial audit and for a clearer division of labour in markets for advice—at least, for the time being.

In summary, the recent history of the financial auditing field suggests that during the late 1980s and early 1990s accounting practitioners were looking to elaborate and extend their expertise in the area of internal controls design and assurance as a stand-alone 'governance' advisory service. In part this was to do with the re-engineering of the audit process and its broader positioning as business risk analysis. Internal control as an emerging regulatory and managerial object was re-imagined within the audit process as a window on the client organization, on its risk management and on its strategy. The corporate governance explosion in the 1990s had transformed internal control into a generic regulatory and public policy object and created opportunities to develop new consulting markets in a self-reinforcing process. By the mid-1990s internal control had a regulatory, managerial, and conceptual life of its own as a benchmark of good governance.

Internal Control as Risk Management

The previous two sections have identified two pressures for the increased significance of internal control and management systems, namely their critical role in supporting the realization of more nuanced, graduated forms of regulatory enforcement intervention, and their consequent emergence as a stand-alone advisory area in the external auditing field. The two pressures are mutually reinforcing: a regulatory emphasis on *external* audit and inspection has shifted in part to an emphasis on the observability of internal mechanisms and agencies of control. While external auditing remains an important feature of corporate governance, a new model of partnership between internal and external inspection and audit has been created as an explicit form of 'meta-regulation' or 'control of control'. How this partnership operates in practice is an important matter for empirical investigation which goes to the heart of the so-called risk-based regulation ideal. There will no doubt be considerable variation in practice across regulatory fields. However, such variation is to be understood against a broadly based consensus in which the internal control function has assumed a new regulatory significance and has come to be regarded as co-extensive with risk management.

'Internal control' is itself simply a category under which a variety of control processes can be described. The theory of 'dynamic nominalism' discussed in chapter 1 reminds us that new categories can give rise to new conceptions of practice and action. In order to appreciate the transformation in the status and significance of the category of internal control, it is important to understand that, beyond statutory requirements to keep proper books and records in general company law, such control was for many years a private commercial matter with little interest to the regulatory system and of little scholarly interest—notwithstanding conceptual links with control theory. The history of internal control is largely stylized as a 'natural' function of growing organizational complexity and the definition has varied considerably over time as the preferred scope of work of accountants and auditors changed (Hay, 1993; Mills, 1997).

As noted above, in the 1980s aspects of the internal control system of financial institutions became matters of regulatory concern following a number of scandals. Specific requirements to monitor capital adequacy and to separate client money, became increasingly significant aspects of the formal regulation of internal control in the financial sector. However, such requirements were piecemeal and did not relate to the internal control system as a whole until corporate governance principles demanded a systematic and all-encompassing approach. Significantly, the first 'conceptual framework' was published in 1992 in the USA (COSO, 1992). Following a congressional inquiry into fraudulent financial reporting, the Committee of Sponsoring Organizations of the Treadway Committee (COSO) published *Internal Control—Integrated Framework*. Although technical guidance for external auditors on the subject of internal control was in existence, this was the first broad, formal design covering not just controls relating to financial accounting, the typical focus of auditors, but also regulatory compliance matters and operations more generally. This expansion and formalization of the internal control agenda by COSO was a critical development in the category, and established a baseline framework for subsequent guidance to management across the world. COSO has become widely diffused as a significant reference point and resource for regulatory design in many areas.[18]

The COSO approach requires that the design and operation of controls be linked to, and follow from, a prior process of risk assessment. The framework came to be represented as a 'pyramid' and then as a 'cube' of elements which define an integrated approach. Control design is explicitly related to the assessment of risk to entity objectives and sub-objectives. From the early 1990s onwards, internal control activity could be understood and imagined in relation to organizational objectives and strategy. The COSO framework is symptomatic of the more general trend in claims for the 'strategic' significance of control functions and their coding as opportunities rather than costs, as described in Chapter 1. COSO (1992) delineates a broad conceptual map for internal control, which simultaneously opens up a space for the new advisory services as discussed above, not least in assisting organizations to understand their 'control environments'. The idea of control environment or culture has become widely regarded as important, particularly by regulators, and equally widely regarded as difficult to measure and control. COSO places internal control into a new regulatory space; it is now much more than a collection of control routines and tests—it sets the ethical 'tone' of the organization, and is the formal manifestation of trustworthiness as discussed earlier.[19]

The COSO framework set the stage for a new transnational discourse about internal control and its place in governance.[20] In 1995, the Canadian Institute of Certified Accountant's sub-committee, the Criteria of Control Board (CoCo), published *Guidance on Control*. This document extended the strategic significance of risk-based control activities to encompass the entire organization and not just the areas of financial reporting, compliance, and operations. In addition, CoCo places greater emphasis on values, ethics, and learning than the COSO framework (Kinney, 2000). While these frameworks are in some sense competitive and representatives seek to differentiate them from one another, they are also mutually supportive in constructing the regulatory significance for internal control as a managerial process of fundamental importance to organizational governance (IFAC, 2006).

In the UK, while the Cadbury report had affirmed the principle of Directors' responsibilities for internal control, efforts to address the content of this requirement in more detail were delayed until the publication of the 'Turnbull' Report (ICAEW, 1999a), the UK's own, shorter, version of COSO's risk-based approach to internal control. The identification of internal control and risk management in the Turnbull report firmly established a broader accountability and governance context for technical risk analysis (Page and Spira, 2002: 642). Like Cadbury, the Turnbull report became a reference point well beyond its original intentions by becoming an all-purpose blueprint for risk management for housing associations, universities, hospitals, and many other organizations in addition to listed companies.[21] Insurers and their professional associations found in Turnbull a key point of reference and leverage with insured entities. It became a platform for insurance brokers to extend their risk management and mitigation advisory practices beyond selling insurance. By the late-1990s organizations like Marsh and Aon were competing directly with firms like PricewaterhouseCoopers and KPMG in the 'Turnbull space'. Non-governmental bodies and associations have also used the Turnbull guidance to promote engagement in the name of governance. In short, the 'Turnbull' report effect in the UK was and remains extensive.[22]

The emergence of internal control has not been confined to the accounting field. Of equal significance for management and regulatory thinking has been the development of standards for management systems in general. Having its origins in an engineering-technocratic conception of quality control for industrial process, the creation of a generic management standard—BS5750— by the British Standards Institute (BSI) in 1979 marked a profound shift in the quality agenda from the prescription of minimal acceptable technical specifications to an emphasis on management process. In effect, BSI created a basic management system blueprint which formed the basis for ISO 9000 and has been widely adopted and adapted throughout the world (Tate, 2001). ISO 9000 in turn gave rise to a series of tailored versions of quality assurance, notably the ISO 14000 series of norms for environmental management systems which has become a significant reference point in environmental regulation.[23] Applications of this general model are visible in workplace safety (Hood et al., 1992: 162) forestry management (Meidinger, 2002) and many other fields.

The production of norms about control systems in the area of technical operations was already part of the operational landscape of firms in the early 1980s, drawing its intellectual foundations from systems theory and homeostatic models of control (Hood, 1996). System performance is conceptualized as self-monitoring in relation to exogenously determined triggers. This model and its related practices constituted a managerial disciplinary field, which was largely distinct from the field of controls over financial reporting until the concept of internal control was expanded by COSO. This overlap and convergence, made possible by shared implicit systems models, created opportunities for accountants to populate new management areas. For example, it became possible for accountants to target the environmental auditing field as part of the expansion of assurance services more generally (Brewer and Mills, 1994; Power, 1997a). Competition between accountants and process engineers as quality or environmental systems certifiers was only possible because of the conceptual similarity between internal controls and quality management systems. Indeed, internal control in the accountants' sense can be understood as a quality control process for financial statements. So, regardless of detailed differences and origins, both COSO and ISO 9000 share a formal structure as cybernetic models which embody a statement of function with monitoring and feedback, and subject to a generic audit of their effectiveness (Karapetrovic and Wilborn, 2000).

Quality management systems have been realized in different ways (Casper and Hancke, 1999), but their operational abstraction has enabled the rapid diffusion and adoption of the standard as an organizing idea in both management and regulation (Furusten, 2000; Coglianese and Lazer, 2003). In addition to the environmental field, quality assurance approaches are visible in many other areas, such as hospital management and university teaching. It is therefore no surprise that the quality management systems model was formally extended to encompass risk management, since 'risk' and 'quality' are two increasingly overlapping categories for organizing the management of uncertainty, and both have been mobilized by similar logics of opportunity and enterprise. In 1995 the first national-level risk management standard was published jointly by the Australian and New Zealand standards organizations and was used as a blueprint for controls assurance in the UK National Health Service. Notwithstanding differences in detail, this standard and its subsequent versions, share a similar conception of risk management design as COSO, CoCo, and Turnbull. This design is explicitly intended to be certifiable and auditable.

It has been argued that the publication of COSO transformed fundamental criticisms of the accountancy profession by the Treadway commission into new product opportunities for that same profession (Brilloff, 2001). The Cadbury code has been interpreted in similar terms (Freedman, 1993) and critics of quality management systems argue that their self-evidence belies a new phase in the bureaucratic control of labour and has more to do with discipline than enterprise and autonomy (Wilkinson and Willmott, 1995). From these different viewpoints it is clear that the rise of internal control systems as a core feature of organizational governance is more than a minor administrative matter; it is a carrier of values. Internal control lies at the heart of a complex political economy of organization and regulation. More and better control and risk management systems are demanded in the wake of scandals and failure as an 'administrative fix' which intensifies the need to make such systems auditable. Yet the internal control system has also become invested with values of enterprise which characterize organizational virtue. Within governance discourses, internal control systems have become regarded as the formal responsibility of management.

In summary, in a relatively short period of time, the private world of organizational internal control systems has been turned inside out, made public, codified, standardized, and recategorized as risk management, thereby also creating a renewed object of research interest (Maijoor, 2000; Kinney, 2000). During the 1990s internal control came to be thought of in the broadest terms as an 'enterprise-wide' practice and as the foundation for an explicitly risk-based approach to control. Regulatory strategies for working with the grain of organizational control systems sought to build on the business incentives for controls in a wide variety of areas, such as solvency, capital adequacy, health, safety, environment, business continuity, teaching, waste management. From a mixture of conceptual elements, internal control has been constructed as a regulatory resource, as an advisory opportunity, as a strategic necessity and as a way of governing the management of risk. A blueprint for extending the reach of risk management into every aspect of organizational life has been created (Power, 2004c). The essential variety of organizational and individual activity can now be re-described in terms of a meta-process for handling risk. The logical end point of this process of turning organizations inside out is a public reporting function focused on internal controls and risk management. However, this has also been one of the most sensitive areas for development.

Going Public on Private Control

Specific risk and control related disclosures for corporations have existed since the 1990s. Many jurisdictions require disclosures about derivatives, going concern, contingencies, and provisions. In the USA, the operating and financial review and other filing requirements contain risk disclosure provisions and many banks provide much more information as part of industry practice.[24] In the UK, there has been considerable discussion about risk reporting (ICAEW, 1997b; 1999b) and an Operating and Financial Review (OFR) was proposed which requires organizations to disclose key risk indicators (ASB, 2005). Although the OFR was formally abolished in November 2005, it is likely that risk disclosure practices will emerge (ASB, 2005; Power, 2007). In Germany, the Control and Transparency Act (KonTrAG) strengthened the role of supervisory boards by requiring them to establish a monitoring system for risk identification (Pausenberger and Nassauer, 2000; Weber and Liekweg, 2000). The newly formed German Accounting Standards Board (GASB) also published German Accounting Standard (GAS) 5 in 2001 which takes its lead from COSO and defines risk management as a 'comprehensive set of control procedures'. Like the ill-fated UK OFR, the standard requires a single report on risks 'affecting future developments' and a description of the system in the management report (Dobler, 2005).

All these various specific disclosures could be said to relate to specific risk 'objects'; they contain no requirement to comment on the effectiveness of the risk management system as a whole, as the original principles of the Cadbury Code require (paragraph 4.4). When the Code was published, there followed much practitioner debate both about the meaning and 'auditability' of 'internal control effectiveness' from the point of view of an external auditor, and about the nature of any public opinion on such matters. In the UK, the Rutteman report in 1994 had proposed a form of limited reporting on internal control, but the proposal stalled (ICAEW, 1994; 1995). In the United States, the Public Oversight Board (of the AICPA) published *In the Public Interest* in 1993 which recommended public reporting on internal control to the SEC; subsequently the POB Board published its *Audit Effectiveness Report* (The O'Malley Report) recommending that audit committees spend more time on internal control. The General Accounting Office Report on the Accounting Profession in 1996 also supported internal control reporting, and there were ongoing pressures for reporting on the effectiveness of internal control in Canada, led by the Toronto Stock Exchange. In 1998 the UK Audit Practices Board published a discussion document on the subject of providing assurance on internal control which builds on the COSO framework (APB, 1998) and the ICAEW (1999b) proposed the publication of a statement of business risk as some version of the organizational risk map (see Chapter 3). Caveats and caution can be read between the lines in all these documents reflecting an institutionalized unwillingness by both directors and auditors to venture a public opinion on effectiveness as a 'hostage to fortune' (Spira and Page, 2003: 648). When the dust settled on the debate, UK Directors were required only to report on whether they had completed a review of effectiveness, rather than on its substance.

While private advisory services for internal control and risk management began to thrive in the 1990s, and were marketed in terms of opportunity, value and enterprise, public reporting on these matters was shrouded in caution and blame avoidance (Hermanson, 2000). Slowly, qualitative non-mandated public disclosures about internal control and risk management grew as part of governance reporting more generally. The fact of Directors' responsibility for maintaining a sound system of internal control became a standard assertion, as did caveats about the necessary limitations of any system of control. Internal control systems slowly became a more prominent object of public disclosure despite the reluctance to make general statements on control effectiveness. Then the world changed. Enron and other companies collapsed and the rapid passing of Sarbanes–Oxley legislation created new public certification requirements.[25] Corporate risk management had been seen to fail (Rosen, 2003b) and companies were now forced to do something they had previously avoided and had regarded as difficult, costly and boring (Chan et al., 2006).

It is no exaggeration to suggest that Sarbox took the existing market for internal controls advice and created an industry, even to the point of stretching the internal resources of the large professional service firms to their limits. A great deal of commentary has been focused on the costs and benefits of section 404 which requires a public certification by senior officers of the effectiveness of internal control systems over financial reporting, meaning that they contain no 'material weaknesses' in their design or operation.[26] Criticisms of the first two years of implementation drew attention to the bureaucracy and cost created by the need to document controls in minute and low-level detail to support 404 certifications, particularly where the spectacular governance lapses have involved much higher levels of control failure.[27] Auditors have been blamed for failing to adopt a risk-based approach, thereby amplifying the requirements. Concern was expressed that some companies may delist and 'go dark' and that these requirements may prove to be an uncompetitive barrier to IPOs. In contrast, enthusiasts held fast to rhetorics of opportunity and argued for the advantages of being able to prove what had hitherto been assumed. They suggested that much of the early cost was fixed in nature and unlikely to recur on this scale.

The SEC conducted consultative reviews of experience in 2005 and 2006 and these discussions, which will stretch into the future, will be further animated as non-US resident SEC registrants report under the legislation for the first time.[28] What cannot be disputed is the role of this legislation in placing internal controls reporting at the very heart of efforts to improve the financial statement aspects of corporate governance. A 'section 404' advisory industry was created at a stroke, hence the nickname for Sarbox as the 'accountant's friend'. The legislation positions internal control systems as part of an operating philosophy of getting things right first time. It remains to be seen whether this emphasis on reporting on the process of producing financial statements will become more significant for regulators than the financial statements themselves; internal control systems now have the potential to become the *primary* regulatory and managerial reporting object.

The rise in the regulatory and managerial significance of internal control systems since the publication of the Cadbury report in 1992 has been dramatic but the question of public reporting on internal control as a risk management system has always been problematic. Even if the problem of incentives might be overcome by drastic legislation, there are continuing issues in determining the meaning of terms like 'effectiveness' and 'material weakness.' Such difficulties in the opinion process apply equally to the internal reporting process as boards consider internal control statements for sign-off. Just as terms like 'true and fair' and 'fairly present' have dogged the interpretation of financial statements, so the concept of effectiveness will also affect the interpretation of internal controls statements. In such cases, it may matter less what such terms mean, as this is a potentially endless discussion. It is more a question of who is trusted in organizations and regulatory fields to determine their meaning. Who, in short, is an internal control and risk expert? An important candidate for this role is the internal auditor.

The Internal Auditor as Risk Manager

For many years, internal auditors have operated in the shadow of the external auditor. Notwithstanding scholarship and commentary in journals such as *Managerial Auditing* and *Internal Auditor*, they have often been thought of as an adjunct of a statutory auditing process. Thus, economic conceptions of internal auditing often trade its costs against savings in external auditing, and early professional guidance focused on the conditions under which reliance might be placed on the internal auditor in conducting that work. Lack of barriers to entry and a fragmented professional status, despite the efforts of the Institute of Internal Auditors (IIA), positioned internal auditors as poor relations. They were a necessary function but with limited organizational and institutional significance (O'Regan, 2001).

All of this began to change with the rise of internal control and the changes in regulatory style described above, something anticipated by ICAS (1993) and a number of other commentators. The large accounting firms sought new markets in outsourced internal auditing in the 1990s, a move which proved highly controversial in the USA (Rittenberg and Covaleski,

2001; Covaleski *et al.*, 2003; Robson *et al.*, 2007) but which also helped to raise the profile of the internal audit function by blurring the methodological boundaries between the two practices; risk-based approaches developed for the external audit were applied in internal audit practices.[29] These market developments have also seen internal audit departments transform themselves into niche consultancies.[30] In the UK the original Turnbull report devoted considerable attention to the internal auditor (and little to the external auditor).

The mutation of the category of internal control into risk management therefore became both a threat and an opportunity for internal auditors to establish a position in the 'system of professions' (Abbott, 1988). On the one hand, it was a threat because the new significance tempted the large accounting firms to offer outsourced internal audit services. On the other hand it was an opportunity for internal auditors to position themselves as risk experts (Rezaee, 1995; McNamee and McNamee, 1995; Selim and McNamee, 1999) providing 'value added' services (ICAEW, 2000a; Nagy and Cenker, 2002). The IIA, a world umbrella organization with many loosely federated member bodies, consistently emphasized the significance of internal auditing in the wake of criticisms of the external audit function. From the mid 1990s onwards the IIA was active in publishing guidance—specifically adopting and promoting risk-based approaches to internal audit and leadership on risk management more generally with a strong operational and IT focus (Colbert and Alderman, 1995).[31]

Prior to this 'metamorphosis' of the concept of internal audit (Spira and Page, 2003), it had been subject to its own internal pressures for reform which can be traced in part back to specific organizational experiences. In the 1970s individuals such as Paul Makosz, head of audit at Gulf Canada, pioneered new participative approaches to internal control under the label of Control Self Assessment (CSA) (see Leech and McCuaig, 1999; Wade, 1999).[32] In this particular case, the dominant engineering-based control culture of the organization came to be regarded as problematic and as a source of operational and control risk. Internal agents of organizational change promoted the ideal of a new kind of control knowledge and Gulf recognized the need to think beyond the idea of internal control as a specialist functional area. CSA promotes a logic of control within organizations which is similar to quality 'ownership'. Questions of risk communication were at the heart of CSA as a 'soft' tool for accessing collective tacit risk knowledge in organizations, and then formalizing it in collectively owned registers. Control became more sensitive to the internal 'sociology' of organizations and CSA workshops functioned to cement individual and organizational commitment to control.

CSA style practices remain a significant resource for regulatory regimes as forms of self-assessment (Russell 1996) and debates about corporate governance provide the CSA specialists with new market potential. For internal auditors, CSA was an opportunity to cast the control and risk agenda much wider than hitherto; CSA co-developed with claims for a new identity for the internal auditor—as teacher, facilitator, and overseer of organizational control more broadly defined (Wynne, 1999). CSA ideas shifted the concept of audit from a disciplinary, backward-facing, transactions-based practice involving narrowly defined expertise to one which was forward-looking, anticipatory, and explicitly risk-based, and which saw itself as providing knowledge leadership and risk management advice in organizations (Leech, 1997). This was a shift from a disciplinary framing of work to one which draws on the tropes and values of enterprise culture. The IIA's policy developments are good examples of the pervasiveness of the logic of opportunity within discourses of control.

Beyond the rhetoric and visionary aspiration for the organizational significance of internal auditors (Spira and Page, 2003: 657–8), much depends in specific cases on their organizational position in relation to other control agents and technical specialists. It was reported that IBM separated periodic risk-based internal audits and more continuous CSA activity (Goble, 1997); whereas Sears gave the internal auditor oversight for the control review of the entire organization (Mercer, 1997). More generally, the internal organizational jurisdiction of the internal auditor can often be unclear and the overlap with CSA work is variable. The case of the internal auditor reflects a more general phenomenon created by the re-description of internal control as risk management, namely the struggle by advisory and control groups for organizational significance, a struggle defined by appeals to the strategic relevance of their control skills (Makosz, 2005). In part, the issue centres on the relations of dependency and sub-contracting which are worked out between accounting and non-accounting expertise in the internal field of risk assurance services (Power, 1996a). In some organizations this leaves internal audit with a higher order oversight or surveying function as internal inspectors and facilitators, a role which may lead to turf battles with human resource specialists who also see CSA as an opportunity for professional redesign. It may also leave the internal auditor with an 'expectations gap' between professional aspirations to become a high level advisor and management demands to detect fraud and errors. To say this is to acknowledge that internal auditing has always worked close to the border territory of many internal disciplines with a claim on the risk management process. A continuing occupational challenge for internal auditors with accounting and systems expertise is their capacity to contribute to the analytical and technical aspects of the management of risk in different sub-fields. Accordingly, their specific organizational significance depends on the local legitimacy of a process-based view of risk management (Selim and McNamee, 1999).

Internal auditors have been exhorted to 'think risk and survive' (Brilliant, 1998), to make the strategic and risk-oriented changes to their practice and to become internal business risk surveyors and 'adders of value' (e.g., Bou-Raad, 2000). However, as the question of internal auditor independence from management has been debated as part of governance more generally, many large organizations now try to separate sharply a risk management function from an independent internal assurance function. The rise of the chief risk officer (chapter 3) may further dilute the internal auditor's claims on advice and facilitation. Practices like CSA are an opportunity to re-engineer the conception of the internal auditor, but there are no great barriers to entry for this kind of work. The internal auditor has also experienced Sarbox as a dilemma. On the one hand, it has been an opportunity to acquire organizational significance by supporting management in its efforts to design and document appropriate internal controls (Cenker and Nagy, 2004; Harrington, 2004). On the other hand, such a role compromises the independent assurance function and gives the impression that the internal auditor owns the process, rather than management.

In summary, we should distinguish carefully between the rise of the category of 'internal control' as a newly public regulatory object, and the fortunes of an existing occupational group who may, or may not, call themselves 'internal auditors'. The category of 'internal audit', which had been perceived as insufficiently enterprising in the 1980s, has made a comeback as a consequence of regulatory institutionalization via the Turnbull report and Sarbox. In the UK, the category has been stabilized by the FSA which has expressed a wish to place greater reliance on the internal audit function. The designation of 'Internal auditor' refers to quasi-regulatory agents in *neoliberal* regulatory and governance regimes who work within organizations via persuasion, interaction and example and who rely on the organic pressure of 'best practice' norms linked to world-level discourses of governance (Rose and Miller, 1992; Pildes and Sunstein, 1995). These discourses now provide the necessary, if not quite the sufficient, conditions for these agents to have a new organizational authority. Yet, internal control has also become more significant than the internal auditor.

Conclusions

Organizations concerned with the production of normative frameworks for governance in general, and corporate governance in particular, have grown rapidly in the 1990s. These frameworks embody two intertwined logics: a neoliberal managerial logic which draws heavily on the intellectual resources of economics and principal-agent theory as well as from practical disciplines such as accounting; and a rights-based participative logic which draws from democratic and critical theories (Drori, 2006). This chapter argues that this explosion of governance has intensified public policy attention to the *internal* organization and design of large entities. While the role of external auditing, monitoring and inspection has not been superseded, demonstrable capacities for self-control and self-observation have grown in regulatory importance. In this way, governance discourse has created a new political economy of internal control; internal control and risk management have become demanded as core values of a new 'grammar' or 'policy paradigm' (Hall, 1989) for corporate governance.

To understand the supply of internal control ideas and designs, we considered a number of specific pressures for change in the financial auditing function. Efforts to redesign the external audit, both to be more business risk-based and also as a platform for further assurance services, created a professional focus on internal controls and led to experimentation in forms of private assurance for the management process. Thus, professional services markets were already positioning themselves in the emerging area of internal governance and control prior to the collapse of Enron. The Sarbanes–Oxley legislation in 2002 accelerated and radicalized these developments.

Throughout the 1990s, ideas about internal control and about risk management were increasingly co-mingled, beginning with COSO (1992) and extending to the Turnbull report in the UK. Despite differences in emphasis among the various governance codes and blueprints published in the 1990s, including those in the field of quality assurance, very similar high-level emphases on internal control as a management process are evident (IFAC, 2006). And notwithstanding the undoubted variation in the implementation of these ideas, the concept of risk-based internal control has come to be a source of isomorphic pressure across organizations, across industries, and across the private–public divide. The idea of risk-based internal control has become both a resource for regulation and, via a number of blueprints to be discussed in Chapter 3, a model for regulation itself. At the transnational level organizations like OECD and the World Bank promote the importance of internal controls in government as part of their own governance.

The rise of internal control and its re-designation as 'risk management' represents a new 'grand narrative' of control. As a source of self-evident, self-supporting authority, the concept of internal control now substitutes for the state. The definition of internal control has always varied in nuance and scope, but this vagueness has been important to its recent significance and allowed it to accommodate the two logics of governance described above. Internal control is a 'boundary object' (see Chapter 1) in so far as policy-makers in many domains can think of 'better internal control' as a desirable solution path. Managerial and insurance practices also see the concept of internal control as a basis for rethinking and representing themselves with a renewed strategic importance; and stakeholder organizations can hold organizations to account for the quality of their self-control.

The emergence of internal control as depicted in this chapter is an attempt to tell a story of the dynamics of an idea, how this idea comes to shape the way in which control practices depict themselves and how practitioner understandings are reframed, often via intense circuits of discourse, such as conferences. From this point of view, defining a fixed concept of internal control is less interesting than observing the capacity of the idea in its various institutional manifestations to shape managerial and regulatory practices, practices which will produce definitions for their own operational purposes. As a methodological prescription 'dynamic nominalism' demands that we view 'internal control' and 'risk management' not as descriptive categories which refer to a clear object, but as contested stakes in an internal regulatory space, a space in which the internal auditors and others seek representation collectively and individually. Internal control is something which these different groups seek to perform, codify in rational form, and own.

The topic of internal control in organizations has never been part of mainstream management research, reflecting no doubt its position in the hierarchy of management knowledge and its primary association with auditing. Compared with the body of scholarship on management accounting and management control more generally this is surprising since there is considerable overlap. For many years, the subject of internal control has been a private matter for a sub-group of technical control and assurance specialists, a largely pragmatic field populated by technical journals. Control systems and monitoring may figure abstractly in principal-agent theories of organizational design, but the practice by which corporations, corner shops, clubs, and churches maintain a basic level of financial and non-financial control over resources, has hardly been worthy of serious intellectual attention.

Today, in 2006, the new governing centrality of internal control is such a part of common-sense that we forget the very short period of time over which it has come about. Internal control systems and their presumed effectiveness are now issues for public policy and formal law. Over a fifteen-year period, *private* organization internal control has come to play a very significant external *public* role in regulatory programmes. Organizations ranging from major companies to universities continue to be turned 'inside out' on the basis of rational designs for control. Internal control has been fashioned as a mode of organizing and processing uncertainty which demands the *externalization,* justification, and auditability of organizational control arrangements.

This transformation and transition in the institutional life of the organizational internal control system, from humble adjunct of management to a blueprint for the management of enterprise-wide risk, illustrates the generic shift from risk analysis to risk governance mentioned in Chapter 1. Internal control and management systems translate primary or first order risks into systems and control risks. Diverse risk content gets transformed into auditable process via warning mechanisms, compliance violation alerts and 'near miss' reports. Many varied sources of uncertainty get represented and made governable by organizational processes of control (although indicators for rare but serious events are the most significant challenge as we shall see in Chapter 4). For example, the BSE crisis gave rise to a renewed regulatory emphasis on farm management systems; the regulation of GM crops has focused on systems for traceability; the experience of earthquakes has intensified concerns with systems for enforcing building regulations. In the medical field, clinical risk management was originally conceptualized in terms of accidental harms done to patients during the care delivery process. Now it is part of a regulatory regime concerned with the effectiveness of health care in general, a matter of health care organizational control systems rather than specific clinicians (Walshe and Sheldon, 1998).

Internal control is much more than an instrument of control; it has become a form of governing rationality for the organization of organizations, including the agencies of the regulatory state. Internal control does not simply make governance 'better', it brings a certain style of governance into existence which reaches into every corner of organizational life. Internal control instrumentalizes neoliberal logics of governance. Good internal control is regarded as a signal of a certain kind of organizational virtue, and a potential platform for the representation and coordination of external interests.[33] Rationalized control systems will continue to be regarded as a legitimate response to crisis, even as their limitations are recognized, because they express this dominant logic of governing.

Notes

1. The original recommendations for companies were subsequently refined. In 1995 the Greenbury report introduced provisions on remuneration. The code was revised by the Hampel Committee in 1998 which also framed governance in terms of a logic of opportunity and value; corporate governance may have had its origins in scandal, but it was to be 'good for business'. In 2003, the Higgs report dealt with the role of non-executive directors and a new consolidated code was produced—the Combined Code (FSA, 2003).

2. For example, in Canada the Dey Committee published its recommendations in 1994; France published a code in 1995—the Vienot Report; the OECD published generic principles of corporate governance in 1999; a code of best practice for Quoted German Companies was published in July 2000. See also, Cheffins (2000) on Britain as an exporter of governance codes, Vinten (1998) and Drori (2006) on the role of transnational institutes for disseminating corporate governance 'scripts'.

3. See Boli and Thomas (1999); Hutter (2006); Djelic and Sahlin-Andersson (2006a); Ericson and Doyle (2004); Drori (2006).

4. In the areas of 'treating customers fairly' (TCF) and financial crime.

5. The deterrent ideal is to secure conformity to social or legal norms by regulating to detect and punish violators. It is essentially an *ex post* function and is argued to be the most effective regulatory option when it is necessary to control the behaviour of discrete and dispersed individuals by acting as a disincentive to violation.

6. It has been argued that this is an effective ideal for controlling the behaviour of individuals in organized activities where there is a distinct and definable population of potential violators who can be monitored According to Reiss (1984: 32): 'the basic systems of surveillance by inspection and of investigation, including audit, are far less restricted in compliance than in deterrence based systems. What we wish to emphasize here is that techniques of detection and proof that are considerably restricted in deterrence based systems are far more likely to be legitimated in compliance based systems, especially where one seeks to control the behaviour of organizations or of organized activity.' See also Parker (2000) who defines the compliance mode somewhat differently in terms of a tight definition of desired regulatory outcome coupled to flexibility regarding the methods of achieving this outcome.

7. See 'Bank recruits to bolster supervision role', *Financial Times*, 11 November 1996.

8. For a discussion of the tensions facing reporting accountants who must manage duties to both regulators and to clients, see Dewing and Russell (2005).

9. Shapiro also includes other control measures, such as liability systems and forms of collateral security, to provide agents with incentives for compliance. Although liability systems can be regarded as a deterrence strategy, insurance companies increasingly impose compliance systems on the insured as a condition of liability cover.

10. I owe this point to Christine Parker.

11. See Skidmore *et al.* (2003).

12. See also: ICAS/ICAEW, (1989); ICAS, (1993); APB, (1994); CIPFA, (1994); Hatherly, (1995); Elliott, (1995); ICAEW, (1997a), (1997b); AICPA, (1996).

13. Elliott (1995) distinguishes in a similar way between rethinking the audit and 'line extensions' of basic audit competences into the wider arena of assurance services.

14. See also Roger Davis, 'Time May be Ripe for a "Fourth Generation Audit" ', *Financial Times*, 10 August 1995.

15. These efforts to redesign the financial audit intensified concerns by practitioners to articulate and defend their independence. For example, in North America the Independence Standards Board was created to articulate principles of independence as a 'core' professional value (Kinney, 1999). So the redesign of financial auditing, by threatening independence, has also intensified regulatory and professional concerns with it. In the post-Enron world, independence has acquired a new value and status.

16. The Business Risk Audit (BRA) did not suddenly appear. It was a reconceptualization of older practices of controls assurance, such as SEADOC in the 1970s and 1980s (Systems Evaluation Approach: Documentation of Controls). I am grateful to Keith Robson for pointing this out to me.

17. In cooperation with academics at the University of Illinois at Urbana-Champaign, KPMG backed this initiative with a research programme. See also Robson *et al.* (2007).

18. For example, see various public speeches by Governor Susan Schmidt Bies of the Federal Reserve Board at http://www.federalreserve.gov/boarddocs/speeches/2006/. COSO has also been a significant framework in fields of health and clinical governance.

19. The significance of the control environment has led to many efforts to devise proxies, risk factors and red flags which create auditability and actionability for the concept.

20. For a Dutch interpretation of the implications of COSO, see Hartman (1994).

21. In 1990 the Business Support Group of the ICAEW published: 'Managing Business Risk'. This document reflected generic concepts of business risk management long before the production of formal standards as discussed in Chapter 3.

22. The report was revised in 2005 by a committee chaired by Douglas Flint. The revision stopped short of requiring public reporting on internal control but urged companies to say more in this area.

23. Critics have argued that these system standards are of doubtful benefit to the natural environment. See Aalders (1993); Watson and Emery (2004).

24. While there is considerable content in the form of financial risk disclosures by banks and other financial institutions, analysts argue that this information is not standardized and it is very difficult to compare results even for apparently similar practices, such as VaR. Thus, whereas accounting has achieved a good deal of standardization and hence comparability, risk disclosure has not (Woods *et al.*, 2004).

25. These requirements were not new in concept; the Cohen Commission in the 1970s had recommended something similar. See Chan *et al.* (2006: 3).

26. A similar requirement to section 404 has been proposed in Canada.

27. See Ira Solomon and Mark Peecher, 'SOS 404—A Billion Here, a Billion There', *Wall Street Journal Manager's Journal*, B1 9 November 2004.

28. See Solomon and Peecher, note 27; Tackett *et al.* (2006). See also 'Under Fire: Auditing Standard Number Two', *CFO.com* 8 May 2006; 'Panel: Don't "Audit Low Level Risks"', *CFO.com* 10 May 2006; 'Sarbox Rollback Bill Introduced', *CFO.com* 17 May 2006. For the SEC 2006 briefing see http://www.sec.gov/spotlight/soxcomp/soxcomp-briefing0506.htm.

29. See, 'Internal Audit Moves Out', *Accountancy Age*, 24 July 1997. Outsourcing of internal auditing also became significant in the public sector. See Bowerman *et al.* (2000) and Goodwin (2004).

30. For the case of Specialist Audit Services, see 'Into the Audit Action with SAS', *Accountancy Age*, 9 October 1997, 26.

31. See IIA publications at http://www.theiia.org.

32. Makosz subsequently chaired the Criteria of Control board in Canada.

33. See Shamir (2004; 2005) who vigorously contests the neoliberal accommodation of CSR. See also Parker (forthcoming) for a response to his critique.

3

Standardizing Risk Management: Making up Processes and People

Chapter 2 traced the emerging regulatory significance of internal control and its reframing as risk management. The COSO, CoCo, and Turnbull frameworks are standards which formalize fundamental design principles for the organizational self-management of risk, and which establish normative baselines against which organizations must evaluate themselves. Indeed, the field of risk management in all its variety is symptomatic of the emerging 'world of standards' (Brunnson and Jacobsson, 2000) which permeates organizations of all shapes and sizes. Reformist discourses of organizational governance have generated an industry of norm production for organizational conduct. Recent decades have witnessed an expansion of organizing in general via a multiplicity of transnational organizations who codify, formalize, and publish standards of practice (Meyer, 2002).

Scholarly and policy interest in the nature of these diverse norm production processes, whether characterized as 'private government' or 'soft law', 'decentred regulation' or 'global governance', have grown in response to these developments (Boli and Thomas, 1999; Djelic and Sahlin-Andersson, 2006b). Work in many social scientific fields such as international relations, political science, law, economics, management, and accounting, has become preoccupied with transnational organizations, their role in projects of standardization, their relationships with states and formal law, and their capacity to generate conformity, acceptance, and compliance. Boundaries between disciplines and organization types have become blurred as a result of converging interest in the private production of rules and standards, a production process embedded within broader programmatic discourses of, and pressures for, 'better' organizational governance (Drori, 2006). This chapter examines a specific sub-sector of this world of standards, namely the development, mobilization, and standardization of something commonly referred to under the umbrella concept of Enterprise Risk Management (ERM).

While industry technical guidance on the management of specific risks existed prior to 1995, that year saw the publication of the first explicitly generic risk management standard—a joint document by the Australian and New Zealand Standards organizations which built on earlier global standards for quality management systems. This was quickly followed by counterparts in Canada, UK, and Japan. In addition, professional associations and firms entered the field of standard setting for risk management.[1] ISO has developed standards for common risk management terminology (ISO/IEC, 2002) and broad process standards have been reapplied to specific areas, such as information security (e.g., COBIT). Most recently, COSO (2004) updated its earlier guidance on internal control and reframed it as a standard for 'enterprise' risk management. The risk management field is now awash with generic norms, standards and guidance which have been reapplied and adapted in specific sectors.

ERM has emerged as a significant category for rethinking the organization of risk management activities and there has been a conspicuous growth of normative and technical texts on the topic.[2] However, while there are various attempts to own the category, ERM should be understood as referring to any broadly based conception of risk management, encompassing ideas of 'holistic' (Hopkin, 2002), 'integrated' (Nottingham, 1997; AIRMIC, 1999; Doherty, 2000), and 'business' risk management (PwC/IFAC, 1999). The specific category of ERM is increasingly prominent and plays a critical discursive role. It signifies any aspiration for a form of risk management practice which is all encompassing in scope, business-focused, and is suggestive of a bird's eye view of organizational life. We should not assume that ERM refers unequivocally to a coherent set of practices. ERM as used in this setting must be understood from the outset as a label for a mixed bag of reformist, organizing sensibilities in the name of risk which have gathered momentum since the mid-1990s. Far from being a simple or unitary category referring to well understood processes and procedures, it would be better to regard

ERM as a semi-popular managerial discourse which exists at the interface between regulators, finance specialists, insurers, and accountants. The idea of ERM speaks to their varied interests as agents of organizational change and accountability.

If ERM is not uniquely owned, it is also not a single standard of the kind that is normally discussed in professional circles. It signifies an emergent and hybrid programme in Rose and Miller's (1992) sense, a programme of control in search of expression via clear standards of risk management as norms of organizing. ERM is an imagined organization-wide process of handling uncertainty and a category which mobilizes a number of projects of writing directed at standardizing the foundations of organizational control and governance. ERM signifies a basis for a new way of talking about control in organizations, one which appeals to enterprise rather than discipline. It is a discourse which envisages the integration of control and organizational strategy.

The discussion begins by recapping the conception of risk management as an essentially calculative practice, as discussed in Chapter 1. Ideas of ERM as developed in the fields of finance and insurance are considered, and the analysis focuses on the specific case of value at risk (VaR) as a risk measurement technology. This version of ERM is premised on the regulating ideal of calculating firm-wide economic capital, an ideal which runs up against many practical limitations, particularly in the area of operational risk (chapter 4), but which still retains a hold on the imagination of a sub-class of practitioners in the financial world. In contrast to this calculative 'grammar' of risk management, section 3 deals with an aspect of ERM thinking which is continuous with the transformation of internal control discussed in Chapter 2 and with the corporate governance reform discourse of the early 1990s. Here, risk analysis and measurement issues are subsumed within a broader risk governance process. While a number of different versions of this concept of ERM exist, the discussion will focus on the example of the COSO principles for internal control and their rewriting as a standard for something now explicitly called 'enterprise risk management' or ERM (COSO, 2004).

Section 4 analyses the emergence of new organizational agents of ERM, notably the chief risk officer role. Where Chapter 2 had considered the role of internal auditors in an increasingly crowded risk management field, this discussion focuses on the nature and jurisdiction of a head of risk, a role which accompanies the rise of audit and risk committees. It is argued that the

CRO role must contend with a number of operational conflicts in being a change agent for ERM. Regulatory systems, particularly in the field of financial services, increasingly require a head of risk and conformity to an accepted ERM framework, such as COSO (2004) or Turnbull. Section 5 argues that regulatory systems which seek to rely on organizational risk management practice also re-import this knowledge as a framework for their own role. Thus, ideas of risk-based regulation are discussed as a particular dimension of the ERM standardization process, namely the increasing isomorphism between regulatory and regulated organizational processes. ERM must therefore be understood as a body of popular organizational knowledge which is simultaneously managerial and regulatory.

Taken together, these four strands of argument suggest that the category of ERM is now prominent as an umbrella for a world-level organizational model, with more general significance for a new risk-based 'moral economy' of organizational life in general. ERM is 'global' both in the sense of being all-encompassing in ambition and also in being transnational in reach (Drori, 2006: 113). The rise of ERM is also an administrative manifestation of neoliberal pressures to transfer the conception of risk management from the negative space of the risk society to that of the 'opportunity' society populated by risk-taking entrepreneurs. In addition while ERM posits risk and its management as a fundamental constituent of the production of value, it also recodes calculative and administrative processes within a new kind of organizational 'actorhood' in which the 'ownership' of, and accountability for, risk, rather like quality in the 1980s, defines a domain of responsibility and virtue.

ERM as Risk Calculation

As noted in Chapter 1, the history of risk management has come to be associated with ever greater technical and calculative mastery of regularities in the natural world and human affairs. The emergence of probability theory, and the rise of institutions for gathering population statistics formed the bedrock of the actuarial sciences and the foundations of life insurance (Alborn, 1996; Ericson and Doyle, 2004: chapter 2). In the 1960s, risk analysis came to be understood as a discipline in its own right and during the 1980s and 1990s the emergence of financial economics, coupled to developments in information technology, intensified the management of financial risk (Hacking, 2003; Whitley, 1986; Rosen, 2003a). Risk was to be studied, analysed, and calculated as volatility in financial returns based on the mathematics of mean-variance analysis.

While it is well known in both theory and practice that risk calculation depends at critical junctures on human judgement, a technical ideal of risk understood as a product of the likelihood and impact of an event has been at the centre of the risk management collective imagination, defining a broad community of specialists united in the belief that managing risk demands measurement. For this community ERM signifies nothing less than a programme to develop a 'whole of enterprise' risk metric. Pressures for such a whole of business view became evident in the field of insurance when assumptions of risk transfer came to be challenged by large companies. Critical of their existing, fragmented insurance strategies, and with an advanced grasp of their own loss experiences, some organizations preferred to retain and self-manage many risks which they might previously have transferred. Insurance organizations responded by developing risk management consultancy and advisory practices which, in the name of reducing client risk and premiums, increasingly focused on governance and risk control.[3] Companies like BP Amoco in the 1990s calculated that premiums could be reduced by consolidating hitherto separate insurance lines.[4] In this way ERM, as a demand for the identification of all collective risks that affect company value as a whole, could take into account the diversification benefits of viewing risks together which were traditionally managed and insured as separately defined 'lines'. ERM was managerially constructed in terms of improved recognition of 'natural hedges' and 'unanticipated correlations' across financial risk categories within organizations (Rouyer, 2002). As a consequence, new multi-risk policies developed and led to a calculable benefit in the form of reduced premium costs (Meulbroek, 2002b: 58), something which gave economic substance to the logic of opportunity inherent in ERM. More generally, the conception of an enterprise as a portfolio of asset classes with corresponding risks is central to the idea of ERM as risk calculation and blurs the practical distinction between financing and insuring.

The financial risk management function has a recent history rooted in specific organizational experiences which were externalized and projected as a field of technical expertise (Field, 2002a). For example, material losses on mortgage-backed securities suffered at Merrill Lynch in March 1987 resulted in the creation of one of the first dedicated risk management units in a financial organization, albeit defensively oriented to prevent future events of a similar kind. In 1987, very few organizations had an explicit and formal risk management strategy; the role lacked credibility and a collectivized organizational memory or dramatology of risk events did not yet exist. In this early period the risk management function was more or less that of transaction clearance with right of veto, and there were no immediate pressures to institutionalize a new trans-organizational function. Indeed, over time the new unit created at Merrill lost power and existing techniques of risk analysis were relatively slow to find an operational basis in firms (Wood, 2002b).

The analysis of financial risk changed fundamentally in the 1990s for a number of reasons, not least perceptions about the potential for technology to support the applications of finance theory, challenges to regulatory conservatism for calculating capital, and pressures for a new performance culture for financial institutions as part of a popular reform discourse. Accordingly to Doherty (2000: 9–10), the fundamental theory of finance, in which returns on assets are always relative to risk, had made risk management a conceptually thinkable part of the corporate value creation process since the 1960s. However, though thinkable, that model had to wait until the early 1990s for an institutional climate of financialization which was receptive to the general extension of advanced finance theory to organizational practice, such as the modeling of 'real options' for strategic purposes (Rosen, 2003a; Ciborra, 2006; Shiller, 2003: chapter 5).[5]

An important event was the publication by J. P. Morgan in 1993 of its *RiskMetrics* technology for calculating capital at risk—the first attempt at the 'standardization' of 'value-at-risk' (Kavanagh, 2003; Scaillet, 2003). This came at a time when banking regulators were discussing the potential to recognize 'in-house' risk models as a basis for assessing adequacy of capital for banks and other financial institutions. The traditional approach to regulating the capital adequacy of financial institutions by the hierarchical prescription of detailed rules, rules which in any case provided opportunities for creative arbitrage, was also being criticized for being anti-competitive and arbitrary (Mengle, 2003b). *RiskMetrics* was a treatise on the application of 'value at risk' techniques and an attempt to create an industry standard by a powerful organization.

Like most techniques of risk analysis, VaR is a hybrid, has many different definitions and can be operationalized in a variety of ways—leading to difficulties in interpreting public disclosures (Wood et al., 2004). The general aspiration is to provide a measure of the potential trading financial loss to a portfolio of assets arising from adverse market movements (Wilson, 1995). VaR calculation seeks to show value 'at risk' in terms of a distribution of expected portfolio returns and expected losses over a holding period subject to a confidence level. The idea of VaR has become increasingly recognized as legitimate for regulatory purposes as a form of decentralized risk assessment. According to Jorion (2001a; 2001b), VaR is a simple integrating technology for risk management. Beyond its immediate application to market risk, it also has generic potential to provide a common financial measurement framework for the 'economic capital' of a firm, understood both as capital at risk and as a buffer for unexpected shocks. As a quantification of enterprise risk exposure over a period of time subject to a confidence level, it is argued that the results of VaR modelling are relatively easily understood and visualizable for senior management in financial institutions. Numerous applied textbooks have been published on VaR, texts which represent efforts to standardize applied thinking in the area.

While some of the motivation for VaR as a standard for risk management was to counter regulatory conservatism, it had more to do with improving divisional control in financial organizations and charging activities and transactions with a required return hurdle for risk. The case of Chase Manhattan (now J. P. Morgan Chase) Corporation in 1998 is an instructive example of this motivation. The bank became concerned that its assets were growing too fast and that its sales force was not making an appropriate trade-off between risk and reward in developing new business.[6] In particular, traders were not relating their new business to the risk capital required to support it. Consequently, the bank decided to introduce the practice of 'Shareholder value-added' (SVA), a technique by which the profit of any business unit within the bank would be charged for capital, a variant of residual income methods for divisional control purposes. Thus, the 'free' cash flow that supports shareholder value was reconceptualized as 'free' only after charging units for the portion of risk capital they required the business as a whole to keep in reserve. The capital base on which such charges were computed was an allocated portion of the firm level risk, and this was calculated by two principal methods: value at risk (VaR) and related stress testing for different classes of asset exposure (Bhasali, 2003). Thus, the organizational and institutional significance of VaR analysis extends beyond the calculation of capital at risk at the level of a portfolio of assets. VaR has origins in organizational demands for transaction control. The principles are simple: profit of a unit is calculated after a charge for capital at risk (Jorion, 2001b: 96) and this is commonly known as a risk adjusted return on capital (RAROC). The method presupposes and requires the quantification of capital at risk (e.g., using value at risk methodologies), which in turn allows the performance of different units/ traders to be compared in terms of a ratio of net return to risk capital.

A wave of conferences and concept papers on RAROC in the early 1990s led to demands for a more 'rigorous' RAROC practice which 'feeds off a bank's underlying risk models and data'.[7] At the level of implementation, matters were complex: 'if line managers can't understand the approach ... RAROC can't gain acceptance across a bank' (Jameson, 2001a). Managers must become 'comfortable' with capital allocations based on RAROC and this is 'partly a problem of bank politics and balance: making sure that senior managers support RAROC projects, that business lines are involved and that RAROC figures are neither rejected out of hand nor used uncritically' (Jameson, 2001a: 5). So, RAROC as an integrative risk measurement technology appears to have started life as part of a complex organizational politics, one potential tool among others in constraining decisions (Mikes, 2005): '... while it is important to get the formula right, RAROC analyses are part of a longer term battle for the hearts and minds in an institution' (Jameson, 2001a: 5). In reality getting traders in financial firms to accept VaR based or other determinations of economic capital was, initially at least, a significant behavioural constraint on their operationalization. Capital attribution to business units needs to be perceived as legitimate and an extensive practitioner literature suggests that these representations of capital at risk, even down to the level of individual transactions, can be highly adversarial within organizations. Consequently, normative commentaries continually emphasize the *social* support for measurement practices, namely the role of senior management buy-in, cultural commitment, and the need for champions of change (e.g., Cumming and Hirtle, 2001; Sullivan, 2001; Nash et al., 2002). From this point of view, RAROC measures illustrate the general claim that risk analysis is not a self-sufficient practice of calculation.

The observation that rational calculation must be 'sold' to practitioners is not new. Studies of new accounting systems demonstrate the complex micro-politics of accounting change and the barriers to local institutionalization (Miller, 1994). The implementation of RAROC and economic capital systems based on VaR challenged existing practices and related power relations in banking organizations, just as divisional performance measurement has done more generally (Mikes, 2005). From this point of view RAROC was, and is, more than a technical device for calculating a return. It is also a high-level idea for managerial control which has acquired legitimacy *irrespective* of its implementation frictions. RAROC principles have become part of 'best practice', codified and standardized in textbooks. In RAROC and the idea of 'risk adjusted capital and returns', the interests of regulators and of business can be linked. Through the idea of an integrative, calculative technology, regulatory objectives for system safety via a capital cushion could be imagined and aligned with managerial objectives for the efficient allocation of resources and for performance appraisal. Both VaR and RAROC techniques in their most abstracted form have become calculative bearers of the enforced self-regulation ideal discussed in Chapter 2.[8] Under the Basel 2 regulations banks have been permitted to use their own in-house models for determining a capital cushion for market risks since 1996. Although supervisors constrain the use of these in-house models, and apply arbitrary multipliers to capital levels, the changes in regulatory philosophy have brought about increasing conceptual convergence between regulatory management of economic capital and internal business models.[9]

Changes in techniques co-construct organizational fields and professional identities (Robson *et al.*, 2007) and the rise of the tools of VaR and RAROC have led to the creation of new agencies of calculation in organizations (Callon, 1998) and to a shift in the power and visibility of experts in organizations, armed with data and the authority to interpret. Because of its basis in financial mathematics, a new expert class of risk calculators in financial organizations has been created (Mikes, 2006), whose hand has been strengthened by regulatory demands. Financial organizations import much more than techniques; VaR and RAROC characterize a potential sub-culture in the form of teams of calculative experts and risk modelers with a distinctive technocratic conception of the risk management task. This calculative and analytical culture naturally extends its reach into new areas and new domains of model applicability—such as operational risk where a distinctive politics of calculation has come about (Chapter 4). Even though VaR techniques are heavily dependent on the availability of high frequency data sets and have developed most rapidly in the domain of 'market risk', their successful establishment as a body of abstract knowledge motivates their extension to other areas in an attempt to develop measures of 'true economic risk' for an enterprise. From this point of view VaR and RAROC are categories of practice which have made the relationship between shareholder value and risk management newly thinkable and actionable during the 1990s, providing a clear application of the logic and language of risk-return and a value or opportunity-based grammar for risk management in general.

The operational meaning of ERM for many risk specialists in financial institutions is paradigmatically identified with risk capital metrics based on a version of VaR modelling. VaR is more than a technique; it represents the *financialization of governance*. It is an idea which represents a risk-capital based concept of organizational control presided over by a new class of chief risk officers who talk up the organizational value of risk management. The calculative basis for VaR predates its increasing operational significance in the 1990s for a variety of reasons. First, the interest in VaR was in part a rational response to volatility in financial markets and the need to manage asset growth and trader behaviour more carefully in large financial institutions by calculating risk-based returns. Second, it became institutionalized because of its appeal as a unifying, whole of entity approach aligned with the popular philosophy of shareholder value management. Third, it provided financial organizations with a rational basis for contesting imposed regulatory capital requirements, resulting eventually in the regulatory recognition of in-house models for determining economic capital in the mid-1990s. Fourth, VaR and RAROC signified an expansionary potential for abstract risk-metrics in new domains, an expansion made possible by the increasing liquidity of markets for a broader set of financial instruments, thereby extending the boundaries for risk transfer and for the securitization of new assets, such as 'weather bonds' (Meulbroek, 2001; Porter, 2003). Yet, just as trends for financialization placed no limit in principle to the mechanics of securitization or to what can be made into an insurable risk, demands for the governance and oversight of these processes also grew. Risk metrics like VaR, though originally conceived as calculative governance, would need to be embedded in an organizational accountability framework.

ERM as Organizational Process

For many years, lone pioneers and critics of risk management practice bemoaned its 'balkanization', its insurance based preoccupation with risk as a negative factor to be avoided and transferred, and its bias towards the measurable (see e.g., Kloman, 1976; 1992; 2005). Notwithstanding, the historical development of the techniques of risk management (Bernstein, 1986a; 1986b), calculation alone has not been regarded by many as a sufficient basis for a whole of business approach which encompasses a wide range of risks and uncertainties. Consequently, managerial demands for risk control via back office monitoring have always made activity in financial markets more bureaucratic than is commonly imagined (Clark and Thrift, 2005). From this point of view, the potential for ERM is not primarily measurement or risk analysis focused; it is fundamentally about the governance of risk metrics as these tools have evolved and have generated 'self-made' risks of their own. For example, following financial scandals involving the use of derivatives by public bodies in the early 1990s (Nicholls, 2003b; Shapiro, 2003) there was much discussion about their controllability. The fact that derivatives are only understood (or not) by a small number of experts makes senior management oversight difficult, if not impossible. Derivatives came to be problematized as a governance issue rather than a calculative risk measurement issue and the G30 group published a control framework for them, adapting elements of the COSO standard (Group of Thirty, 1993). A risk-based controls framework for derivatives came to be articulated as a high level management and governance process (e.g., Touche Ross, 1994; Mengle, 2003a).

The COSO framework for internal control discussed in Chapter 2 was one of the first systematic conceptual frameworks and standards for internal control. Since 1992, COSO established itself as a standing coalition of professional associations to provide oversight for specific technical projects in common.[10] The 1992 guidance was redrafted under the concept of ERM and drew on an architecture developed by PricewaterhouseCoopers (e.g., PwC/IFAC, 1998). In stark contrast to risk metrics based ideas, ERM has been defined as: '... a process, effected by an entity's board of directors, management, and other personnel, applied in strategy setting and across the enterprise, designed to identify potential events that may affect the entity, and manage risks to be within its risk appetite, to provide reasonable assurance regarding the achievement of entity objectives' (COSO, 2004: 2). Written with the explicit intention being a 'standard', COSO (2004) codifies the discrete elements or stages of an ideal-typical ERM process which owes much to cybernetic systems thinking. The standard requires demonstrable organizational attention to all of the following 'managerial objects' in an idealized sequence as follows:

1. The *internal environment* or tone of an organization, which is regarded as the general foundation of all specific risk and control activity. This idea has a longer history in the concept of 'general' controls and speaks directly to popular sensibilities about risk governance as well as organizational scholarship on the problems created by 'normalized deviance'.

2. *Objective setting* reflects the conventional wisdom of 'top-down' analysis, namely that all risk management activity is to be explicitly related to organizational mission and sub-objectives in the service of that mission. The implication is that, without clarity of mission, the entire risk management process is undermined.

3. *Event identification.* Whereas VaR techniques are premised on high frequency event identification systems for market prices, data availability of this kind cannot be assumed for many other risk categories and objects. The emphasis on event identification systems reflects a climate of concern during the 1990s for risks which are not be easily captured and understood by conventional information systems, particularly operational (Chapter 4) and reputational (Chapter 5) risks. The psychology of fear and anxiety is directly relevant to the identification process and the active search for risk.

4. *Risk assessment.* Quantitative methods of risk analysis, such as VaR, remain important under this concept of ERM but they are implicitly positioned as one method within a wider suite of analytical and assessment techniques, many of which may be highly judgemental. Thus, COSO is inherently pluralistic about assessment methods and includes qualitative techniques, such as focus groups, for populating risk maps.

5. *Risk response.* This is regarded as the set of managerial action possibilities in terms of risk avoidance, reduction, sharing, and acceptance. Specific choices will reflect what has come to be known as the 'risk appetite' of organizations. Such an 'appetite' is in the first instance revealed by what organizations actually do (rather than what they claim to do).

The COSO framework formalizes a requirement for organizations to become more explicit about defining and monitoring their risk appetite, thereby creating a new managerial and regulatory object of attention.

6. *Control activities.* Controls of various kinds must no longer have, as critics have often observed, a life of their own as part of organizational 'common-sense'. Rather, they are to be designed explicitly in relation to risk response above. Accordingly traditional internal control activities, such as segregation of duties, arithmetic and accuracy checks, and authority controls are now to be subsumed within a larger ERM process and justified by reference to their mitigation of risks to the fundamental purpose of organizations.

7. *Information and communication* are positioned as an essential feature of ERM although, as Chapter 2 indicated, the nature of risk reporting is a major organizational challenge. This part of the standard appeals to popular management ideas that risk communication must be appropriate to the expectations of groups and individuals. The perceived quality of information and communication is taken as a proxy for a good control environment. Hence, elements of the ERM standard are related in ways which are not captured by sequential presentation.

8. *Monitoring.* As with the earlier framework for internal control in 1992, the ERM structure prescribes organizational self-observation and evaluation in much the same way as quality management systems do. The internal auditor claims an important monitoring and feedback role within this concept of ERM, which is in essence a self-observing system. This feature is critical since it governs all the other elements with a logic of auditability.

The COSO standard also articulates the roles and responsibilities of the various organizational agents who must realize ERM: the board and executive management must set the 'tone' of an organization, and the chief financial officer, risk officers, and internal auditors 'must know their responsibilities and the limits of their authority'. In short, the COSO framework for ERM represents a control process concept in which risk management is related in ambition to entity objectives, to the production of value and thereby to organizational strategy. It is defined as a process requiring senior management direction, extends across the whole organization and signifies a new organizational consciousness of 'risk appetite', and assurance. ERM defines and instrumentalizes governance.

Although the COSO standard acknowledges the limitations of control systems (collusion, ability to override), its representation of the risk management process is open to criticism on a number of fronts. As a prescription, it is manifestly hierarchical and its underlying cybernetic form may not be suitably descriptive of organizational realities. It posits risk appetite as fixed rather than emergent, and relies on an unrealistic degree of self-observation. Implementation deficits will be the norm and official risk tolerances may be ignored. It is also argued that 'top-down' approaches like this may be relevant in emergencies or with regard to specific material transactions, but they lack relevance for the day to day, and are out of touch with the forms of local autonomy with which contemporary organizations of necessity operate. A more pragmatic prescription would be a 'bottom-up' approach based on freedoms to expand and trade subject to central tracking that these activities remain within risk profile. Clarity of risk appetite and a technology for monitoring it, would replace the inherently Taylorist architecture of ERM.[11]

The general challenge is that the COSO standard embodies simplistic organization theory. Hood (1996b) argues for a style of risk management which institutionalizes conflict and works more realistically with the grain of organizational politics in a way which makes lower demands on organizational rationality and thereby leads to less disappointment. Like ISO 9000, the COSO version of ERM projects an image of design clarity and order which has little or no relationship to existing academic scholarship on organizations (Furusten, 2000). Yet the durability of 'homeostatic' conceptions of control like ERM is not really a surprise. The ERM framework as articulated by COSO could only become a significant reference point in regulatory and management discourse precisely because of its abstraction from organizational realities. However, this is a different kind of abstraction to that of finance theory; it is a systems-theoretic abstraction which is a blueprint for an auditable risk management process. It constructs a mode of self-presentation for senior management which is required by broader values of accountability and governance, values which have little capacity to recognize and work with organizational politics. As Hood admits, the weakness of the institutionalized conflict approach is that it lacks targetability and is difficult to engineer. By contrast, ERM signifies a distinctive organizational optimism in the possibility of control.

The COSO framework is one among several but for the purposes of the present argument their similarities are more striking and significant than their differences. COSO can be taken as representative of a style of standard making in the risk field. First, risk is defined in terms of both opportunity and harm, an essential aspirational strategy for reconceptualizing the value-enhancing dimension of control activities and consistent with finance-based conceptions of risk as variance. Second, great emphasis is placed on risk communication rather than on specific measurement techniques, which may be diverse. In particular, some standards (not so much COSO) recommend communication with a wide range of stakeholders, signaling the need for sensitivity to the variations in risk perceptions of groups external to the enterprise (see Chapter 5). Third, ERM is part of a responsibility allocation process which establishes risk accountability and authority. Here the parallels with quality ownership are evident. There is a similar emphasis on the documentation and auditability of process (Power, 1999; chapter 6; Furusten, 2000). Fourth, the emphasis on risk identification systems gives technologies of risk visualization or 'mapping' a more central position in the management process than risk calculation; governance requires overview instruments.

Risk maps have been an established element of risk analysis for many years, particularly in areas of environmental damage and epidemiology. As a more generic senior management tool, they came to prominence in the 1990s and have become a standard device for the qualitative identification and evaluation of risk categories. At their simplest, risk maps are defined by the two traditional axes of probability and impact, often calibrated in qualitative terms of high, medium, and low. The 'space' defined by the map is populated by various risks which may or may not be collectively identified by some form of CSA process (Chapter 2). Risk maps are not formal models and are usually the result of efforts to tap the 'folk risk intelligence' in an organization. As such, their objectivity consists in a kind of organizational consensus emerging from processes of challenge. As decision aids, risk maps visualize and often calibrate risks in terms of colour coding (red, green, amber), thereby directing management to develop action plans for the gross risks with high impact and probability. Enthusiasts argue that maps can make explicit and visible the relation between risks and organizational objectives and can create a conversation where none had existed before. And, as discussed below, risk maps can function as an operating matrix for regulatory agencies.

ERM and risk-mapping have become highly standardized practices which define the ability of organizations to identify the risks they face. Many large organizations now display considerable ability in being able to document the *content* of risk as a consequence. However, while mapping risk in this way has become institutionalized as a tool for senior management, the actionability of risk maps is much less clear. Organizations have difficulty in articulating and implementing action plans; action columns in risk spreadsheets are often cosmetic unless they reflect pre-existing work streams (Sharman, 2006). For low-probability, high-impact risks, the problem of actionability is particularly acute (Chapter 4). However, the legitimacy of standard routines, like risk maps, may have little to do with their capacity to generate managerial actions, actions which will in any case be a complex function of motivational and cognitive factors (Shapira, 1995). Rather, they create representations of a rational, hyper-rational perhaps, risk management process for governance purposes. The densely populated risk map makes an organization 'readable' by its senior officers and provides a risk 'accounting' statement. This representation also constitutes a trail of evidence for regulators and is part of making the risk management process auditable. To say that such devices have limited functionality for organizations (e.g., Samad-Khan, 2005) is to miss the point that they allow boards of directors to articulate abstract conceptions of risk. This is functional for governance purposes even if not for internal decision making.[12]

COSO (2004) and other similar risk management standards exemplify a generic control based tradition of ERM thinking. The ERM concept of a risk management process is a sequence of elements which is homeostatic in form. Even though accountants, engineers, and others might add different nuances to this model, they share a common framing of the risk management process. ERM is continuous with earlier internal control and quality assurance frameworks and increasingly defines the language of governance and senior management responsibility. These designs tend to be undented by the much documented complications of management within organizational and political scholarship. As rationalizations their appeal lies in a capacity to represent popular and persistent systems-based management ideals.

ERM and the Rise of the Chief Risk Officer

The argument so far suggests that conceptions of enterprise-wide risk management have their origins in organizational change programmes which have become attached to world-level ideas of good governance. In addition to these standardization processes, new governing actors and change agents must be envisaged and 'made up' (Hacking, 1986), such as the Chief Risk Officer (CRO). In 1993 James Lam became CRO at GE Capital, claiming to be the first to hold a formal role with that title (Lam, 2000; Hanley, 2002). Since then practitioner and scholarly discourse includes numerous surveys of emerging ERM practice. They suggest that the CRO role or its equivalent is growing and is defined by responsibility for the oversight of a wide range of risk management and internal assurance activities. In conception, the CRO operates in a much broader framework than the purchase of insurance (Dickinson, 2001; Lam, 2000; 2003a; 2003b).[13]

CROs have become more prominent as a senior occupational category with main board representation or at least direct reporting lines to the Chief Executive. By 2001 it could be argued that the concept of a head of risk management had evolved from back office defensive 'Cop' to, at least in aspiration, a front office partner and adviser in risk-taking (Wood, 2002a). As the risk management model shifted slowly from its low status back office role towards ERM, and came to be represented as having strategic significance, the CRO category grew in parallel. The CRO was to be the 'voice of risk' in the organization (Hanley, 2002; Mikes, 2006) and, while the precise form and status of the role remains dependent on specific organizational factors, the category became firmly established and institutionalized. CROs and the risk committees they service, have become part of the architecture of good organizational governance.

Mikes (2006) identifies three different types and levels of risk manager in her analysis of ERM practice in two banks, namely risk capital calculators (the VaR specialists discussed above), risk silo managers concerned with specific risk categories and their departmental equivalents and the CRO role with a senior governing oversight role. The nature of this oversight role has been subject to extensive practitioner discussion (e.g., Butterworth, 2000; Falkenstein, 2001; Fishkin, 2001). It is commonly argued that the CRO is not an 'owner' of risk. Rather the CRO and her staff support and enhance the management of risk as a responsibility of line management. The role is more that of 'coordinator and advisor' (AIRMIC, 1999), risk strategist, analyst, and catalyst for change, developer of best practice, policy designer and communicator, and a multidisciplinary coordinator.[14] That CROs might not be managers of risk at all (Ward, 2001) has created some issues in securing an institutional 'definition' but has also helped to elevate the category. Yet the CRO is also a new kind of risky position (Douglas, 1999) in so far as seniority means accountability for perceived failure and potential blame.[15]

Allocating responsibility for the management of risk to business heads requires the CRO to have capacity for oversight.[16] CROs must also work hard to create representations of their own effectiveness and performance, something inherently difficult in the light of the essential counterfactuality of their role; equally they must work hard to establish the claim that they are not directly managers or owners of risk, a strategy subject to considerable internal and external 'expectations gaps' between their own account of what they do and how this is understood elsewhere in the organization. Weiat's (1993) empirical study of the development of the compliance officer following the UK Financial Services Act 1986 is generically instructive. As 'distinct organizational actors' officers must establish internal authority by preaching integrationist ideals and articulating the business case for their functional area. Accordingly, such officers need to enlist internal actors with 'win-win' rhetorics to mobilize change in highly political organizational settings.[17] Weiat (1993) argues in the case of compliance officers that 'departments able to render themselves in some sense critical to the firm's success will achieve authority.' But what is critical is not absolute; criticality and relevance (Power, 1997) must be constructed by CROs in an internal political pitch, in which they represent themselves as 'modernizers', as moral guardians of legitimate values of good corporate governance and as spokespersons for a new logic of opportunity for risk and compliance functions.

The politics of the CRO role described above exists because, as Abbott (1988, p. 126) suggests more generally, aspiring super-ordinate roles, such as headships of risk, will seek to offload 'dangerously routine' activities. The stakes are therefore high for 'the ability to define old problems in new ways' (Abbott, 1988: 30), in this instance to establish ERM as an organizational rearrangement and repositioning of existing tasks. Old routines must be located under a new umbrella, an umbrella which gives the CRO in principle a central role. CROs are the human embodiment of the value proposition for risk management, and must work hard to make it prestigious. Metrics, such as VaR discussed above, which provide links between control activities and value propositions are important persuasive resources for them. As Abbott (1998: 103) suggests, 'expert action without any formalization' is perceived as craft knowledge and as lacking legitimacy. From this point of view, hierarchies of quantification are important (Chapter 4) since the existence of 'high level' analytical metrics such as VaR and RAROC can be important to the legitimacy and aura of risk management agents, even if not actually used.

Vaughan (2005) argues that NASA engineers worked in a craftlike fashion rather than in terms of hard science, and the same is likely to be true for CROs as they report their own work. But the symbolic backing of the image of science can be an essential feature of claims for organizational effectiveness and rationality by these agents. Abbott posits a critical difference between 'descriptivist' expertise and elite mathematical inference as basis for practitioner status; CROs in banks are normally capable of elite mathematical inference, and promote this as an ideal, but in fact such work is usually done by a small group of calculative experts. The senior risk people spend most of their time in descriptivist, mapping and communication mode. Agents of governance cannot be embroiled in risk analytics.

As a 'risk governor', the CRO is charged with 'organizing' the way in which an organization identifies and processes uncertainties, creating actionable response paths. In Vaughan's (2005) terms, CROs preside over organizational 'clean-up' work to produce organizational facts (registers and spreadsheets) about risk for the consumption of senior management and regulators. In this way, they are at the center of a process in which accounts of the manageability of risk are produced via ERM scripts of process. Like other internal agents, CROs must create an 'immaculate image' and must represent risk management as an integrative and 'productive function' (Weiat, 1993). This representation of the management of risk is part of a more generally observable phenomenon in which policing and regulatory activities are being reinvented with value propositions, turning them into new products.

The CRO is an emergent category which began life as a hybrid (Kurunmaki, 1999; Miller et al., 2006) and is becoming rapidly institutionalized. The rise of the Chief Finance Officer (CFO) was a not dissimilar phenomenon and went hand in hand with the emergence of the finance conception of the organization (Fligstein, 1990). CROs may in due course challenge the professional pre-eminence of the CFO with a risk-based concept of the organization, so the CRO/CFO interface is a possible fault line in the logic of organizing.[18] The control of professional language which, according to Abbott, makes work appear 'more coherent and effective than it really is', will be a critical factor, and here there have been significant developments in the field of risk management which support the rise of the CRO. New categories of management attention, like operational and reputational risk, may allow CROs to 'seize residual areas' (Abbott, 1988: 235) in the name of risk management, thus expanding their internal jurisdiction and influence at the expense of more traditional functions. The emergence of a conception of risk management with an enterprise-wide reach, and its administrative technology, also creates a platform for CROs to claim their place as a profession: 'To say a profession exists is to make it one' (Abbott, 1988: 81) and numerous references to the risk management 'professional' in practitioner conferences and articles have this performative quality.[19]

The CRO is the latest manifestation of a standard organizational innovation, namely the creation of a dedicated officership with hybrid regulatory and managerial functions. The organizational legitimacy of these officerships increases as the category becomes embedded in legal and other forms of external regulation; the quasi-legal aura of the term 'officer' is an essential and not an accidental feature of this process. Creating a dedicated officership category is both part of problem definition and organizational responsibility allocation. Health and Safety officers (Beaumont et al., 1982; Hutter, 1988); environmental risk officers (Rehbinder, 1991) compliance officers (Weiat, 1993), and chief operating officers (Dobbin et al., 2001) all have a history reaching back many years. In addition to the CRO, recent innovations include ethics and corporate governance officers and knowledge officers. Officerships provide internal organizational representations of norms, rules, and standards which may or may not be legally mandated; they are a standardized response to uncertainties in organizational environments. While officerships are likely to increase the internal 'legalization' of organization (Sitkin and Bies, 1994b), they are also held out as neoliberal agents of 'reflexive governance' and of 'meta-regulation' (Parker, 2002, chapter 9). From this point of view, the rise of CRO role exemplifies the shift in regulatory discourse discussed in Chapter 2. To return to Hacking's concept of 'dynamic nominalism', the invention of the CRO category is coextensive with the creation of new spaces of managerial action.

Functional explanations of the rise of the CRO role, and indeed for risk management itself, suggest that they are a rational organizational response to increased risk in the environment of organizations, and to the cross functional nature of these potential threats. Volatility in financial markets, anti-corporate activism, adversarial legal environments (the so-called compensation and blame culture), and growing awareness of ignorance in the face of high impact operational risks, all support the creation of a dedicated risk function with a broad remit. Increasing market completeness in new areas with more contracting possibilities drives a need for greater monitoring of returns on newly visible and vulnerable assets. And the credit downturn in the early 1990s, together with the mid-1990s financial scandals demanded a rational organizational response to capital maintenance. As Wood (2002a) argues, CRO roles emerged to fine-tune the calculation of economic capital for organizational control purposes. Put simply, it can be argued that CROs have come into being because of the way the world is, a view supported by the internal history of CROs (Lam, 2003).

Without discounting these explanations in specific cases, particularly for 'first movers', the category of CRO has also become institutionalized as a standardized role for large organizations, particularly in the financial and energy sectors. It is less a response to specific risks and more a feature of what it is to be a legitimate (large) organization. The head of risk role is part of good governance design in addition to audit committees and internal auditors.[20] CROs are a new mode of structuring risk expertise and symbolize high-level organizational commitment to rational risk management. Individual CROs may have organizationally idiosyncratic histories, but the generic role is becoming institutionalized well beyond any originating economic rationale. The CRO is becoming part of a 'standard managerial corpus' (Dobbin et al., 2001) and regulators expect to interact with these people.

ERM and the Standardization of Regulators

The previous three sections suggest that the idea of ERM is a hybrid of elements linked by a common 'whole-of-organization' risk approach overseen by a new class of actors—CROs. Metrics based conceptions of ERM have been subsumed within reformist discourses focusing on internal control and quality management ideas. Risk management and internal control are understood as a process and this process in turn has come to be constitutive of good organizational governance and accountability. Notwithstanding the different nuances of ERM, it has come to be a significant regulatory resource in its various manifestations. For example, the COSO framework has come to play an important role for the Securities and Exchange Commission.

As governance discourses and ideas have swept through central and local government organizations, business risk management ideas have been grafted on to internal control frameworks for public bodies. In the United Kingdom, there has been a specific change programme to this effect led by a central government which is 'currently awash with initiatives to promote risk management' (Black, 2005: 512). ERM ideas, as expressed in the UK Turnbull Report, have come to be part of a public change programme not dissimilar in scope to the collection of neoliberal ideas embodied in the 'new public management'. Public organizations must internalize a model of business risk assessment which demands that risks to strategy are considered. As Black puts it, this is now the new public *risk* management. Risk is becoming the organizing principle for change and challenge in public services, a development which merits further examination from public administration scholars.[21] An important subset of public bodies where such changes are particularly pertinent are regulatory organizations themselves; risk management is becoming part of the rules for being a 'good' state regulator (Marcussen, 2000).

As discussed above and in Chapter 2, a family of convergent regulatory strategies now demands explicit articulation and proof of internal control and risk management systems. From this point of view, ERM in all its variety is a potential regulatory resource and a basis for regulatory oversight or meta-regulation. However, the emergence of control-based and business risk management standards like Turnbull and COSO has also come to influence the framing of the architecture of regulation itself. Thus, one of the more profound aspects of the organizational significance of risk management is now evident in the widespread diffusion of the idea that regulatory practices of many different kinds must be 'risk-based' and must import the language and concepts of risk management standards to do this. From being a regulatory resource, ERM has been transformed into a model of regulatory process itself. ERM has become part of reformist discourses for regulators themselves, informing conceptions of what good regulatory process should look like (e.g., IOSCO, 1998).[22]

To grasp this development, it is useful to understand the number and variety of regulatory bodies to manage risks to the public in the UK. A recent report lists 63 national bodies (HM Treasury, 2005) and Hood *et al.* (2001) have identified critical sources of diversity in risk regulation. In the broadest terms, each regulatory body has its own methodologies for data gathering and has always been 'risk-based' in the sense of employing dedicated risk analysts, many of whom would have relevant scientific training in specific risk techniques (Black, 2005: 516; Rothstein *et al.*, 2006b). So the pressure for change being described here is less directly to do with these different forms of technical risk analysis in themselves, and more to do with demands for greater transparency and accountability of regulatory operations and decision-making in general. In part this is the result of greater pressures to democratize regulatory science in specific fields and of claims that risk acceptance or tolerance issues are not the sole preserve of experts (Rothstein *et al.*, 2006a). In part the pressure has also been for greater justification of the regulatory process in the face of 'red-tape' arguments, particularly for super-regulatory bodies created as a result of consolidation (Hutter, 2005). This has led to the development of principles of good regulation as a high-level standard embodying prescriptions that interventions must be targeted and proportionate to the risks to the public. Formal elements of business risk or ERM thinking have, to varying degrees, been imported as part of this pressure for regulatory justification.

In the UK, the Health and Safety Executive published an account of its decision-making process and drew attention to its analytical approach (HSE, 2001). ERM ideas are visible in this account. The HSE process approach begins with deciding whether the issue is properly one for them and ends with evaluating the effectiveness of action taken. This is a prescription of an ideal cybernetic process, which corresponds very closely to that of COSO and quality management. In another example, the Nuclear Energy Agency of the OECD published a discussion document *Improving Nuclear Regulatory Effectiveness* (OECD, 2001) which draws explicitly on quality management systems and ideas of continuous improvement. The mission of the agency is the starting point for evaluating everything its does and how it manages risk to the public, its efficiency and added value. In these two examples, risk-based regulation is close to meaning *mission-based* regulation, reflecting the quality origins of ERM thinking. Perhaps the clearest example of the internalization of ERM ideas by a regulatory body is to be found in the self-description of the mission of UK Financial Services Authority (FSA 2000). The FSA has explicitly designed a regulatory approach in terms of risks to its statutorily defined objectives. This is a successor to the RATE system (Bank of England 1997a) and the assessment of regulated entities has become framed under a risk assessment framework (ARROW) explicitly in terms of the risks posed to these objectives (Black, 2005; Hutter, 2005).[23] The approach has been internalized and interactions between FSA and regulated entities are structured by an assessment of the risks they pose to the statutory objectives of the regulator.

Two issues are of particular significance in the emergence of risk-based regulation. First, a subtle but important translation has taken place in the conception of public risk management. The idea of managing risks to the public in different domains is now mediated by the idea of risks to the objectives of the regulatory body, their mission risk (Power, 2004c; Black, 2005). This translation epitomizes the accountability and governance framework within which risk management and risk-based ideas of regulation now operate. ERM creates a new basis for self-justification and formal account giving in the face of secondary, reputational, or institutional risk (Rothstein et al., 2006a)—understood as the risk of sanction and blame in the wider institutional environment. Regulator specific versions of ERM may have varying degrees of operational and decision making purchase in regulatory agencies, but claims to a risk-based approach provide a common language of justification and rationalization of method (Hutter, 2005). ERM as the capacity to defend process in terms of recognizable, abstracted institutionalized elements underlies the legitimacy of all organizations—including those organizations whose task is to regulate.

The explicitly risk-based nature of regulation in many domains in the UK no doubt overlies considerable variation in practice, but it provides a frame for a potential new 'politics of uncertainty', one in which the possibility of failure and imperfection is accepted and made public. Risk-based regulation modeled in ERM terms necessarily and logically embodies the idea that failures are possible; there is a long history of similar qualifications to the effectiveness of internal control systems. However, as Rothstein et al. (2006a) argue, risk-based operating philosophies are ambivalent resources for regulatory bodies. On the one hand, the possibility of no-blame failure can be articulated. On the other hand, risk has become reflexively applied to regulatory bodies themselves; risk-based approaches become central to an active blame management process via the ability to demonstrate a rational process trail (Chapter 6). Existing political and public discourses sit uneasily with a risk-based ethos and tend to have a more 'zero-tolerance' character. There may be good distributive reasons for this. For example, the demise of Equitable Life in the UK, which could be regarded as 'tolerable' from the impersonal point of view of systemic financial risk, was in fact experienced by large numbers of people as a life-changing catastrophe. So business risk-based approaches which translate public risk into mission risk for the regulator do not necessarily avoid the politics of risk distribution and of varying public attitudes to risk. All this means that an *ex ante* public acceptance of the possibility of failure embodied in risk-based regulatory mission statements can never fully control *ex post* public reaction to actual failure. Regulatory bodies claiming to be risk-based are always inherently exposed to political reactions to major events.

This brings the argument to the second important issue regarding risk-based regulation. It was noted above that for regulatory bodies such as HSE with an established risk analysis community, being risk-based primarily means being more public and more formal about the process of analysis, or at least about some scripted account of that process. However, a prior process of risk analysis or meta-risk analysis is required by regulators in order to decide where to focus more technical risk analysis. In short, the business risk top-down approach is intended to focus analytical methods based on some kind of provisional *ex ante* risk assessment. This was evident in the structure of Business Risk Auditing (Chapter 2) and is no less the case in risk-based regulation. The problem for auditors was the fixed cost of developing business models of the client and its economic environment so that work could be targeted. The same is true of regulators applying this approach, particularly those with large populations of regulated entities or individuals (Black, 2005: 518–19). The initial challenge is to develop reporting instruments capable of providing baseline information about entities and individuals which enable a risk assessment to be made and inspection or enforcement resources to be targeted accordingly. The FSA in the UK currently uses a self-assessment return (RMAR) in the retail financial services area to build a risk profile of the entity over time. Something analogous is necessary in all such systems but the capacity to develop such baselines may be heavily constrained. Another significant challenge is that any risk-based approach is necessarily resource-constrained, so much so that some regulators would prefer it to be described as 'resource-based regulation' to manage public expectations more appropriately. Of course, while this category might be more descriptive, it would also be less legitimate and more threatening to governance ideals. Finally, political considerations may require that areas deemed low risk to a particular regulator's mission must be examined and allocated resource.[24]

It is clear from the above that while the idea of risk-based regulation has become significant in the UK, it has a cluster of different meanings: transparency (and auditability) of risk assessment processes, efficiency of methods to allocate limited regulatory resource, risk to regulatory mission and objectives. These different meanings feature in the broad ERM frameworks discussed above. Regulatory organizations are subject to isomorphic pressures to become, at least at the level of formal mission and purpose, more like the organizations they regulate. Regulators are simply organizations whose distinctive purpose is to regulate, and accounts of their operating philosophies have necessarily become risk-based, because this is what is expected of a properly governed regulator. By analogy with the discussion in Chapter 2, risk-based regulation is part of the 'turning inside-out' of regulatory agencies, of being explicit about limited resources and the need to direct them to where they are needed most, e.g. failing schools, unsafe industrial facilities, banks with weak controls. ERM has become a design blueprint for resource constrained risk regulators (IOSCO, 1998).

The regulatory state is becoming a risk management state, both in its reliance on risk management systems in organizations and in its reflexive internalization of risk management to characterize the operating process of regulatory agencies. Elements of ERM have filtered into regulatory organizations not because such organizations have a deficit of risk assessment tools and methods, but as a blueprint for the governance and accountability of the regulatory decision process. Risk-based regulation adds little that is new to the analytical capacities of the large regulators; it rather provides them with a new encompassing strategic rationality for justification, for resource allocation, for focus, and for relating mission to activities. As a consequence, regulators are more like the business organizations they regulate and are increasingly regulated themselves (Jacobsson, 2006). How this risk-based rationality plays out in practice will be varied, but such variety will be assessed against the benchmark of a risk management ideal which is much more than analysis and marks a new 'logic of organizing' (Powell, 2003: 54) in the regulation of public risks.

The Moral Economy of Risk Management

The preceding four sections have sought to convey the sense in which risk management, understood as a process framework, has become a highly institutionalized organizational form involving the creation of new categories of organizational actor. Standards for risk management procedures have been produced by many trade bodies (IIA, AIRMIC) and transnational organizations (COSO, ISO). Some of these bodies have an explicit norm production mandate, others are the public arm of private organizations. What is evident from these developments is that there is no single ERM standard, notwithstanding the profile of COSO (2004). Rather ERM is a web of norms which has 'cropped-up' across many different organizations and fields with little to do with each other (Brunsson, 2000) but which characterizes common ways of talking about organizations and risk. There is no doubt competition between centres of standard setting (Mattli, 2001; Mattli and Buethe, 2003), but this competition takes place on a global field which has already been populated by ERM ideas.

The standardization of ERM bears a resemblance to Berger and Luckman's (1966) analysis of institutionalization. This begins with pressures to disembed, make explicit and *externalize* customary and pragmatic elements of practice. This gives way to the organization and *objectivization* of these elements under the umbrella of abstract categories as bodies of formal knowledge and as standards for practice. These standards are subsequently *re-internalized* in a newly rationalized and disciplinary form, subject to local editing, as standards of accountability. The development of RiskMetrics mentioned above illustrates these three stages of institutionalization. More generally, this is how ERM and internal control have turned organizational life inside out. Within this web of rationalized thinking, particular individuals—academics and practitioners—have acquired almost guru status and their texts have become standards in themselves. The role of the CRO, though highly varied in practice, has also emerged as a standard of good organization—and most large organizations in the private and public sectors now have a high-level risk committee as part of the furniture of governance. The wide diffusion of ERM standards and recommendations, encompassing regulatory organizations, is facilitated by the new position of risk in popular management discourses, making the standardization of risk management not simply the prescription of techniques but a new system of rules for *talking* about organizations. As Brunsson (2000) argues, new talk is easier to diffuse than new practice as it is unencumbered by the frictions of implementation. The growth of explicit 'risk-based' representations of regulatory practice is a new kind of regulatory common-sense, notwithstanding the considerable empirical variety in the mandate of such bodies. As the previous section suggests, claims to a risk-based regulatory strategy are now made in areas such as finance, health and safety, policing, medicine, social policy, and many others.

The language and high-level architecture of process-based risk management has become standardized and widely diffused as a reform discourse. A new 'moral economy' of organizational risk has been created which recognizes that the assumptions which structure ideas of VaR and 'tolerable safety' must be explicitly located in a new frame of values. Risk management is to be governed and accounts of this process must be possible which conform to rational designs. In part, ERM has created a heightened internal *responsibilization* for risk within organizations; senior managers must routinely consider risks to strategic objectives and 'risk owners' must be specified. Risk management has entered the formal job descriptions of many organizational actors and ERM standards provide boards, audit committees, internal and external auditors, with frameworks through which to evaluate, monitor, and account for organizational processes. This is a much broader and more fundamental remit than traditional risk analysis. Risk management has come to be merged with management more generally (Hood *et al.*, 1992: 150).

While this intensification of organizational responsibility structures is an important feature of the phenomenon, the new moral economy of risk management also has to do with internal control and risk management systems bearing the burden of projecting a fictional organizational unity. The idea of an economy or public sector as a collection of autonomous discrete legal units has been firmly dispelled by practitioner and scholarly literatures on networks, strategic alliances, outsourcing and hybrids (e.g., Miller *et al.*, 2006). And management, like regulation itself, has undergone significant critiques of the 'command and control' idea in the form of appeals to 'flat' hierarchies, empowerment, and stakeholder communication. The material on these topics is vast and points to the managerial design challenges posed by varying degrees of fragmentation and uncertainty in organizational forms and practices, challenges for which new unifying concepts and categories are invented. ERM in its most general form projects an organizational unity composed of procedural elements. It is a fiction which expresses abstract principles of organizational commonality and unity underlying popular slogans like: 'risk is everyone's business'. The COSO standard is a successfully diffused organizational blueprint not because it provides more effective management of risk (though this is often claimed). Rather, its power resides in the representation of a new form of (risk-based) administrative objectivity. This is broadly consistent with Douglas and Wildavsky's (1982) thesis that social risk handling is less about the realities of danger and more about forms of life and the construction of institutions.

To replicate the thought experiment posited by Meyer *et al.* (1997), if we were to imagine the creation of a new organization of a significant size, we know that it could not be founded without rapidly adopting the mission and principles of an ERM-informed framework. It would very quickly appoint a CRO together with a number of other structures. This is because, as Meyer suggests, ideas of actorhood, whether of individuals or of organizations, are cultural in form, that is, they express notions of what it is to be a legitimate and proper actor, regardless of values of functionality or efficiency. As suggested in Chapter 2, being a good or proper organization has come to be strongly identified with establishing, and being able to demonstrate conformity with, the principles of risk management. ERM in this sense is a potential 'world-level' norm or web of norms of proper organizational actorhood. These norms also shape regulatory principles and actions because they are rules for talking about management and regulation.

To suggest that ERM has the characteristics of a world model in Meyer's sense is entirely consistent with empirical recognition of the variety of risk management practices organized in its name. As stated in Chapter 1, practices are a shifting and dynamic assembly of routines animated by concepts and ideas. The apparent coherence of the COSO version of ERM belies its many different sources (Deragon, 2000) which get filtered and re-expressed in highly rationalized form. VaR is also an idea of whole-of-entity risk management which has many versions and implementation difficulties. The point is not that these ideal forms are unrealistic or cannot be readily implemented without local scripts. This is obviously true.[25] It is rather that they establish a normative climate and a new basis for the description and representation of action. This is a neoliberal moral economy in which organizations must increasingly give internal and external accounts of the conformity between management practices and ERM ideas. This sense of 'moral economy' is not to be confused with business ethics programmes. Such programmes have undoubtedly grown in significance since the late 1980s but they have been made possible by the rise of a governance concept embodying logics of both managerial and social responsibility. A new organizational platform for ethics has been created by ideas of good governance and by ERM as a projection of the possibility of organizational virtue and corporate 'citizenship' (Boli, 2006). We shall return to these themes in later chapters.

The rise of corporate governance and its associated demands means that internal control and risk management have become the basis by which organizations show *how* they govern themselves rather than *what* they do. The former can be presented in ready-made standardized and managerial forms, whereas the latter, the content of risk management, cannot. It is no accident that the public disclosure of generic statements about the risk management process have grown as substantive risk disclosures, such as VaR, remain inconsistent and problematic (Woods *et al.*, 2004). So while critics may argue that control-based ERM embodies an unrealistic and unworkable model of organizations, it must also be understood that the power of the idea is precisely its unreality. ERM standards represent, and are based on, a 'cultural principle, a vision which is weakly anchored in local circumstance . . .' (Meyer *et al.*, 1997: 156). The formal and standardized unreality of ERM principles is simultaneously the source of their strength in expressing 'myths of control' which serve to 'organize organizations'. Even as they are criticized at the level of implementation, frameworks like COSO have acquired self-evidence as the kind of thing expected in a 'proper' organization. From this point of view, surveys of ERM practices (e.g., Tillinghast-Towers Perrin, 2001; 2002), which, on the surface, point to an implementation deficit, simultaneously constitute and perform ERM as a programme which is organizationally transcendent and with claims to universal applicability. So called 'adopters' of risk management standards are already in an important sense ready-made and 'made-up' as ERM actors (cf. Henning, 2000).

Uncertainty has been organized by the discourse of ERM in such a way that the historically visible anxieties and pressures for the democratization of risk analysis as discussed in Chapter 1, and visible in the work of scholars like Jasanoff and Wynne, have come to be reframed by the neoliberal managerial logic of internal control and quality systems. In place of the alleged scientific positivism of risk analysis, which still preoccupies science studies scholars, a new kind of administrative positivism has entered the stage. The rise of ERM represents a moral displacement of science by that of management and administration; the positive knowledge of the accountant and process engineer are now organizationally and culturally ascendant (Porter, 1992). The questions of causality and agency which have traditionally concerned risk analysis (Jasanoff, 1999) have been displaced and 'made managerial' by ERM frameworks. For example, consultation and transparency as the hoped for basis for a new 'risk science' have been conceptually translated by ERM frameworks into 'stakeholder analysis'. This is the distinctive epistemological character of the moral economy of ERM: it is both more open and responsive to external voices than previous science-based risk management thinking. Yet it is also closed around organizational control processes which constitute a 'complex web of mutual legitimation' (Loya and Boli, 1999: 192). Public policy issues may enter into organizational discourses, but tend to be internalized and organized under the category of reputation management (see Chapter 5). In a neoliberal, post-command and control world more dimensions of social risk are mediated by organizational management systems, including those of regulators.

Standards for ERM may be the latest, and certainly not the last, in a long line of 'world-level' frames for organizational control. In the 1980s and 1990s, ideas of audit and of 'new public management' emerged as models which could be made to look self-evidently functional and whose cultural legitimacy was relatively immune to micro-cultural problems of implementation and professional protest. However, while nation states were important actors in these earlier programmes, the institutionalization of risk management and ERM have emerged at a transnational level where a multiplicity of organizations can now claim legitimacy as actors in the creation of collective goods and broad meaning systems (Meyer et al., 1997). A number of these transnational actors have been mentioned above: Chase Manhattan and J. P. Morgan (now one entity); COSO and PricewaterhouseCoopers; national and international standards organizations; the Basel Committee on Banking regulation; the OECD, the World Bank, professional associations like the IIA, and legitimized human actors, such as academics and practitioner commentators. Some so-called 'global' corporations are unwitting world actors and standardizers. Even though they do not actively participate in the creation of collective meaning systems, their operations are written up and disseminated as case studies by business academics and consultants as carriers of knowledge.

All these different sources have provided convergent pressures for ERM not just as a set of technical routines but as a unifying and governing force, a collective and popular set of managerial sensibilities. In this apparent world of voluntary and private standard setting, world level actors themselves adopt very similar strategies to authorize their production of norms. They all argue for the positive effects of standards, their necessity and rationality; they all seek to place risk management standards and organizational actors in a new moral economy of organizational opportunity and efficiency.[26] Yet, is this belief in the possibility of rational risk governance in fact an elaborate technocratic fantasy and a bureaucratic defence against anxiety of disorder (cf. Clarke, 1999)? We shall return to this question in Chapter 7.

Conclusion

This chapter has analysed four critical 'moments' or themes in the institutionalization of an enterprise-wide or business-oriented risk management design which has emerged since 1995. The first concerns continuing efforts to develop whole-of-enterprise RiskMetrics, a calculative endeavour typified by the emergence of value at risk (VaR) modelling. The second, encompassing the first, concerns the production of standards for enterprise risk management which are process-based and continuous with the internal control and quality management projects discussed in Chapter 2. The third moment concerns the transformations in the field of expertise around ERM and the emergence of a corresponding whole of enterprise role, namely the chief risk officer. The fourth moment concerns the partial and continuing re-internalization of ERM or business risk concepts by regulatory agencies themselves.

Although ideas about an enterprise-wide or business approaches to the management of risk predate the development of recent standards and textbooks on the subject (e.g. Kloman, 1976; 1992; Haines, 1992), these four moments represent a distinctive formalization and normalization of ERM from 1995 onwards. Key events have catalyzed regulatory and managerial interest in rational principles for risk management design. This is much more than the extension of technical virtuosity and signifies the creation of a new moral economy for organizations. World-level governance values have created a social necessity for giving an account of how risk is managed. Risk management information is a signal of good governance and is increasingly coextensive with the language of accountability.

ERM is a model for the reorganization and coordination of existing risk management sub-disciplines; it is a programme for 'de-balkanization' (Kloman, 1992) which creates new rational relations between risk management, control activities, organizational objectives, and strategy. Popular claims for functionality may or may not be realized but the point of ERM, as realized and legitimized in standards, texts, and now regulations is to project the possibility of governing risk management processes and hence risk. ERM is an illusion of control which may be a necessary illusion because it reconstitutes a possible unity for a fragmented management field. As the rational re-organization of uncertainty, ERM displaces the much discussed 'technological fix' of risk analysis and science studies with something more powerful and far reaching—an 'organizational and governance fix'.

As argued in Chapter 1, organizations are centrally, even definitionally, concerned with the management of uncertainty and the coordination of resources to create forms of order for identifying risk and making decisions (March and Simon, 1958). The family of frameworks informed by ERM constitute another in a long line of programmes for repositioning the relationship between management, as the production of order, and uncertainty. ERM in this sense has been transformed from the preoccupation of a small number of critical observers and pioneers, into a broadly based and popular managerial and regulatory discourse. As a potential world model without apparent origins ERM has acquired the quality of a self-evident set of principles which do not only constitute a way of managing risk but also shape conceptions of proper organizational actorhood. Hence, the argument that ERM delineates a risk-based moral economy of organizational life.

This chapter has been concerned primarily with the emerging logic of ERM as a web of normativity about risk handling, its formalization in standards and its status as a world-level model of good governance. It has not been directly concerned with empirical questions of adoption and implementation or with the kind of political and distributional issues which concern political scientists and critics of neoliberalism. A few things can be sensibly anticipated about what such studies will show, based on work in other areas. First, there can be no doubt that any implementation of ERM systems is laden with organizational politics and negotiation, that objectives which should shape risk management activity will become shaped by it, that traders will resist arbitrary capital charges and so on. So the official sequencing of ERM processes as represented in standards should not be assumed to be at all descriptive, and internal competition between various organizational actors, not least between the CFO and the CRO, and their respective professional bodies, should be expected. For enthusiasts of collibrational techniques, such conflict is also to be preferred to the anaemic logic of ERM (Dunsire, 1990; 1993; Hood, 1996b).

Second, ERM standards will become implicated in the legalization and proceduralization of organizations (Sitkin and Bies, 1994), notwithstanding the enabling logic of opportunity within which ERM is framed (Chapter 6). As regulatory systems depend increasingly on ERM at the organizational level, ERM and good organizational governance will become increasingly co-defined. Third, we should expect to see, and do see, an active advisory market for ERM and its customized variants, a market in which consultants articulate proprietorial versions of generic principles. New models of organization and regulation have emerged and consultants and professional service firms are conspicuously the creators and carriers of templates for managing risk, sensing opportunities for using risk to re-define their strategic significance.[27] From, this point of view standards and surveys exist in part to scare organizations about imagined futures and are indicative of the 'managerial turn' in both risk management and regulation. They contribute to greater formal articulation and visibility of internal processes and translate critical governance themes, such as stakeholder analysis, into matters of internal control.

We began by suggesting that, despite its universalistic pretensions, ERM was an assemblage of different elements and ideas, a formulation which suggests something temporary. Some critics argue that continuing organizational barriers to the full implementation of ERM will diminish its legitimacy over time, reducing it to the status of transient fad (Banham, 1999; Brunsson, 2000; Deragon, 2000). These difficulties may feed back and be registered at the world-level, namely the global conference circuit, the practice survey, consulting templates, handbooks of best practice, and world-level standard setting bodies. As a language of organizational self-description, ERM and its variants may be replaced by something else precisely because there is no enduring rational way to deal with the management of enterprise and change is inevitable (Simon, 2002). Against this scepticism some durability in the idea should be expected, irrespective of apparent specific failures and frictions, precisely because it is grounded in world-level ideas and norms and is thereby relatively unencumbered by the contingencies of action.

Notes

This chapter is partly based on material and arguments in Power (2004a) and Power (2005c).

1. See AS/NZS (1995), now AS/NZS (2000); CSA (1997); BSI (1999); (JSA, 2001); AIRMIC/ALARM/IRM (2002); Coopers and Lybrand International (1996). In Germany the *Deutsches Institüt für Normierung* (DIN) has not to date issued a generic risk management document, reflecting a revealed German preference for product and service specific standards. See also ISO/IEC (2002) which attempts to standardize risk vocabulary.

2. See for example EIU (1995); Banks (2004); Deloach and Temple (2000); Miccolis *et al.* (2001); Barton *et al.* (2001); Gregory and Nokes (2002); Walker *et al.* (2002); FEI Research Foundation (2002); Lam (2003); Choudhry and Joannas (2003); Shimpi (2000); Zech (2001). See also many specific papers and articles on ERM e.g., Berry and Phillips (1998).

3. The Turnbull principles became important to insurers and brokers as a basis for framing and marketing their advisory services.

4. See 'Meet the Riskmongers', *The Economist*, 18 July 1998: 93–4. See also *Risk Management Reports*, December 1999, pp. 4–5.

5. While it is not possible to develop this argument in full, it is likely that it would parallel Miller's (1991) account of the rise of DCF in investment appraisal techniques. In contrast to Shiller, the Miller argument suggests that technological capacity is insufficient to explain the emergence of practical applications of finance theory. This has more to do with broader cultural trends towards the financialization of organizational life and with the cultural power of a conception of an enterprise as a 'portfolio' of assets.

6. This case is based on Barton *et al.* (2001, chapter 3).

7. Jameson (2001a) bases his comments on interviews with a number of CROs.

8. For a critique of regulators' reliance on VaR see Danielsson (2001).

9. The Basel Committee leading the reform of banking supervision (Basel Committee on Banking Supervision, 2003a) is a key resource for conceptualizing risk management in financial markets and publishes regular surveys of 'risk aggregation' practices which realize the theoretical idea of ERM (See Basel Committee on Banking Supervision, 2003b; 2003c).

10. The sponsors of COSO include: The American Institute of Certified Public Accountants; The Institute of Internal Auditors; the Financial Executives International, the Institute of Management Accountants, and the American Accounting Association).

11. These observations are based on a conversation with Hugo Banziger, Head of Risk, Deutsche Bank, 4 April 2006.

12. In fairness, regulatory bodies have become more concerned with management action plans than this suggests. Notably, they are focusing increasingly on management action plans under extreme scenarios as part of the capital assessment process.

13. See Ward (1998); *Risk Management Reports* 28(6), June 2001; Conference Board of Canada (2001); Oliver Wyman and Company (2002); Miccolis *et al.* (2001); Tillinghast-Towers Perrin (2002). See also *Risk Management Reports* 28(9) September 2001 pp. 3–5.

14. According to Lee (2000: 2), 'the problem has been determining just what this new creature should look like. That is, what is the right role, the right responsibilities and the right competencies for a CRO? At first look, it seems the CRO should be a master technician, someone who commands the technical expertise of every sub-discipline of risk management in their organization, from credit, to market to operational risk. But it turns out this is not the case. In the first place, that model of universal expertise exists in very few, if any, individuals. Second, the sheer accumulation of analytic detail...is not really what the organization needs...What is required is someone who can coordinate the company's risk management efforts...It is more of a synthetic rather than an analytic task...a leader, facilitator and integrator. In this role, the CRO serves as a coordinator, more than a manager, of risks.'

15. It is argued that the creation of dedicated officerships may lead others to relax their risk management efforts, leading to higher risk overall.

16. There are limits to internal sign-off as a basis for responsibilizing agents. If actionability is limited, such delegated responsibilities will tend to lose internal legitimacy. I am grateful to Bill Tonks for this point.

17. In the setting of managing securities traders, Willman *et al.* (2002) observe similar barriers to the integration of control and business objectives.

18. It has been argued that intra-organizational conflict involving CROs is inevitable, particularly between risk taking and risk managing functions, and that it is functional to institutionalize this conflict in separate roles which bargain with each other (Wood, 2002a). The organization control model is that of 'collibration' (Dunsire, 1993; Hood, 1996). Mikes' (2006) empirical study of ERM suggests that risk-based and accounting-based definitions of the firm come to the fore at different times in a firm's history depending on which model of control is pre-eminent.

19. A number of risk management associations now exist and the Conference Board of Canada has created a Council of Chief Risk Officers.

20. Institutional and economic explanations are not mutually exclusive, especially for a practice which unfolds over time (Dobbin *et al.*, 2001). Adoption of the CRO role may initially depend on a variety of specific factors, such as whether CEOs see risk as discrete area, the impact of industry scandals and regulatory changes. But the explanatory purchase of any such variables, including economic ones, diminishes as the level of industry adoption increases (Tolbert and Zucker, 1983).

21. See NAO (2000); Cabinet Office (2002). In 2003, the central government risk programme published a 'risk management assessment framework' as a 'tool for departments' and backed this up with an awareness raising change process.

22. For example, in the case of the World Bank, ERM functions to manage the risk to the Bank of not fulfilling its mission, rather than the risk to developing countries directly. The latter is reframed and internalized by ERM relative to the entity that is the World Bank

organization. The World Bank may be concerned with the governance of developing countries, but the adoption of ERM also signifies a focus on its own organizational governance.

23. See also Audit Commission (2003) for the case of UK local government.

24. This paragraph is based on comments by heads of regulatory bodies at a workshop on risk-based regulation held at the Centre for Analysis of Risk and Regulation (CARR), London School of Economics and Political Science, 18 January 2006.

25. Surveys suggests considerable barriers to a broad risk vision within insurance companies and a strong cultural bias to quantitative analysis. For example, 'Overall the positive correlation between which risks are covered by ERM and satisfaction with the tools to manage those risks ... suggests that risks may be included in an ERM program based on their ease of quantification more than their degree of importance' (Tillinghast-Towers Perrin, 2002: 6–7). With the exception of Canadian insurers, the general picture is one of a robust actuarial culture defining ERM to suit its own terms. This suggests that the concrete realization of the ideal elements of ERM is partial and subject to micro-cultural forms of resistance, such as intra-organizational turf wars, and a bias towards measurement in operationalizing ERM.

26. See Tamm Hallstroem (2004). See also Suddaby and Greenwood (2005) for more discussion of generic rhetorical strategies.

27. For example, see PwC/IFAC (1999).

4

Putting Categories to Work: The Invention of Operational Risk

Sometime during the 1990s, the category of 'operational risk' emerged as a taken for granted label in banking and insurance discourses worldwide. Operational risk was conceived as a composite term for a wide variety of organizational and behavioural risk issues which were traditionally excluded from formal definitions of market and credit risk. The explosion of operational risk discourse gave new structure and rationality to what had traditionally been regarded as a risk management residual and negatively described as 'non-financial risk'. Banking industry mythology, as propagated in conference speeches and consulting pitches, closely associates the crystallization of operational risk sensitivities with a specific event, namely the collapse of Barings Bank in 1995. This case became central to a new public dramatology of risk and to the managerial construction of a basket of business threats which had been ignored and under-managed. Although the category of operational risk pre-existed the collapse of Barings, particularly in high reliability process industries where it characterizes risks associated with organizational infrastructure and technical systems (Group of Thirty, 1993), the Barings event was the platform for its rationalization, expansion, and institutionalization.

Operational risk has quickly become a prominent focus for organizational and regulatory reform discussions, despite being problematic to define. The definition of operational risk settled upon by the Basel Committee, the transnational policy body for banking supervision, is very general: the risk of loss resulting from inadequate or failed internal processes, people, and systems or from external events. The broad nature of this definition enables it to appeal to a wide range of sub-groups within organizations and to function as an umbrella for many different interests. The category of operational risk is a 'boundary object' as discussed in Chapter 1, i.e. it is a discursive object which gives diverse expert communities a common basis for self-description. It posits the unity of an abstract community composed of a range of managerial practices focused on a portfolio of risks. The story of operational risk illustrates the thesis of 'dynamic nominalism' described in previous chapters and shows how management categories, involving new definitions and related formalizations of practice, go hand in hand with the creation of new identities for practitioners and the construction of new practices. Operational risk also represents a programme to develop formalized risk knowledge in areas which are traditionally resistant to calculability.

This chapter analyses the early trajectory of 'operational risk'. First, the emergence of the concept is traced to major regulatory changes facing the world banking industry. Second, we consider the interests and issues at stake in the development of a definition of operational risk. Third, we consider early concerns from practitioners about the implementation of operational risk management, not so much as an analysis of the frictions of implementation, but more for what these concerns reveal about different cultural preferences for quantification and modeling as an ideal in risk management. This discussion suggests that different attitudes to risk calculation and governance co-exist uneasily in the space of operational risk.

Banking Regulation and the Rise of Operational Risk

The regulatory regime for banking has evolved over many years, mainly understood as a series of responses to specific crises (e.g., Moran, 1986; 1989). While national legislative frameworks continue to be significant in the regulation of banking, there has also been a marked growth of regulatory knowledge at the level of transnational networks and institutions. This began at the industry level as a programme for global coordination in key areas of mutual advantage, not least that of cross-border settlements. In 1974, a 'club' of central bankers, the Basel Committee on Banking Supervision, was formed which consolidated and formalized an existing network with the aim to coordinate global policy for banking supervision. The Basel Committee is a meta-organization in so far as its members are other organizations (Ahrne and Brunsson, 2006). It has no national regulatory authority directly, but has de facto power via the implementation of its recommendations by the national supervisory bodies who are its organizational members (Marcussen, 2006). In 1988 the committee, located within and administered via the Bank for International Settlements, devised a system for regulating the adequacy of the capital base in banks—Basel 1.

The management of capital is the foundation of prudential banking and is of central concern to all regulatory systems. There has always been a strong business case for banks to maintain a buffer of resources adequate to enable them to survive unexpected losses. However, the nature and level of this buffer has come to be an object of acute regulatory interest, both for the protection of customers and the banking system as a whole. By regulating capital to prevent failure at the individual bank level, it is argued that this mitigates 'systemic' risk, that is, the risk that the failure of a single institution could create failures elsewhere in the system, because of the interconnectedness of transactions and credit. Accordingly, the regulation of the 'adequacy' of capital has become paradigmatic, part of the deep logic of prudential knowledge in the field (Blattner, 1995).

The process of determining specific levels of capital for regulatory purposes is far from being merely technical. The minimum ratio of capital to assets was set originally at eight per cent, a level which reflected the prevailing practice and interests of Anglo-American banks and effectively disfavoured German banks (which typically operated with much higher ratios) and Japanese banks (which were required to reduce assets to comply).[1] The ratio of capital to assets is a second-order calculation based on accounting numbers, and the lack of standardization of underlying national accounting systems has always been a source of conflict and debate. The 'mark to market' proposals for derivatives by the International Accounting Standards Board (IAS 39) created controversy at the highest levels in government (Shin, 2004). So, from at least the beginning of the first Basel accord, the regulation of capital has been a contested area for individual banks and nations.

The capital base for a specific bank is normally determined by a national banking supervisor, usually the central bank or a dedicated regulatory body, and is calculated on the basis of disclosed balance sheet items weighted according to judgements about their underlying risks. During the 1990s, banks complained about the calculative basis of the charge, arguing that it was arbitrary and did not discriminate sufficiently between the different risk profiles of specific banks, or between different risks within a single bank. In addition, as noted in Chapter 3, the large banks were developing their own models as a basis for having better control over trading activity. By comparison with these models, the 1988 Basel accord was not regarded as sufficiently risk sensitive (Vieten, 1996). Banks who felt that their risk management processes were good believed that the regulation placed them at a competitive disadvantage by requiring too much capital to be maintained.

The Basel Committee began to revise its 1988 approach during the early 1990s. Central to this revision process was the growing recognition of the use of risk models developed by banks for the calculation of their regulatory capital. This increasing regulatory receptivity to so-called 'in-house' models included the acceptance of VaR and scenario analysis as the basis for calculating capital. The major change occurred in 1996, when the Basel Committee rules were adapted to permit the use of in-house models for the purpose of reserving capital against market risk exposure. This was a big shift in policy style and strategy, from a command-and-control approach which prescribed conservative risk weights to assets to one with the flavour of 'enforced self-regulation' as discussed in Chapter 2. Banks would calculate capital according to their own models subject to regulatory oversight and discretionary 'add-ons'.

Traditional concerns about regulatory moral hazard (individual banks are better placed than regulators to understand their exposures) were transformed within a new logic of opportunity and banks' self-interest was nurtured with the promise of graduated forms of inspection. As in the more general case of internal control, this strategy is attractive to regulatory agencies who can shift costs to regulated entities. 1996 therefore also marks an important shift in the political economy of banking regulation, with powerful actors being transformed from lobbying outsiders to insiders in regulatory knowledge production with representation on significant transnational technical committees. Indeed, the development of banking regulation perfectly illustrates Meyer and Rowan's (1977) thesis about how powerful organizations come to externalize their own rules as governing institutions for a field.

In addition to the capital charging philosophy and the emergence of new rules for the use of in-house modelling for market risk ('Pillar 1'), a second strand of regulatory approach was developed which relates to the theme of the supervisory review process by regulatory bodies ('Pillar 2'). Here the emphasis is on the aspects of internal control and management oversight discussed in Chapter 2 which are understood as benchmarks of a 'sound capital assessment *process.*' A requirement for internal control systems has been a part of banking legislation and regulatory philosophy since the 1980s (e.g., the UK Banking Act 1987, s 39). Over time, as the self-management of regulatory capital has become more established, supervisory systems and approaches have been re-designed to take account of internal controls (Basel Committee on Banking Supervision, 1994; 1998a; 2001c). In particular, supervisors usually set capital levels in excess of the regulatory minimum to reflect judgements about a bank's control environment. Pillar 2 provides more structure, but does not eliminate, this discretion. Threshold standards for internal control have been defined by reference to world-level standards, such as the COSO framework, and are becoming required as a condition of using advanced approaches for calculating capital. Thus where Pillar 1 relates to risk calculation and risk analysis, Pillar 2 is a prescription for an oversight and auditing process capable of being modulated according to an assessment of the risk management process. In short, Pillar 2 is concerned with the control environment of the risk analysis process in banks. It is about the production of evidence for good governance.

This changing climate and style of banking regulation describes the context within which the category of operational risk came to be institutionalized from the mid-1990s onwards.[2] If operational risk scarcely existed as a category of practitioner thinking in the early 1990s, by the end of the decade, banking regulators and practitioners could talk of little else.[3] There was a rapid expansion of books and conferences on the subject and the role of 'operational risk manager' was created by a number of banks as a specialist reporting to the CRO. These developments led some to talk of an 'operational risk' profession and in the UK the Institute of Operational Risk (IOR) was formed.

It is tempting to regard Nicholas Leeson, the 'rogue' trader attributed with the destruction of Barings Bank in 1995, as the true author and unwitting inventor of 'operational risk'. Most discussions of the topic refer to this case as a defining moment and Leeson dramatizes operational risk as Maxwell did for corporate governance; both are part of an iconography of regulatory failure (Tickell, 1996; Hogan, 1997; Nicholls, 2003a). However, the Basel Committee itself already recognized the significance of 'operations risk' earlier in 1994, understanding it in terms of 'deficiencies in information systems or internal controls' giving rise to unexpected losses.[4] It was also revisiting the scope of its 1988 guidance well before the Barings scandal (Basel Committee on Banking Supervision, 1994).[5] So it is more historically accurate to say that the history of Barings (and many other financial scandals in the mid-1990s, such as Daiwa) were retrospectively constructed and represented as 'operational risk' management failures.[6] By the late 1990s it could be argued that that many banking scandals and failures had been misdescribed and diagnosed in terms of credit or market risk. They had to be reinterpreted as failures of management oversight of operations (Tschoegl, 2000).

Basel 2 is a regulatory programme (Rose and Miller, 1992) at the heart of which is the paradigm of capital as a buffer for both measured (credit and market) and 'non-measured' risks (see Basel Committee on Banking Supervision, 2003a). The idea of a category of risks which could not be measured, empirically if not in principle, was implicit in the conservatism of the original 1988 accord. The emergence of the category of 'operational risk' signalled a regulatory intent to give greater visibility and manageability to these risks under Pillar 2. And with this greater accent on management, also came the question of the measurability and modelability of these risks under Pillar 1.

The Basel 2 proposals began with an 'evolutionary' approach to measuring operational risk for capital adequacy purposes. Banks were encouraged to develop their approaches to operational risk management along a one-way, increasingly risk-sensitive continuum. Three classes of approach have been envisaged: basic, standardized, and an advanced measurement approach (AMA) differentiated in terms of degree of calculative elaboration and specificity. The intention was that, once a bank qualifies to use a 'higher' approach, it would become mandatory for it to do so. In order to encourage this evolutionary process, Basel 2 originally set 20 per cent of current minimum regulatory capital as an opening benchmark for the new operational risk (OR) capital charge, a ratio derived from observed practice. This was subsequently reduced to 12 per cent, and the original details of the standardized and advanced measurement approaches were also modified.

The process of developing these rules for measuring operational risk capital has been, and remains at the time of writing, subject to considerable industry negotiation, featuring 'road shows', marketing of best practice by the Basel Committee staff (e.g., Basel Committee on Banking Supervision, 2001b), and a succession of quantitative studies of the impact of the regulations on overall banking capital. By 2006, five quantitative impact studies (QIS) had been published which investigate how the new capital rules would be implemented, focusing on the incentives for banks to use advanced approaches and the effect on total capital in the banking system.[7] In addition there have been specific exercises focusing on operational risk loss data. The many years in development suggest that Basel 2 has the features of a genuine regulatory experiment (Millo and Lezaun, 2006). The ambition of Basel 2 as a regulatory project of control may be without precedent in its attempt to reach into the micro-managerial world of banks.[8] Frequent postponements and revisions to the implementation timetable indicate the complexity of the task. The sub-agenda for 'operational risk' typifies a politics of banking regulation in which rules cannot simply be imposed from above, but must be represented and marketed as a consolidation and formalization of existing practices. The British Bankers Association website typifies this strategy by stating in 2004 that: 'Operational risk is not a new risk ... However, the idea that operational risk management is a discipline with its own management structure, tools and processes ... is new.'

In keeping with a need to create industry consensus, the regulatory agenda for operational risk management was slowly grafted on to the existing technical interests of different occupational groups, groups who could begin to see the operational risk agenda as a new opportunity for significance. For example, in June 2001, the 4th Annual Global Financial Industry Forum addressed the topic of 'Managing operational risk and latest developments in achieving operations, settlements and payments efficiencies'. In the setting of this particular event, the concept of operational risk was positioned within a community of credit risk managers with very specific interests in the integrity of settlement systems.[9] Operational risk was rapidly promoted as a world-level category precisely because it could be managerialized in specific ways within different fields of expertise populated by agents who could translate and elevate their own concerns in its name.

The Basel 2 proposals in general and the launch of a deliberately under-specified category of operational risk had three critical effects. First, they permitted the institutionalization and acceptance of a concept at the level of principle unencumbered by practical considerations. In this way, the idea of operational risk management was implemented and legitimated prior to practice and its inevitable complexities (Brunsson, 2000). Second, they created a new and potentially competitive space for diverse control agents inside financial organizations, for whom acting in the name of operational risk management presented opportunities for occupational advancement. Third, the Pillar 2 focus on internal control and supervisory processes overlaps considerably with operational risk issues, understood as including management oversight capacity. This means that operational risk is not the same kind of category as market and credit risk, it has greater purchase on matters of organizational governance. This makes the definition of operational risk an important stake in the political economy of Basel 2.

Defining Operational Risk

According to Beck (1992: 56) 'demands, and thus markets, of a completely new type can be created by varying the definition of risk, especially the demand for the avoidance of risk'. As we have seen in previous chapters, the organization of uncertainty around transformed definitions of internal control and enterprise risk management has been a conspicuous feature of the risk management field since 1995. As outlined in Chapter 1, an important theme in this book is the role of classification and categorization in the intellectual organization of risk management, particularly as a basis for the writing of standards of risk accountability. However, new classifications of areas of work do not simply reflect natural or functional divisions of labour. They constitute explicit efforts to create new forms of managerial and regulatory intervention, efforts which simultaneously challenge existing practitioner identities, create new ones and re-partition the map of professional knowledge (Abbott, 1988).

The link between practical efforts to fix the meaning of key terms and issues in the jurisdiction of expertise and bodies of practical knowledge is very evident in the case of operational risk. The regulatory and organizational definition of operational risk is much more than a project of re-labelling a number of existing fields of work or of clarifying the meaning of a regulatory concept. It concerns the constitution of a new practical and managerial narrative, and the creation of a field in which different interests and ambitions can be re-represented. In this respect, the question of defining operational risk depends on who is reinventing themselves in its name. Definitions are endogenous to the political economy of regulation.

Within early regulatory discourses on the subject, operational risk was regarded as simply a residual category for 'other risks' not covered by market risk and credit risk. From the mid-1990s, it became clear that this was an inadequate basis for regulatory and managerial attention and efforts began to define and determine its scope more positively. While the importance of so-called 'non-financial' sources of risk was recognized, operational risk proved 'extremely hard to define' (Goodhart, 2001) and gave rise to considerable debate (see Hoffman, 2002, chapter 3). At stake in these discussions were boundary issues, such as the place of business risk as characterized by ERM and the emerging role of reputation (Chapter 5). In addition, a distinction was drawn between internal and external sources of operational risk. Thus, the space of operational risk was inherently contestable with fuzzy boundaries (Jameson, 1998; Kuritzkes, 2002).

The Basel 2 regulation initially settled on the narrowly construed definition of operational risk mentioned in the introduction: 'the risk of direct or indirect loss resulting from inadequate or failed internal processes, people and systems or from external events' (Basel Committee on Banking Supervision, 2001a: 2).[10] This definition reflects a long process of discussion and, while it is slightly broader than the 1994 definition of operations risk which was influenced by COSO, it specifically excludes reputational and strategic business risks. The manifest intention was to give operational risk a clear, actionable and ownable focus on loss causing events although this still left open a range of interpretations of the scope of operational risk which different groups could exploit. For example, the element of the definition focusing on systems failures (an internal event) was an opportunity for IT systems specialists and chief information officers (CIOs) to acquire a new significance, which was further enhanced by a focus on business continuity and critical systems in the wake of the September 11th bombings in New York.

Other aspects of the definition encompass potential sources of loss which escape the obvious ownership of an existing department. Accordingly, organizational change in the name of operational risk has been an opportunity for sub-groups to makes claims for relevance and importance but has also involved turf issues. For example, compliance and legal functions have undergone reinvention.[11] In particular, 'legal risk' has obtained 'conceptual leverage' from the umbrella of operation risk to become a stand-alone management category. Legal risk objects include 'exposures to fines, penalties, or punitive damages resulting from supervisory actions, as well as private settlements' and new roles for legal departments in banks are envisaged, not least in managing systems for logging issues which may create legal exposure (McCormick, 2004a; 2004b; 2006). It is clear that potential losses from regulatory non-compliance and other legal actions have always existed as risk objects. However, the emergence of 'legal risk' as a practice category is new and expands its network of significance. Operational risk has given in-house lawyers a capacity and legitimacy to ask for information about loss events, and a stake in the emerging risk management agenda.[12] The websites of many large law firms also offer legal risk management as a new service line, suggesting that this practitioner sub-category has become a significant mobilizing force in the organization of uncertainty.

If operational risk has given lawyers a foothold in risk management, accountants have taken the familiar concept of internal control as discussed in Chapter 2 as their starting point (Wilson, 2001). A continuing issue in the operational risk field is the role of frameworks like COSO for providing its intellectual organization. This framework has implications for the status of the operational risk category. It is not quite a functionally discrete area alongside market or credit risk under Pillar 1; it has some of the higher order governance status under Pillar 2. For example, while stress testing market risk models is part of first order market risk management practice, failure to stress test market risk models against extreme market movements (allegedly in the case of Long Term Capital Management) is a form of operational risk, that is, a second order failure of internal controls over the stress testing function. From the accountants' point of view, far from being a residual, operational risk management is closely identifiable with internal control and therefore with the oversight of the organizational environment of market and credit risk management. Operational risk is a governance category.

Definitional work is undertaken by different organizational agents interested in constructing risk management in terms of their own concepts, protocols and related interpretations of risk phenomena. In addition to lawyers and accountants, IT specialists, human resource managers, and compliance officers have all sought to redefine and reposition their work in terms of risk management. The definition of operational risk is therefore a stake in the micro-politics of professional mobilization and responsibility allocation.

Douglas (1992a) argues that the classification of organizational dangers is necessarily a forensic and social process, that is, one that also defines a system of accountabilities and potential blame. This suggests that definitions of operational risk embody, intentionally or otherwise, intuitions about responsibilities. For example, minor systems failures and payment errors may be laid at the door of technical operatives directly responsible for these systems. However, the unauthorized trading and cover-ups which occurred at Daiwa and Barings in 1995 were ultimately interpreted as a failure of senior management oversight. Indeed, documents in the early 1990s (Group of Thirty, 1993; Basel Committee on Banking Supervision, 1994) made much of senior management responsibility for risk management systems, as indeed did the corporate governance discourses in 1991 (see Chapter 2).

Accordingly, while nuances may vary according to professional cultures, the concept of operational risk as defined by Basel 2 is part of a larger regulatory discourse directed at emphasizing and positioning the responsibility of senior management for the risk management architecture of firms (Gray and Hamilton, 2006). Defining operational risk is also about making management responsible. The breadth of the Basel 2 definition reflects a deliberate strategy to 'responsibilize' Boards and the most senior levels of management for a wide variety of newly visible and relevant operational areas. The parallels with the emergence of internal control as a regulatory object, discussed in Chapter 2, are evident. For example, in the UK the FSA (2005: para. 2.6) envisages the elements of an operational risk management system in much the same cybernetic way as the COSO and ERM frameworks discussed in Chapter 3. This makes the scope of operational risk much more than technical; it is an organizational governance concept. Indeed, the FSA are relaxed about risk categorization per se provided that all significant risks enter a management system (FSA 2005: para. 3.4).

Definitions of key concepts are an intimate and central part of the logic of any practice and the identity of its practitioners. Without a system of concepts and taxonomies, any practice of intervention is blind, disorganized, and of questionable legitimacy. Definitions are attention-directing devices with an 'as-if' status and a product of strategies which determine objects of managerial and regulatory interest. Definitions create boundary objects which are initially vague and ambivalent, enabling their widespread mobilization, but which become determinate through the processes of intervention and control conceived in their name. In this sense definitions are endogenous and 'kick-start' new practices. The definition of operational risk is a major regulatory and managerial innovation which has created the conceptual conditions of possibility for a new kind of discipline. Operational risk is more than the sum of its established constituents.

Organizing Operational Risk Practice

How organizations define and 'cleanse' errors are part of their rituals of managing (Vaughan, 2005). While the category of operational risk was rapidly institutionalized and implemented at the level of idea, debates about material implementation were predictably heated. These issues concerned the organization of data collection and the role of technology in that process. The design of some systems gravitated towards available historic loss data. However, there was also much discussion of near misses and potential losses as sources of operational risk knowledge which are well-established in high reliability industries like airlines (MaCrae, 2006).[13] Near-miss conceptions of operational risk management develop the insight that accidents and crises are generally preceded by a build up of signs and anomalies (Muerman and Oktem, 2002; Phimster et al., 2003). Operational risk reporting systems can in principle be designed to capture risks as they 'incubate' (Turner and Pidgeon, 1997). Internal anomalies, such as non-compliance with organization rules and public regulations, have a renewed significance in the financial services industry as a form of near miss management embedded in compliance programmes. The concept of 'near miss' also challenges the neat distinction between capital as a reserve for unexpected losses and accounting provisions to cover 'expected' losses. On closer inspection, near misses may be causally related to 'unexpected' loss and, if unremediated, make the latter more 'expectable'.

The Basel Committee itself recognized that 'there is often a high degree of ambiguity inherent in the process of categorizing losses and costs' (Basel Committee on Banking Supervision, 2001a, para. 8). The problem is compounded by the fact that if the prospect of sudden catastrophic events is in fact mitigated by preventative internal controls and business resilience plans, or possibly transferred by insurance, then successful management interventions will create fewer historic internal data points, whether of loss or near loss. In any event, the issue is not simply one of data per se, but also of organizational capacities to interpret and act on data. In the case of Barings, internal control weaknesses and initial losses could not be acted upon because they were not regarded as anomalous by the management. The Barings case also shows that, as they incubate, risks cross existing conceptual and managerial boundaries leading to misdiagnosis and misanalysis (Cagan, 2001). And if management is unable or unwilling to respond to cues, no amount of capital provides protection since it will simply be run down without corrective action being taken.

These issues show that efforts to create data infrastructures for managing operational risk are necessarily embedded in organizational rituals and cultures for defining and dealing with error. Definitions, responsibilities, concepts of error and of loss, and potential risk management jurisdictions are mutually constitutive. How operational risk data is defined has implications for who is legitimized to act in its name. Vaughan (2005) analyses how technology populates the operational world of air traffic controllers with data about aircraft separation giving material reality to the idea of 'near miss'. However, compared with high reliability industries and their histories of accident and incidents, the emerging world of operational risk management lacks data of this kind and depth. The Barings paradigm of the uncontrolled employee, a high impact and low probability event, by its very nature lacks rich historical data, even at the industry level. Large loss experiences are rare and adequate time series for operational losses and their causes need to be actively constructed. The distinctive challenge of operational risk management is to make manageable, and collect data on, 'tail' events at the limits of systematic managerial knowledge.

In its early studies, the Basel Committee admitted that the current state of knowledge and loss data was so poor that the internal measurement of operational risk was 'still in the dark' (1998b). Appropriate data was absent for all but a handful of banks, and industry standards for such data were lacking (Cagan, 2001). Hence the early days of operational management are characterized by data poverty where it is most needed, that is, for heterogeneous catastrophic events, and by data availability for normal classes of error, for example, transactions processing. Although work on rare events in distribution tails has developed, some enthusiasts of extreme value theory doubt whether it can really travel to operational risk management (Kuritzkes, 2002).

The fact of loss is often silent on causation and probability of loss is not a given based on historical frequency data, but can be influenced by management. Probability in these settings is space for social action and is behavioural and reflexive in form, rather than simply technical (Wynne, 2003).[14] Within operational risk discourses, some practitioners are also unconvinced about how any database for losses could be coupled to the internal control environment, since serious operational risk events may not be linked to transactions or earnings volatility in a clear way (Moody's Investor Service, 2002).

Demonstrable adherence to corporate governance standards as prescribed under Pillar 2 should lead, in theory, to an adjustment factor by the Basel 2 regulations, especially as good controls are a prerequisite for the use of advanced approaches. The Committee was initially hesitant to develop explicit scores for internal controls on the grounds that they would not be 'objective' and because good internal control would translate into lower loss experience in later years. However, banks complained that they would be required to have a higher minimum capital than their controls merit because they only get credit *ex-post* via lower loss experiences and by being permitted to use advanced measurement approaches. All this gave rise to an extended regulatory politics about how and when banks could gain capital reserving advantages from loss preventing investments. This was a politics of the boundaries between Pillar 1 and Pillar 2, but it was also a politics of verification. The entire capital charging structure underpinning Pillar 1 is weighted towards the recognition of concrete, verifiable *ex-post* events as data points, such as direct losses and write downs. From this point of view, anticipatory and preventative investments in internal controls get valued in so far as they impact on the future loss experience of the bank.

Another dimension of the early experience of operational risk management is that organizational agents, faced with the task of inventing a new management practice, tend to choose a pragmatic path of collecting data which is collectable, rather than that which is necessarily relevant. The development of operational risk management activity in financial institutions focused initially on routine systems errors, malfunctions, and losses where accounting and information systems were most established, extending and rationalizing existing data sets about the operational performance of systems. So early experiences of operational risk management replaced the burden of managing potentially unknowable risks, such as rogue traders, with easier tasks and with more routine and expected areas of loss which may in aggregate be economically significant on a recurrent basis. Thus, fines for mis-selling financial products, fines imposed on some US investment banks in 2003, and credit card fraud losses have given the operational risk management agenda its early flavour. A strong emphasis on routine fraud and on the management of legal and regulatory liability also gave legal risks an important role in the development of operational risk (Wood, 2003). In these areas, it becomes possible in principle to apply and adapt modelling techniques which are accepted in the areas of market and credit risk analysis.

An institutional solution to the data infrequency problem has been the pooling of loss data across banks to generate richer databases and a top-down approach to operational risk at the industry level. There have been experiments with databank consortia to improve collective information resource, experiments which reveal a tension between confidentiality and collectivity.[15] However, these approaches, which are still developing, have the effect of making an internal approach to operational risk measurement *de facto* external, thereby blunting the risk-sensitivity to specific organizations, which is the whole purpose of the advanced approach. So pooling of loss data may provide comfort about aggregate capital levels in the system, but is potentially contradictory for a regulatory practice explicitly committed to a capital charge for operational risk which reflects the experience and risk profile of an individual bank.

The data collection process for operational risk has other important behavioural dimensions, most obviously the problem of action and incentives to report relevant events where they are likely to increase the capital charge to a business unit. As Hood et al. (1992: 158) put it, 'complex systems can only function efficiently if all incentives to hide information about errors are removed so that near-misses and minor malfunctions can be fully analysed and discussed so as to head off major malfunctions'. While internal agents such as in-house lawyers and human resource specialists may have no disincentive to report near misses (because they enhance their own role by doing so), operational departments may wish to hide these events, or 'translate' them into other risk categories, such as credit and market risk. Equally, risks and losses may be reported and overstated as part of an argument to secure more resources. At its worst, data collection methods used 'in order to limit the adverse effects of an event, may result in incentives which would increase the number of such events themselves' (Goodhart, 2001: 12), making data collection a perverse and contradictory activity for banks. From this point of view, the management of operational risk is itself an operational risk (Mestchian, 2003).

An additional dimension to the debate concerns the role of insurance in mitigating operational risk. Critics argue that Basel 2 overstates the applicability of the capital cushion philosophy and understates the role of insurance and internal process controls in risk management (e.g., Calomiris and Herring, 2002; Kuritzkes, 2002; Kuritzkes and Scott, 2005). It is argued that insurance is part of the overall risk management process and that the focus of capital adequacy should be on residual risks after insurance. While there is some allowance for insurance under AMAs, banking supervisors remained cautious about the recognition of insurance transfers of operational risk. Operational risk management might be transferred to an insurance market which it considers to be under-capitalized, thereby increasing systemic risk. And given the problems of data definition and frequency discussed above, the actuarial base for operational risk insurance must be suspect (Goodhart, 2001). Notwithstanding the inventiveness of underwriters in taking a bet on new insurable objects (Ericson and Doyle, 2003), the data issue is simply shifted by insurance and there may be no rational basis for correlating premiums and operational risk despite the development of new basket policies (Ashby and Young, 2003). Questions exist for regulators about the scope of policies and how claims might be paid, subject to reinsurance risk. Insurance policies for operational events can have many idiosyncratic features, such as deductibles and limits, which make them difficult to value and one large loss on an operational risk policy could eradicate the entire market for cover.

These different discussions within the emerging operational risk field show how the data collection needed for more advanced calculations of risk demands the creation of new institutions and units (Power, 2004b). It is well known that organizations tend to collect the data that they can, given legacy information systems, rather than the data they want or need. Organizations also frame and construct notions of error and its management which fit existing institutionalized patterns of information gathering and demands for modelling, while other significant anomalies may go unnoticed (Vaughan, 1996; 2005). So the material realization of operational risk management is therefore far from being a simple technocratic process involving risk identification and data collection. Data collection is a constitutive and performative process, which identifies and makes visible organizational categories of error, mistake, and anomaly, and locates them as risks for decision-making purposes.

New forms of data collection are always a behavioural challenge. The 'buy-in' by staff, and the organizational capacity to use 'new' data sets to challenge prevailing cultures and norms, are persistent themes in operational risk discourses. This is the puzzle of the managerialization of operational risk: on the one hand, it is an emergent managerial and supervisory category drama-tized by the historical experience of low probability, high impact events, that is, the Barings rogue trader paradigm. On the other hand, the material practice of operational risk management is necessarily shaped and constrained by existing patterns of risk management work by private internal agents who routinely act in a world of low impact and medium to high probability events. These agents, such as lawyers, compliance officers, and internal auditors, tend to define the operational risk agenda according to their own bodies of knowledge, collect the data relevant to their working practices, and construct notions of error which can reasonably be managed and, crucially, audited. In this way, agents necessarily seek to frame, shape, and 'tame' new categories of organizational danger within institutionally defined paths. Yet categories, like operational risk, also move in a space of regulatory discourse which is unencumbered by these local frictions of implementation.

Capital and Calculation

The emergence of operational risk management in the banking industry has taken place within a broader business and regulatory context. As we saw in Chapter 3 considerable investment in the development and application of economic capital measurement techniques was motivated in part by a need to gain more risk-based control over transactions by charging businesses with the cost of risk capital. In theory, the sum of all such capital requirements calculated on a bottom-up transactions basis represents the economic capital at risk of the firm as a whole (subject to diversification allowances) and provides a guide to reserving requirements for unexpected losses. Measures of capital at risk, such as *Riskmetrics*, grew in external importance and formed the basis for a new kind of dialogue between banks and regulators about capital adequacy.

Pillar 1 of the new Basel accord defines a discursive space within which regulators and managers may disagree about specific aspects of calculating risk capital but share an underlying assumption that management demands measurement. As noted in Chapter 3, VaR is not only significant for its capacity to calculate specific numbers for capital at risk, subject to assumptions. It also represents an ideal of regulatory and managerial control based on capital as a common language for internal and supervisory management. Whatever the micro-politics of implementation and variability of method, calculating capital is a deep-seated aspiration which establishes the possibilities of discourse between banks and regulators. However, while the field of banking risk management seems to exhibit a profound 'trust in numbers' (Porter, 1995) (more accurately, a trust in models), on deeper inspection this trust is more complex and varied.

The ideal implicit in Pillar 1 is that capital measurement methodologies which have been accepted in the field of market and credit risk management can and should be extended to operational risk. Operational risk is a new category in need of being populated by institutionalized forms of calculation (Alexander, 2003). The need to calculate a VaR equivalent for operational risk quickly defined a new sub-community of interest in the risk management field, namely *calculative idealists* committed to extending the broad calculative logics of RAROC and VaR. Calculative idealists typically regard numbers as aiming to represent the true cost of economic capital based on high quality frequency data, and to induce correct economic behaviour in the light of these risk measures. Operational risk must be made to fit this knowledge paradigm of risk measurement defined by a market risk benchmark.

Calculative idealists are *reductivists*. They hold a deeply non-pluralist view of operational risk management and worry constantly about the 'robust' and 'hard' nature of operational risk analysis. They may be cautious about specific methods but they refer often to the 'immature' nature of risk modelling for operational risk and are dismissive of scorecards as anything but a temporary measure. Their knowledge base in financial economics exhibits deep-seated assumptions about calculation as an ideal and they have a dislike for the messy, recalcitrant nature of operational risk and its data poverty.[16] They ignore or look down on internal auditors and regard COSO as a muddled and misleading basis for risk management (e.g., Samad-Khan, 2005).

In contrast, practitioner debates about operational risk reveal another class of commentator which may be called *calculative pragmatists*. They are more sceptical about the role of numbers in managing operational risk, especially legal risks (Kuritzkes and Scott, 2005). They typically regard them as attention-directing devices with no intrinsic claims to represent reality, or at best as a very partial representation of enterprise risks.[17] Calculative pragmatists are more tolerant about risk and control scoring systems and crude approximations of capital provided they help to steer behaviour and action in the right direction. They are more pluralistic about operational risk management, partly because they think capital should not be the sole foundation of risk management practice: 'operational risk management is about internal controls, not about quantification and capitalization'; the quantification of operational risk is just one tool for controlling it (Cagan, 2001). Indeed, 'given the difficulty of quantifying aspects of operational risk, the reliance on a single number may itself be an operational risk' (Wilson, 2001).[18]

Calculative pragmatists regard operational risk as more akin to a craft than a science. They place much greater emphasis on the role of preventative internal controls than idealists (e.g., Mestchian et al., 2005). Core knowledge is based in the disciplines of audit, of credit control and settlement systems management, in business processes and in human resource management.[19] Calculative pragmatism, commonly referred to by idealists as 'soft' risk management, makes sense in environments where it is critical to identify and catalogue risks which lie at the limits of formal knowledge. Many calculative pragmatists believe that VaR models do not transfer well to operational risk, prefer probabilistic scenarios, and tolerate self-assessment where completeness of risk identification is critical. Scoring systems which emerge from consultative, focus group processes make risk identification and mapping a semi-expert practice which presupposes a 'knowledge and wisdom base in all organizations that can provide powerful feedback for the purpose of mapping risks' (Cagan, 2001). For calculative pragmatists, scoring systems for economic capital which generate crude but directionally effective RAROC numbers have the critical behavioural merit of reminding line managers about the cost of capital.[20]

The distinction between calculative idealists and pragmatists has been somewhat exaggerated to make a point about two logics of calculation and two practitioner identities in the field of operational risk. The observable differences are naturally more subtle than this. Idealists may behave as pragmatists in the short run, waiting for the day when operational risk 'matures'. They tolerate scoring systems as a way of constructing the field and they may display scepticism about models, but this is more for practical than fundamental reasons. Idealists may also realize that it is smart to make appropriate statements about governance and internal control. On the other side pragmatists do not think that calculation has no place in operational risk management; so they will support its development enthusiastically. However, they will tend to construct operational risk management with the help of standards such as COSO as the management of risk management and see it as having a higher order governance role, standing in a hierarchical relation to the calculative idealism of market and credit risk management functions (e.g., Aerts, 2001). Pillar 2 appeals to pragmatists because a philosophy of relying on 'solid management processes' seeks to activate senior management responsibility for the self-assessment of risk, that is, the 'management of risk management'. However, it should not be forgotten that pragmatists and idealists are likely both to share a distrust of arbitrary supervisor discretion, either through judgements about the quality of internal controls in the second pillar, or by orders to modify banks' own calculations of economic capital. Nevertheless, there is a fault line within operational risk discourse which runs deep and reflects antagonisms about the role of measurement in management.[21] The two contrasting styles of approach to operational risk represent competing knowledge discourses or 'logics of practice', a 'tug of war' (Hoffman, 2002: 186). Basel 2 accommodates these logics in Pillar 1 and Pillar 2, the difference between which broadly reflects the difference between risk analysis and the narratives of risk governance as discussed in Chapter 1. Concrete realizations of operational risk management embody these deeper tensions between different constellations of quantitative expertise in organizations.

The tension between calculative pragmatism and idealism also reflects a disciplinary collision between different bodies of knowledge with a claim on the management of uncertainty: auditing and finance. The former is a pragmatic craft, despite a history of scientific pretensions, and the latter draws upon advanced mathematical techniques to model 'market' and 'credit' risks.[22] So the differences *within* notions of economic calculation which are visible in the operational risk debate also correspond to competing occupational mobility projects. The case of operational risk shows how private actors enlisted in support of the 'enforced self regulatory' ideal of Basel 2 compete to construct the manageability of risk in their own image.

A growing body of work in the social studies of finance emphasizes the performative character of calculation. By this is meant the fact that calculative technologies co-produce the risk objects that they measure, such as value (Mackenzie and Millo, 2003; Mackenzie, 2005; Kaltoff, 2005: 75). This chapter has shown how spaces for calculation, and demands for risk calibration, must themselves be constructed by systems of concepts and categories. The category of operational risk became institutionalized and accepted before any particular calculative construction of it, just as institutional demands for 'efficiency' or 'value-added' came to be accepted as ideas before their realization in specific projects of calculation (Burchell *et al.*, 1985). The case of operational risk also reveals additional complexity and shows how material realizations of operational risk remain varied because its management can be 'performed' according to different calculative pathways. The authors of Basel 2 sensibly sought to accommodate and formalize this diversity in the difference between Pillar 1 and Pillar 2 prescriptions without fully realizing that the category of operational risk would become a stake in the competition for pre-eminence within management hierarchies.

To summarize: practitioner debates about operational risk are informed by wider presumptions about the calculation of economic capital. Like discussions about market risk management, they refer extensively to issues of quantification, but not in a consistent manner. The reason for this inconsistency lies in a fundamental difference between two philosophies of calculation. Idealists regard managing operational risk as no different in principle from market risk or credit risk; they assume it is a monster to be ultimately tamed within these frameworks. Pragmatists accept much of the idealists' need to model where this is possible, that is, in restricted cases of homogenous, high frequency data sets, but they place greater emphasis on management processes and internal controls as the foundation of operational risk management. Although these ideal differences are rarely manifest in a pure form, they surface constantly in policy discussions about Basel 2 and in variations in the approaches adopted by particular banks.

Conclusions: Operational Risk and the Construction of Manageability

New regulatory practices involve the production and negotiation of ideas, the development of classificatory schemes, and the writing of blueprints for best practice. Multiple agents with overlapping interests in forms of organizational practice and ordering contribute to these discursive processes (Leyshon and Thrift, 1997: chapter 8). Possibilities and aspirations for control and order are materialized in a wealth of discussion documents, codes of practice, guidance manuals and laws, but are always in part visionary or programmatic, and always subject to contests about meaning at the local level. Furthermore, theories of regulation and finance are also part of this discursive process, and get mobilized to structure a political economy of regulation which is increasingly knowledge and information based (Thrift, 1994) and which increasingly relies on the expertise of private actor coalitions (Tsingou, 2003; 2007) operating beyond the state and constructing regulatory reform programmes, such as Basel 2 (Rose and Miller, 1992).

Perhaps nowhere is the discursive character of regulatory change more visible than in the example of operational risk.[23] The process of naming, defining, developing, implementing, and supervising operational risk management in banks is continually evolving (Mercer Oliver Wyman, 2004). However, the most difficult and decisive part of that process occurred in the late 1990s with the rapid institutionalization of 'operational risk' as a category of regulatory intervention and as a new object for senior management attention. The regulatory process began to articulate new languages, maps, and ideas for banking organizations in the early 1990s. However, this vision required a further catalyst to frame the issue for management, namely the radical uncertainty generated by the spectre of a single employee destroying an entire organization. The rise of operational risk shows how the rhetoric of a 'killer' event became translated into routines, regulations, and data collection processes. The epistemological anxiety of extreme events came to be tamed and managerialized by naming, scoring, and framing in the rational language of probability.

The organizing power of the operational risk category lies in its boundary-spanning capacity to create a linked constellation of interests (Burchell et al., 1985) uniting apparently disparate concerns with fraud, processing error, business discontinuity, human resource management, and legal liability. Notwithstanding the formal exclusion of reputational and strategic risk management, these concerns constantly leak into the operational risk agendas of organizations—partly because that is an easy place for them to go. The category of operational risk defines a space of policy and managerial attention where a framework based on deeply-held beliefs about the role of calculating economic capital at risk overlaps with other beliefs about a risk governance process rooted in frameworks for internal control and management oversight. The rise of operational risk also provides an instructive normative case study for policy-makers. Given the necessity of relying on private knowledge production for the detailed implementation of a rule, regulators may find that the invention of concepts and principles is more than just their best bet; it can be a powerful technology of change in its own right. Regulators should be 'dynamic nominalists'.

To suggest that operational risk has been 'invented' is not entirely metaphorical. Businesses have always understood sources of hazard and uncertainty arising from diverse sources, such as defective information technology and infrastructure; employee fraud; business disruption; legal exposure. However, the institutional visibility of these risk objects has been re-constructed within the discourse of operational risk. They have a new conceptual location and status for managerial and regulatory purposes. Basel 2 also defines connections between the management of operational risk and good corporate governance in such a way as to position these 'old' risks in a new space of regulatory, political and social expectations. The invention of operational risk provides yet another example of how discourses of good governance and risk management are increasingly intertwined and co-extensive.

Operational risk is no simple or self-evident category; it is a label for a diverse range of practices, a vision of control and regulation in an evolving field, and an imperative to manage and be responsible for a newly visible range of problems. It is both a name for a set of problems and interests, and a promise of a new way of intervening in, and determining, the internal structure of financial organizations. Out of these different elements a new hybrid body of management knowledge has been created with its own texts, emerging disciplines and professional identities. A wide range of organizations must now describe a significant sub-set of their activities in terms of operational risk.

The 'history of the present' of operational risk cannot be definitively concluded. Basel 2 is a global mega-regulatory programme on the grandest of scales, perhaps a regulatory fantasy (Clarke, 1999) which, like the Sarbanes–Oxley legislation, prescribes hyper-rational management for the world banking system. As with Sarbox and internal control, the invention and mobilization of the concept of operational risk, reflects broader political demands for effective regulation and for images of rational control and oversight to underwrite confidence and security in the financial system. This chapter has sought to identify three key themes in the early development of operational risk as a basis for the organization of uncertainty—definitional struggles, efforts to create material infrastructures of data, and competing calculative ideologies. These three themes define the contours of an organizational and regulatory politics of operational risk. While the category of operational risk, like internal control, VaR, and ERM, may remain contested at the level of detail, it has been successful in representing new visibilities in organizations, representations which have created new possibilities for intervention and control in its name. The invention of operational risk is an extended institutional attempt to frame the unframeable, to assuage anxieties and fears about uncontrollable 'rogue others', and to tame the 'man-made' monsters of the financial system.

Notes

This chapter is based on material in Power (2005a).

1. See Underhill (1991) and Leyshon (1994: 137).
2. Indicative evidence for this is provided by a non-systematic sample of ten major banks' annual reports from Australia, France, Germany, UK, and USA between 1995 and 2003. These reports show the first mention of operational risk as a narrative disclosure category from 1998 onwards, with only two mentioning the concept prior to this. For a more systematic treatment, see Helbok and Wagner (2003).
3. In 2000 the Risk Waters group began to publish a weekly newsletter with that title.
4. COSO (1992) also defined 'operations' as an area for internal control distinct from compliance and financial reporting. So the idea of operations as a discrete area for regulation is much broader than its specific use in the banking field.
5. The 1994 Basel Committee document was heavily influenced by Group of Thirty (1993). For more on the wider regulatory influence of the latter, see Tsingou (2003; 2007).
6. I am grateful to Clive Briault for this point.
7. It has been suggested that: 'the new emphasis on operational risk is partly just a smokescreen for a cumulative add-on factor, to offset the reduction that would otherwise occur from the move towards more sophisticated measurement of the other kinds of risk' (Goodhart, 2001: 14).
8. Half the banks in an early survey (Basel Committee on Banking Supervision, 1998b) had created an operational risk manager independent of the business lines, e.g., in the Royal Bank of Scotland where a Head of Group Operational Risk (subsequently a Head of Group Enterprise Risk) reported to the Director of Group Risk, alongside the heads of credit and market risk. The creation of dedicated roles with senior reporting lines reflects an organizational positioning of operational risk in a broader space than regulatory compliance (see also RMA, 1999).

9. This series of conferences started in 1998. While the Basel 2 reforms are not the only point of reference in the proceedings, it is clear that they cast a shadow over the entire event. Such conferences act as important platforms for knowledge leadership and promotion by consultants offering masterclasses and similar packages. Ernst and Young, one of the sponsors of the event, were active in positioning themselves in the advisory market for operational risk related services (e.g., Ernst and Young, 2001).

10. The words 'direct or indirect' were later removed.

11. The practitioner journal *Operational Risk* founded in 1999 has since changed its name to *Operational Risk and Compliance*.

12. It is argued that legal risk, like reputational risk, is not diagnostic. Legal risk is properly understood as a consequence within an operational risk pipeline (see Wood, 2003).

13. For an explicit recommendation for near miss analysis in the chemical industry, see Phimster *et al.* (2003).

14. According to John Thirlwell (private correspondence with the author), 'operational risk is a social rather than a mathematical science'.

15. This was also true of the development of mortality tables in the nineteenth century which were regarded as proprietorial assets for life insurance businesses (Alborn, 1996).

16. An academic colleague in the field of finance once told me that operational risk was very interesting but too 'risky' a topic for research because the lack of available data (of the kind available to study market risk) constrained the possibility of a publication in the *Journal of Finance*.

17. A good generic example of calculative pragmatism is Simon's (1999) risk calculator technology, a tool which generates qualitative scores for the riskiness of different functional areas. The tool generates scores which 'become objective' by virtue of being used by management and by virtue of being attention-directing. The process has nothing to do with measuring risk in terms of frequencies and has little connection with a process of measuring subjective 'degrees of belief' (Gigerenzer, 2001: 26–7). Simon admits that 'the risk exposure calculator is not a precise tool…' and its results are 'directional' only (Simon, 1999: 86).

18. An article by the risk officer at Enron had the title 'Aiming for a Single Metric'. It has been argued that '…operational risk measurement is not the same as operational risk management. Quantifying those operational risks that lend themselves to quantification and neglecting the rest does not constitute best practice…' (Cagan, 2001).

19. Agency-theoretic analyses of operational risk can be classed as pragmatism for these purposes because they conceptualize the control problem as essentially behavioural and calculative devices only have a role in contracts to incentivize agents (e.g., Sheedy, 1999).

20. For example, Bankers Trust, identified as a pioneer in risk management by Jorion (2001: 96), allocated capital to operational risk based on scoring for a range of factors including inherent risk, control risk, and actual loss experience (Hoffman, 2002; Wilson, 1995). Chase Manhattan bank in 1999 also adapted the COSO (1991) framework for its operational risk processes (Barton *et al.*, 2001: chapter 3). In another early experiment, the chief risk officer at ANZ bank, Mark Lawrence, used a scorecard system, claiming it was a forward-looking and rational basis for allocating economic capital to business units (Jameson, 2001b).

21. These antagonisms have been explored by a critical accounting literature for nearly thirty years, particularly in the context of public sector reform processes (see Miller, 1994).

22. For the purposes of this contrast, legal disciplines can be located on the auditing side of the distinction.

23. The complete Basel 2 proposals and related materials can be accessed at the Basel Committee website at www.bis.org/bcbs.

5

Governing Reputations: The Outside Comes in

Just as 1995 was a critical year for the category of operational risk, it is also important for the emergence and intensification of managerial discourses about organizational reputation. Efforts to create a distinctive practice of 'reputational management' were catalyzed by the experience at Shell in that year (Fombrun and Rindová, 2000). The company planned to dispose of the Brent Spar oil container in the North Sea and had considered the environmental impact of different options at some length in arriving at its decision. However, Shell failed to take account of likely public attitudes to water-based disposal, and of the role of a body like Greenpeace in activating that opinion. The anticipated disposal gave rise to widespread boycotting of Shell products and outlets, particularly in Germany, resulting in financial loss and adverse publicity.

This episode involving a multinational organization came to be regarded as a paradigmatic demonstration of the new power of external groups to use the media and to threaten the legitimacy and value of large organizations (Lofstedt and Renn, 1997). Shell executives and the UK government believed mistakenly that the public, and pressure groups such as Greenpeace, would automatically understand the environmental superiority of water-based disposal. In hindsight, their predominantly technocratic understanding of the problem dominated sensitivity to the diversity of public risk perceptions. The Shell organization survived this event (and criticism of its role in

Nigeria in that same year), but undertook to make significant internal changes as a consequence. Their experience was also something of a 'tipping point' for a new corporate sensibility and fear about reputation and its implications for management.[1]

In the same way as parts of management practice in banking came to be reorganized under the category of 'operational risk', so too did 'reputation' begin to emerge as a discrete category of managerial concern. As we saw in Chapter 4, banking regulators chose to exclude reputational and business risks from the definition of operational risk. They preferred to focus on the underlying causes of loss in systems and behaviour, rather than include a phenomenon which was difficult to define, and was relevant to the consequences of almost every possible area of management practice (Larkin, 2002: chapter 3). However, the potential unmanageability of reputation is its essential nature. Organizational reputation is socially constructed, often by specialist organizations which monitor, evaluate, and measure it. Reputation has come to be imagined as encompassing much more than consumer product or service satisfaction. Organizations which certify and celebrate reputation have grown rapidly in the 1990s to create a crowded institutional environment. Reputation has come to be seen as both at risk and at the limits of conventional management control. It has become a governing risk object for large organizations and is infused with both fear and opportunity. By 2004, the World Economic Forum could declare that 'corporate brand reputation outranks financial performance as the most important measure of corporate success'.

Practices to manage organizational environments in the name of a 'good' name in effect seek to manage and construct social perceptions. This means that the potential scope of efforts to manage reputation is very great and may reach into every corner of organizational life with insistent demands for capacities for external responsiveness and 'reputational attention'. Almost any action can be rationalized and redescribed in terms of its reputational implications. In the next section, it is argued that the idea of reputation is an emergent managerial object shared by a wide variety of organizational practices and perspectives. An active advisory market has imported the idea of reputation to redefine and reposition its service base, making the supply of reputation management services a critical factor in the growing significance of the category. Reputational ideas have travelled and diffused widely as a challenge to organizations to be more sensitive to the organized environments in which they operate, and to create appropriate formal organizational structures.

Section three addresses a core aspect of emerging reputation management ideas, namely the imperative to construct, know, understand, and interact with 'stakeholders'. While discourses of stakeholder and reputation management have become almost co-extensive, stakeholders pose a fundamental challenge to ERM and to process-based conceptions of risk management. Even though such frameworks seek to accommodate stakeholder interests as threats, these interests are endogenous, dynamic, and not easily reducible to process. This challenge reflects the fault-line within risk management between managerial and democratic logics discussed in earlier chapters.

The argument then analyses how reputation is constructed and instrumentalized as a 'risk object' by means of metrics, rankings, and league tables created by external organizations. The institutionalization of these external calculations of reputation accelerate organizational and individual concerns with external perceptions and create incentives for organizational practices and metrics to service externally validated 'reputational constructs'. At this point, organizations are caught up in a self-amplifying game of reputation management to bring the 'outside-in'. Finally, the analysis focuses on the construction of reputational risk management as an assembly of practices and managerial sensibilities. These attempts to govern, normalize, and proceduralize a changing and unruly environment reflect, as in the case of operational risk, a managerial ambition to organize uncertainty, to produce order, and to assuage fear. Yet, the uncertainty of reputation is itself the product of institutions, and is itself organized and envisioned as the purest form of man-made contagion.

The Reputation Constellation

Reputation has been described as a new management 'paradigm' (Davies *et al.* 2002; Jackson 2004), but its significance is hardly new. Concerns with reputation have existed as long as ethics and morality have been discussed, which is a long time. As we shall see, *individual* reputation and conduct, especially that of corporate leaders (Gaines-Ross, 2002), is a facet of recent managerial discourse, but it is not the whole story. Rather, it is the rise of concerns with the reputation of *organizations* which has come to the fore since the mid-1990s. The experiences of Shell and other documented cases have come to be part of a reputational dramatology, often drawing on many of the same events and crises as operational risk commentators but constructing them as *causes célèbres* of reputation mis-management. Like operational risk, the sites for this drama are conferences, surveys and prescriptive texts, and a growing body of advisors exploit reputational concerns to reposition their services as a form of risk management.

The category of 'reputation' has functioned as an analytic construct in the field of economics for some time (Klein, 1997). Social and economic actors rely on many proxies in order to gain assurance that expectations of future performance or product quality will not be disappointed, and reputation is a critical analytical variable in bargaining theory. However, this work within social science is different in kind from more recent prescriptive managerial efforts to organize practices explicitly in the name of reputation. Fombrun and Shanley's (1990) classic study of firms' signalling strategies is something of a bridge between economics and normative business strategy. As practical fields come into existence, it is not unusual for elements of academic thinking to become repackaged as part of the abstract knowledge base of practice (Abbott, 1988). In this way analytic concepts become 'scientized' by specific carriers of knowledge, such as prominent academics and consultants (Sahlin-Andersson and Engwall, 2002; Drori and Meyer, 2006).

Fombrun and Van Riel (1997) observe that there are many different 'languages of reputation' spanning the sub-fields of strategy, marketing, human resources, organizational culture, accounting, sociology, and communications. Within the field of marketing, reputation has come to be articulated primarily in terms of customer perceptions, loyalty, and likelihood to repurchase. In its early marketing manifestation, reputation was understood as an aspect of a more general focus on organizational identity and image management (Schultz et al., 2000). Generic branding strategies consciously aim to create or enhance symbols and identity constructs which would encourage customer loyalty—hence a link between brand and reputation management. Organizations are understood to be active in constructing and validating symbols over and above their specific products. Reputation is the outcome of 'creating an account of an organization, embedding that account in a symbolic universe, and thereby endowing the account with social facticity' (Rao, 1994: 31).

A consequence of this marketing construction of reputation is that it is commonly understood as an 'asset' whose managerial reality is dependent on being recognized, measured, and located within a management control infrastructure (ICAEW, 2000). This instrumental discourse of reputation conceptualizes it as a manageable source of 'excess returns' and competitive advantage, governed by the accountant's 'logic of assethood' (Scott and Walsham, 2005). At the border between marketing and accounting, reputation comes to be registered as an 'intangible asset', a component of goodwill which is itself visible in the difference between the book value and market value of an entity.

During the acquisition intensive period of the 1980s, there was a heated politics of how to account for goodwill in general and valuable brands in particular (Power, 1992). This discourse was more far reaching than technical accounting; it concerned the very nature and significance of 'intangibles' and their perceived centrality to the emerging 'new economy' of the 1990s. Accounting systems were challenged to 'catch-up' with, and recognize commercial realities. Historically, accounting 'goodwill' is a broad category which may encompass the value of a skilled workforce, customer relations, and corporate reputation. These qualities of goodwill were traditionally regarded by accountants as not reliably measurable independently of a specific market transaction. Goodwill continued for years to be a residual which was only visible to accountants when a business was sold. As long as the number attributed to this 'goodwill' factor was small relative to corporate net worth, it posed a theoretical problem of understanding only, and not a practical difficulty. Yet as accounting intangibles came to be by far the largest component of corporate value (as measured by market capitalization), new accountings were demanded to support a management process oriented explicitly towards these sources and drivers of value.

Efforts to represent and value brands within traditional accounting frameworks for financial reporting were part of a mood of experimentation in new systems, embracing 'value reporting' and 'triple bottom line' accounts. These innovations sought to bridge disciplinary differences and create new productive relations between accounting, marketing, business strategy, and social values. Efforts to measure and manage intellectual assets in organizations acquired a new practitioner urgency (Mouritsen, 2001) and ideas of 'reputational asset' and 'brand equity' were mobilized in the re-presentation of marketing as a management practice in the service of shareholder value

(Ambler *et al.* 2001). Marketing was constructed as a reputational building enterprise focused on identifying, measuring, and exploiting sources of value. Marketing conceptions of reputation management were pervaded by a logic of opportunity.[2]

The category of reputation is not simply or only a 'boundary object' spanning management sub-fields like marketing, accounting, and human resources. Crucially, it has also emerged from the continuing conceptual, legal, and ethical dynamic in which the boundary between organizations, their environments, and society as a whole is negotiated. So while the notion of 'reputational asset' suggests a logic of instrumentalization within management practice, in fact this asset derives its value from a complex field of social and economic interdependencies, an institutional field from which organizations derive social legitimacy (Meyer and Rowan, 1977). According to Peters (2000), reputational 'capital' is a 'new intangible' expressing the societal value that an organization puts back into the economy, as well as a return to an old concept: the corporate 'license to operate'. So the accounting problem of intangibles can be taken to reflect more fundamental issues to do with sources of corporate value arising from relationships. These relationships are not only with customers, suppliers, and providers of capital but also with potentially threatening agents like Greenpeace who possess a growing capacity to construct an alternative 'social facticity' of organizational reputation and to challenge it. Thus, there has been a 'progressive broadening' of reputational discourse which provides a new platform for critical corporate social responsibility agendas (Larkin, 2002: 41).

The last three decades have witnessed an expansion of interest in corporate social responsibility (CSR) and in organizations whose mission is to promote it (Boli and Thomas, 1999; Boli, 2006). The focus of CSR has moved beyond health and safety in the workplace to encompass a diverse array of external social and environmental factors, including human rights and corrupt practices. Indeed, CSR now seems to take as its object the entire ethical character of the organization and its governance.[3] Of particular significance in this evolving assembly of ideas and practices is the progressive development of platforms to internalize CSR issues within organizations and the role of so-called 'soft norms' developed by non-governmental organizations in this process. In place of critical social audits conducted by external parties in the 1970s, experiments with new 'socially sensitive' accountings have become evident, such as value-added statements (Burchell *et al.*, 1985), social indicators, eco-balance sheets, triple bottom line accounting, and sustainability reporting (GRI 2000). These experiments, prompted in part by scandals and disasters such as Exxon Valdez and Bhopal, are also indicative of a neoliberal style of regulation and governance in the transnational CSR field (Gouldson and Bebbington, 2007). Efforts are underway to make the activities and impacts of companies more transparent, in effect to make corporate virtues and vices auditable (Accountability, 2002). From this perspective risk management provides an operational platform for processing, transforming, and instrumentalizing moral concerns (Sison, 2000; Power, 2003b), although, for a number of commentators, this also represents the cooptation and commodification of CSR (e.g., Shamir, 2004; 2005).[4]

CSR itself is, and remains, a hybrid concept which directs attention in many specific directions (Larkin, 2002: chapter 6). In addition to the reporting innovations noted above, there are accreditation schemes for ethical management practices, particularly for supply chains, and practices for socially responsible investment. Objects of interest range from the use of child labour to environmental pollution, from operating in corrupt political regimes to diversity policy. More significantly, the CSR agenda as it has come to be framed in the 1990s overlaps with marketing and accounting concerns to understand drivers of corporate value. The concept of reputation is a bridge between traditional critical CSR and management recognition of the risk of failing to meet society's expectations (ABI, 2000). The spectre of threat is cast over new discourses of corporate long-termism and new concerns for reputation preservation have created a transformative potential for a CSR agenda which has traditionally been externalized as critique. Organizations must now think 'outside-in' (Jackson, 2004: chapter 10) and aspects of CSR have been reconstructed as a basis for managing organizational reputation. Despite the continuing role of legal liability as the voice of society within organizations, reputation management has come to articulate and internalize social concerns, thereby promising an alignment of governance, risk, and virtue (e.g., Turner, 2004).

In a space between two logics, fears of legal liability and reputational damage on the one hand and management opportunities for enhanced reputation and shareholder value on the other, earlier critical discourses of CSR have been transformed, interlaced with rhetorics of strategic significance, and have acquired greater currency within large organizations.[5] Institutions for progressing the discourse of CSR outside of national legislative frameworks have been created out of networks and alliances linking large businesses, government, pressure groups, and NGOs. The rise of meta-organizations at the world level which seek to define and write standards for corporate conduct has been conspicuous and represents a new space of transnational governance (Djelic and Sahlin-Andersson, 2006a and b; Boli, 2006), particularly in the risk management field.

Reputation emerged during the 1990s from its status as an analytical and ethical category to become an organizing concept within and across a wide variety of management areas, such as marketing, accounting, and strategy. The concept of reputation blurs boundaries, and creates thinkable relationships between practices which were hitherto distinct. Specifically, reputational discourse has provided a basis for rethinking the ambitions of CSR, bringing many of CSR's underlying agendas closer to the heartland of corporate strategy. Thus, like operational risk, the power of 'reputation' as a catalyzing concept lies in its role in linking distinct interests and practices in a constellation, a kind of circuit of commentary and advice which energizes a new consciousness of threat. This complex reputation constellation delineates an imagined, largely programmatic, convergence within a number of managerial sub-fields. The imperative of managing reputation means that the internal governance of the enterprise must become explicitly more outward facing and more formal; the new roles, processes, and strategies discussed in Chapter 3 constitute an organizational face for public evaluation (Meyer and Rowan, 1977). At the heart of this governing vision stands a key actor in the constellation—the stakeholder.

Holders of Stakes and the Risk Management Process

The moral vocabulary of governance described in Chapter 1 intertwines two logics of organizational control—managerial and democratic (Drori, 2006). Organizational systems of self-governing capacities must, to a degree prescribed by norms and codes, be responsive to elements in organizational environments which include markets, regulators, and social interest groups. So, in addition to the formally defined organizational architecture of the Combined Code and its variants (Chapter 2), organizational governance discourse increasingly implies the need for management understanding of, and engagement with, parties who have a 'stake' in control because they may exercise influence over organizational conduct. Such parties have come to be known broadly as 'stakeholders', and considerable intellectual and practical effort has been expended on analyzing the rights of such stakeholders and the duties of organizations towards them (Clarkson, 1998). It is their *de facto* power which is most relevant to risk management.

The category of stakeholder has been developing over a number of years. In 1975, a UK discussion document recommending a broader concept of corporate reporting did not use the word 'stakeholder' at all, referring instead to the rights to information of multiple 'user groups' (CCAB, 1975). Stakeholders have been defined as groups and individuals 'who can affect and are affected by the achievement of an organization's purpose' (Freeman, 1984: 54), a strategic definition which is relevant to recent risk management thinking. However, the concept does not seem to have gained ground in managerial and political discourse until the late 1990s[6] when it became a point of appeal and boundary object for both managerial and CSR agendas.[7] This moral ambivalence is a significant part of the appeal of the stakeholder concept. While the language of stakeholding can have normative connotations of partnership, the mobilization of the concept also has much to do with strategic responses to the perceived rise of consumer activism and the increasingly organized character of social conscience (Larkin, 2002: chapter 4; Friedman and Miles, 2006).

Newly active organizational actors in the governance universe have come to have rights to speak and act on behalf of society. Since Shell's experience in 1995, these NGOs are perceived as capable of organizing direct and indirect action against companies, a perception heightened by extensive attacks on the character of business and the professions in the UK and overseas in the 1990s, and dramatized by violent anti-capitalism protests at the G8 summits in Seattle and Genoa. These events created and amplified a more defensive climate and context for political and corporate concerns with reputational issues. From this point of view, the rise of concerns with reputation reflects much more than internal concerns with asset recognition. It has much to do with a perceived shift in power from corporations to the representative organizations of 'unpredictable consumers', organizations which are increasingly able to reverse burdens of proof about product safety and quality.

Managerial discourses of corporate reputation are symptomatic of the power of stakeholders to escalate reputation issues very rapidly. Yet, the institutionalization of pressure groups like Greenpeace has also shifted their strategy from a purely antagonistic relation with corporations to one which is more dialogic and which can draw on the ethical resources of corporate governance (Friedman and Miles, 2002). Large organizations like Shell have begun to develop capabilities for stakeholder management and new blue-prints and norms for 'engagement' have been created (Friedman and Miles, 2006: chapter 6). The task has been formalized in principles and guidance and rationalized as the demand for organizations to know *ex ante* who their key stakeholders might be. This demand requires a broad view of the potential *boundaries* of a business or project and the metaphor of 'radar' is often used in prescriptive texts. The limits to manageability posed by anti-corporatism as such (Tucker and Melewar, 2005) has been no bar to the growth of a rich advisory industry in the field of stakeholder management.

During the 1990s corporate reporting began to include a more developed social reporting component, and the perceived erosion of the social authority of, and trust in, large corporations led to many forms of experimental engagement with stakeholder organizations (Hutter and O'Mahony, 2004). The CSR agenda itself became structured as an engagement agenda informed by transnational norms and standards for reporting and by an increasingly rich basis in 'soft' law for CSR (Fombrun, 2005). For example, the Global Reporting Initiative (GRI, 2000) recommends the disclosure of the basis by which stakeholders are defined and of the involvement of such stakeholders in the development of performance indicators relevant to them. GRI initially struggled to gain an organizational foothold, but an emerging mood of concern about reputation has created incentives for more attention to stakeholders and to their internalization in management systems. Many organizations now take seriously the need to manage an active environment of potential claimants, whose interests are filtered by discourses of reputation management, corporate governance, and risk management (ABI, 2001).

Beneath democratic conceptions of stakeholder engagement, and beneath the creation of sub-units with this explicit purpose and mission, organiza-tional discourses also address how public risk perceptions could be a destruc-tive force and an unmanageable source of instability, as the Brent Spar episode seemed to show. From this point of view, and in stark contrast to normative theories, stakeholders are a managerial 'dread factor' and an explicitly recog-nized source of risk to the enterprise and its reputation. Initiatives to codify and develop generic risk management guidance discussed in Chapter 3 put 'stakeholder analysis' at their centre (e.g. CSA, 1997: AS/NZS, 2000; BSI, 1999), thereby standardizing, at least at the level of policy discourse, the need for such analysis as a crucial part of risk identification. Echoing Freeman's earlier strategic definition, a stakeholder for this purpose is any 'individual, group or organization having a vested interest in or influence on the business or its projects'. Stakeholder analysis in this sense recognizes that 'whatever the nature of their interest, the existence of that interest means that they are a potential source of risk to the project and perhaps to the business' and can be 'difficult to understand, control or influence'.

In contrast to a conception of stakeholder engagement informed by social democracy, the category enters formal risk management standards as short-hand for unruly risk perceptions. In risk management, the representation of stakeholders is emptied of moral content, and of any content in terms of the *rights* of individuals and groups external to an organization. Rather, the stakeholder becomes defined, represented, and instrumentalized as part of the expanded risk management mandate to process threats to the business (or project). In risk management thinking about stakeholders, the question is: 'who might blame and thereby damage the organization?' Stakeholder perceptions, as proxies for society's expectations, must be taken seriously even if they are not accepted as true; false beliefs about the environmental and social impacts of corporate activity must be managed.

This risk-based construction of the stakeholder reflects a 'thin theory of stakeholding' and contrasts with the surface normativity of CSR discourse discussed above. One problem with this 'thinness' is a tendency to articulate stakeholders statically with well-defined and stable interests. For ERM processes, the identification of relevant stakeholders is conceptualized as a one-off transaction. Yet, it may be a more effective reputation management strategy for organizations to 'optimize dynamically', that is, to play off stakeholders against each other by constantly re-designing their relationships with them.[8] The stakeholder management model of uncertain and developing relationships is consistent with models of risk management which work with the grain of organizational politics rather than prescribe a hyper-rational design (March and Simon, 1958; Hood, 1996a; 1996b).

Stakeholder organizations are themselves constituted as actors via engagements which require increasing rational management and for which strategic recommendations have been developed (e.g. Friedman and Miles, 2006:

chapter 6). In a world of organizing, stakeholder organizations must also constitute themselves as legitimate representatives of society and as credible dialogue partners, (Larkin, 2002: 136–7). Managing the risks posed by stakeholders is a dynamic in which they in turn must become more formally organized as legitimate representatives of society and as entities to do 'business with'. NGOs may adopt the formal attributes of organizational actorhood of those they seek to influence. Indeed, as many critics of CSR note, NGOs have incentives to make themselves less risky as partners to corporate organizations. Many adopt the very risk management standards which conceptualize them as a threat. Such is the isomorphic and normalizing power of risk management blueprints.

Questions of knowledge of, and responsiveness to, stakeholders and questions of reputational management have become intertwined. Organizations have become conscious of reputation as an asset which can be enhanced or harmed by organized elements called stakeholders. Managerial discourses suggest that stakeholders are 'here to stay' (Browne, 2000a; 2000b), a symptom of declining public trust in experts and science, and of the erosion of traditional authority (Larkin, 2002: chapter 1). Via the corporate recognition of stakeholders and their role in creating or damaging reputation, a distinctive form of risk management has become prominent, and a re-reading of CSR through the lens of risk has become possible (e.g., ABI, 2001). For all its operational ambiguity, reputation forces organizations to develop windows on society which bring the 'outside in'. Yet equally, the relational nature of reputational 'assets' places them beyond managerial control. Indeed, where the power to define reputation is wholly in the hands of stakeholders the necessary inputs from management are unclear. This difficulty is especially evident in external calculations of reputation.

Outside-in: Reputation, Rankings, and the Rise of Secondary Risk Management

The argument so far has considered the way in which discourses of reputation have created new connections between many different aspects of the managerial field. Given the general significance of 'calculative idealism' discussed in Chapter 4, and deep-seated ideas abut the fundamental role of measurement in management, it is no surprise that there have been extensive efforts to develop metrics and instruments to calculate the value of a good name. Many of these tools have been developed from the kind of factor analysis commonly used in marketing and brand valuation. For example, a 'reputation quotient' (Fombrun and Van Riel, 2003) has been developed based on a scoring system for six key drivers of reputation, representing a mix of business, social, and psychological factors.

The significance of reputational metrics is the fact that they are calculated by *external* agencies, often using information provided by organizations but using assumptions to combine them in calculations to yield a composite 'score' or index. These compressed, single-figure calculative representations of reputational 'performance' are, depending on their perceived significance, a new source of man-made risk to organizations. Such ranking systems have grown in institutional significance in the last twenty years. For example, as a feature of public management reforms in the UK, league tables of varying degrees of formality now exist for hospitals, schools, universities, and many other public service organizations. In the USA *Fortune* magazine conducts a survey of 'most admired companies'; in the UK the *Sunday Times* creates a ranking of best employers; and Transparency International has a corruption index for countries. Credit rating organizations may not produce rankings directly but they calibrate and construct creditworthiness in a manner which has the same effect (Sinclair, 2005). Business Schools also compete fiercely with each other on the international stage for preeminence in formal rankings (Wedlin, 2006) and organizations such as Governance Metrics International rank companies and countries in terms of good governance.

In general, there has been a conspicuous growth of organizations and practices whose purpose is to evaluate and rank others. They organize 'contests to evaluate products or firms and rank order participants according to their performance . . . victories in certification contests are small fortuitous events that create a reputation that becomes magnified by positive feedback' (Rao, 1994: 32). Individual organizations may provide a 'data feed' to these organizations but do not control the measures of reputation which are produced. Opportunities to contest a ranking or the construction of an index may be limited and undesirable, and managerial attention comes to focus on the management of the components of an index and their underlying causes. In this way, organizations support legitimated evaluators by supplying the necessary information, even to the extent of internalizing the components of the metric as performance variables. League tables, rankings, and indices construct self-reinforcing circuits of performance evaluation, thereby perpetuating the internal importance of externally constructed reputation and giving to reputation a new governing and disciplinary power.

Organizations, such as hospitals, business schools, and universities increasingly take such rankings seriously and orient internal efforts towards satisfying their criteria and improving their ranking. As organizational performance indicators for internal purposes come to be aligned with those which inform an evaluation or ranking system, issues of reputation and of performance are increasingly elided. Internal 'key performance indicators' and external measures of reputational risk may converge over time. Ranking systems which begin by accommodating local measures of performance necessarily rationalize and formalize these measures which are then reimported for internal use. For example, UK universities (and many individual scholars) have internalized the research productivity key performance indicators by which they will be scored and ranked. In this case, rankings have financial consequences and the basis of the metric can be complex and subject to change, making strategic behaviour difficult. Previous research on the external origins of internal information systems suggests that we should expect external reputational metrics to be reproduced and tracked internally (Burchell et al., 1985). Such systems come to play a significant disciplinary role in an organizational field; organizations are 'at risk' if they do not provide base data returns for the purpose of being ranked. In some cases they have the option to opt out of rankings, in others not.

Surveys and rankings are instruments by which society challenges the organizational 'license to operate'. Reputation is socially constructed by all these institutionalized efforts to make it measurable, visible, and auditable. Whereas concerns with reputation have been dramatized by major adverse events, such as Brent Spar, the growth of external metrics and evaluation platforms creates a more routinized approach to the calculation and visibility of reputation. Large organizations now operate in highly organized environments which routinely demand returns and disclosures of a whole array of attributes: community relations, corporate governance, diversity policy, and many more. Representations of social responsiveness quickly become auditable performance targets. The discourses of ranking now define the ambitions and mission of many organizations to be a 'top 20 university' or, '3 star hospital'. Changes in operational practices are certainly a part of the articulation of such ambitions, but such changes become linked to drivers of key ranking variables. Such variables are institutionally valued primarily for their simplicity, additivity and comparativity, yet it is well known that organizational practices are difficult to represent in abstract systems and 'creative gaming' of crude targets is probable (e.g., Bevan and Hood, 2006).

The growth of calculations of reputational strength which then enter rankings and league tables have become governance mechanisms in modern societies which organizations cannot ignore. Institutions which rank create a new class of risk, which might be called a 'secondary risk' of poor reputational performance as defined by the ranking system. From this perspective, 'reputation management' is an organizational space where new performance fears and perception anxieties must be routinely processed. Research on the 'social amplification of risk' (SAR) suggests that the 'secondary' or institutional effects' of an original risk event can have substantial consequences for organizations (Pidgeon et al., 2003). The question of amplification, and the role of the media, is an empirical one, and in some cases risk attenuation may be the case (Rothstein, 2003). However, much of the motivating discourse and imagination of reputation embodies a composite belief in the risks created both by an adverse event itself and also the social mechanisms and circuits which interpret and represent its significance.[9] Rankings are systems which explicitly interpret and evaluate dimensions of organizational actions.

While many amplification theorists have tended to focus on the role of the media, amplification is also profoundly reflexive and expectational in character. Responsive efforts by organizations to understand the drivers of reputation also construct and *amplify beliefs in amplification*. A history of previous failures to understand the degree of organization of external critical groups has itself been amplified in textbooks and consulting repertoires. Stakeholders are necessarily *internal* constructs within managerial discourses, representations of potential for shock. The argument that organizations constantly run the risk of over-managing and internally amplifying risks to reputation (Dukerich and Carter, 2000), suggests a heightened external responsiveness which may be driven by marketing and communications specialists with interests in magnifying the spectre of being 'front page news' for the wrong reasons. Reputational risk management and ranking systems therefore have a multiplying effect because new agents and units get created internally. In short, risk management practice is itself implicated in the amplification of the phenomenon of reputational risk. Organizations are often unable or unwilling to contest public perceptions of their actions because they have already internalized these perceptions.[10]

As noted in Chapter 3, regulatory organizations are not immune from the need to manage their secondary or reputational risks. Designed to deal with primary risks facing society, regulatory agencies themselves face secondary or 'institutional' risks to the legitimacy of their operations as this is judged by different publics (Rothstein *et al.*, 2006a). Thus, regulating social (first order) and institutional (second order) risks become intertwined in a process of governing which can become increasingly preoccupied with its own legitimacy. From this point of view, the emergence of risk-based approaches to regulation discussed in Chapter 2 is less to do with the substance of assessment techniques and more a part of the management of legitimacy and political reputation. This tension between first order and secondary risk management is likely to increase as the performance of regulatory bodies is subject to detailed performance scrutiny. In the UK there is not yet a ranking or league table system for regulators, but there are enough signs and formal materials on the criteria for good regulation to suggest that this could easily happen. In the emerging field of disparate reputation management practices it is increasingly difficult to distinguish strategies for the management of primary or first order risks to health, safety, environment, solvency and so on, from the management of institutional risks arising from the management process itself. A new kind of risk management has internalized and absorbed this tension; reputation permeates approaches to risk, so much so that the distinction between primary and secondary risk is now unclear. The new risk management is characterized by an emphasis on the possibility of account giving.

Arguably, reputational effects may arise from, and be attributed to, anything and everything. For example, assume that the directors of a very large public company consistently incur, and do not pay personally, parking fines for their company cars. The primary risk to the company, in this case of financial loss, is probably very small in relation to its annual turnover, even allowing for punitive fines. Accountants and auditors might argue that these amounts are *not material*, should not be separately disclosed in the annual report, and should be 'lost' in general expenses. But a fanciful example like this can easily be re-described by agents inside and outside the organization as a reputational issue: 'what would the public think of this behaviour by corporate leaders? How would the media report it if it came to light? What general signals of corporate trustworthiness and governance does this give? How might this affect our corporate trustworthiness index?

Fines and penalties, or indeed any operational or personal activity, can now be registered in a much broader social space than direct economic loss, creating a new interest in managing reputation via the discipline of ethics. Legal compliance has also come to be conceptualized as a reputational issue. Reputation has become significant for its role in reconstituting an entire sensibility or mood which is deeply defensive, despite its marketing framing in a logic of opportunity. This defensive dimension of reputation management may be a function of perceived greater 'anti-capitalist' activism, organized and resourced consumer groups, and a global media system capable of transforming minor local transgressions into major crises. However, it also reflects a certain powerlessness in the face of reputation effects which can travel in accidental and contingent ways, and which challenge capacities for rational management. In the unlikely case of two companies with very similar names, misdemeanours by one may be an irrational source of reputational contagion for the other.[11] Within an industry or network, reputational issues rapidly become systemic. Such phenomena suggest significant limits to the normalization of reputational management in indices and rankings. Reputational phenomena and description constantly overflow organizational capacities and designs for management.

To conclude, externally constructed metrics to instrumentalize and calculate reputational strength, and the league tables in which many such metrics have meaning, are not simply operating tools but construct organizational concerns for reputation. As a construct driven by external perceptions of performance in different areas, reputation is a paradoxical management object in so far as intervention increases managerial attention to largely uncontrollable external perceptions. These perceptions of reputation as embodied and instrumentalized in measures and ranks are a new source of governing discipline for organizations. Many organizations explicitly internalize certification contests in performance measures but not all such ranking systems are equally significant and organizations can often chose whether or not to rate themselves. Yet there are enough of these evaluative practices and bodies (Boli, 2006) to ensure that many organizations feel the need to create units for being more aware of how they are perceived and talked about.

The Construction of Reputational Risk Management

At the beginning of the twenty-first century, surveys suggest that organizational interest in reputation and its management has not declined (Larkin, 2002: chapter 4; EIU, 2005). In 2002, the demise of professional services firm Arthur Andersen provided a new drama of reputation in which the actions of a small group of individuals involved in the audit of Enron could be represented as a 'lightning rod' which destroyed the trust in an entire firm. Private acts of document shredding were able to bring into question the legitimacy of the entire global organization at a sensitive time in the audit renewal season.

Fombrun and Rindova's (2000) analysis of the post Brent Spar and Nigeria reputation recovery and management process at Shell reveals how the company made efforts to identify, comprehend, and internalize stakeholder expectations and to formalize this in a 'stakeholder management system'. This provided an opportunity for the Investor Relations Department at Shell to reconstruct itself and begin the institutionalization of reputation as a discrete object of management concern. The integration of stakeholder 'risk analysis' and management into long-term plans, and an emphasis on dialogue and two-way information flows promises to transform the meaning and practice of public relations, by creating the equivalent of an internal control system for stakeholders. 'Reputation assurance' and 'reputational risk management', as a sub-set of an exploding risk management industry, have been built on the quality control blueprints already described in Chapters 2 and 3. Soft norms prescribe that companies must understand their constituencies, consider their significance and possible impact, and develop and implement a strategy for communicating with them. Stakeholder analysis thereby embodies an ambition to become a risk-based advisory practice in the service of reputation (Friedman and Miles, 2006).

Reputational management practices are hybrid, and often contested, constructions from different elements of knowledge. While this is true to some extent of all managerial practices, the term 'reputation management' is not yet fully institutionalized as a practice category, even for consultancy organizations where this would be expected and where metrics have been developed. Advisory firms seeking competitive advantage prefer to build proprietorial products and to use concepts which can be differentiated

(Gotsi and Wilson, 2001; Deephouse, 2002). Without something like the regulatory backing for operational risk, the field of reputational management remains an archipelago of different labels, categories and sub-areas. For example, product risk strategies have their own emergent pedagogy and look to crisis management traditions of thinking about reputation in relation to legal vulnerability (e.g., see Bezuyen, 1994). Strategies of product recall have come to be reframed as part of broader discourses of reputation and risk management. Johnson and Johnson's handling of the recall of Tylenol is an iconic case for issues management, and it is widely accepted that speed of response, apology, and media handling is critical for managing reputational perceptions in a crisis.[12]

Another sub-area concerns public affairs professionals who have been in search of a legitimate label for their activities in the face of external scepticism. Wartick and Heugens (2003) refer to the fragility of 'issues management' both as a professional field and as an object of academic study. So it is no surprise that reputation provides an opportunity for public affairs departments and officers to stake a claim in the risk management process and in dominant managerial discourses of reputation (e.g., IPR, 2003; Murray and White, 2004). In May 2001, the Institute of Chartered Accountants in England and Wales hosted a conference entitled; 'Measuring and managing corporate reputation: making corporate social responsibility count and assessing its impact on the balance sheet.' Co-sponsors of this event were KPMG (a large professional services firm), AccountAbility (the institute of social and ethical accountability), Business in the Community, and Control Risks Group (a consulting firm). Sessions included such themes as 'winning with integrity'; 'defining and measuring reputational capital'; 'reputational risk management—an investors perspective'. Events like these epitomize the role of diverse carriers of management knowledge at work in jointly creating reputation as a new object of practice (Sahlin-Andersson and Engwall, 2002). This event is also indicative of the power of accountants to create and maintain a dominant, orchestrating role in areas remote from their core expertise.

Over a short period of time, an extensive practical pedagogy has developed around reputational management.[13] Texts refer to the need to develop 'finely-tuned' radars for the outside world, to assess whether credible criticisms can be made of an organization, to understand the risks of certain external risk perceptions, and to analyse issues life-cycles. Checklists and proto-instruments have been proposed to realize these imperatives. In addition, institutional innovations, such as the Reputation Institute and the journal *Corporate Reputation Review* provide a 'world-level' focus for disparate academic communities and a basis for further institutionalization of the practical field. Yet, the very same handbooks which establish the category of reputational risk, also reveal the multiple operational sources of risk to reputation. There is also a fundamental epistemological difficulty in so far as reputation is in essence a constructed *outcome* of many specific practices. In this respect the noun 'reputation' is misleading, as philosophers remind us, despite its mobilizing and performative role in management discourse. Organizations have reputations in large part, but not exclusively as we saw, because of the things they do, and these things can be diverse: product quality, customer handling, environmental impact and so on. So efforts to create a practice for managing an outcome directly and independently of the multiple causes of this outcome is widely admitted to be a misconception. The emergence of 'reputation management' is better understood as a redescription of the portfolio of existing operational practices which are somehow infused with sensibilities about reputational impacts.

Some organizations try to realize new sensibilities to the reputational dimensions of their operations by creating meta-units. In the UK, Barclays Bank, which was criticized for many years for its South African interests, created a 'brand and reputation committee' which unites the heads of risk, investor relations, public policy, and marketing and communications.[14] This suggests that reputational risk and its management is recognized to cut across traditionally separate functional domains in organizations. Reputation is difficult to own in a traditional management system sense and we tend not to see 'reputation managers'. Enthusiasts suggest that reputational risk management is the 'natural successor' to brand management (Larkin, 2002: 47), but while 'brand manager' is an established category, there is no clear pattern of actors certified to manage and own reputation.

For organizations operating in regulated industries or otherwise highly legalized environments, questions of reputation and legitimacy have traditionally focused on the management of compliance. Maintenance of reputation with a regulatory body may be required for a real, and not just a metaphorical, licence to continue in operation, and risks to that licence may be revealed by operational and compliance systems. Moreover, the entire area of compliance in regulated organizations has been newly infused with the language of reputation management—the compliance field has used the discourse of reputation to 'talk itself up' as any cursory internet search will reveal. In the UK, the Financial Services Authority has embarked on a regulatory programme under the banner of Treating Customers Fairly (TCF). The principles of TCF require regulated firms in the retail sector to analyse all their processes from product development to after-sales service from the point of view of customer fairness. In essence, TCF is promoted as a lens, or meta-perspective, on compliance routines which exist already and not as a new set of rules. This example, suggests that reputation is similar to TCF as a 'made-up' management object. TCF ideas reframe organizational control discourses, providing existing routines and processes with a new significance and normativity. Importantly, organizations no longer control the meaning of 'fairly' in treating customers fairly. A significant demand of TCF is that organizations must investigate how they are perceived by their customers, taking seriously perceptions of fairness, however apparently irrational. As the practice develops, it is the regulatory intention that organizations internalize the voice of the customer.

The example of TCF in the UK financial services is symptomatic of a broader regulatory and organizational interest in corporate ethics, and in the intersections between compliance risk management and organizational values. Fombrun and Foss (2004) observe the increasing formalization of ethics, both in terms of the creation of a new ethics officer class, for example, the Chief Ethics Officer at Lockheed Martin, and in terms of increased corporate interest in embedding specific norms in the management process. This involves the creation of formal policies in a wide variety of areas, such as diversity, leading to managerial internalization of the law (Edelman et al., 2001). For senior management, personal behaviour has become newly significant, as the case of Boeing's CEO Stonecipher demonstrated in 2005. For large multinational companies, the focus of reputational concerns may also revolve around perceived problems of corruption, bribery, and involvement in financial crime. The rogue briber is as reputationally dangerous as the rogue trader and management reporting systems are being created to deal with this risk.[15] In all these instances, organizational governance, ethics, reputation, and risk have become intertwined in management processes, meta-units, and board committees.[16]

Reputational management processes within organizations are part of an interconnected, transorganizational assembly of elements including stakeholder and media organizations, in particular the business press; reputation metrics, league tables, and other instrumentalities; specialists in marketing, product recall, contingency management, public relations, and accounting. A rich pedagogy is indicative of a field awash with different recipes and orientations. The fact that key reputational metrics are constructed 'offshore' and beyond the control of most organizations, intensifies the capacity of reputation to mobilize management in the design of new practices. Reputational risk may be a poor diagnostic category in formal terms but, like operational risk, it plays a critical role in the organization of managerial attention and in the re-description of existing operations to bring out their relational implications. It is precisely the archipelago of approaches which gives reputation its distinctive and insistent character as a programme for organizing uncertainty into risk, and which underwrites efforts to make reputation an actionable management object.

Conclusions

Since the mid-1990s, the category of reputation has become more central to managerial agendas, undoubtedly reflecting the continuous 'passion for reinventing' within practice (Chambers, 1999: 3). This chapter has examined the manner in which diverse arenas and management sub-fields have been catalysed by the imagination of risks to reputation. The category of reputation has been actively utilized in discourses which problematize existing organizational practices and the nature of the fields within which they operate. Reputation is a boundary object for different constituencies of interest which offer diverse promises of rational management. Investor relations, communications, accounting, marketing, and issues management have all come to be transformed by an idea which is both moral and instrumental. Reputation has become strong as a motivational force for large organizations, being coopted by specialists in public relations and marketing who seek a seat at the risk management table. The idea of reputation has also facilitated the normalization of CSR in corporate thinking, and given business ethics a foothold within organizations. The operationalization of reputation ideas has produced a hybrid family of practices rather than any single, dominant discipline.

While previous chapters point to pressures for heightened forms of risk *responsibilization* within organizations, reputation overflows efforts to govern it because responsibility attribution is difficult (EIU, 2005) and because key measures may be constructed beyond the boundaries of the organization. Yet, the imperative to organize in the face of uncertainty is strong even as the paradoxes of reputational risk management are most evident. Organizations are actively engaged in creating units, committees, and processes to understand, audit and account for that which is most difficult to manage, i.e. how they are experienced by others. Strategic, technical, and normative dimensions of corporate decision-making are increasingly informed by efforts to internalize outside elements, understood today as stakeholders. Reputation management is often articulated by its protagonists as a new basis for enlightened self-interest in which 'competent' management and 'socially responsible' management are the same thing. The management of reputational risk permeates ideals of governance and creates a new 'organizing potential' for CSR at the very same time as traditional distinctions between moral and instrumental thinking are blurred. Reputational concerns have become another facet of the self-observing, self-regulating organizational capacities described in Chapter 2. Even though it may be odd to make individuals and departments responsible for reputation, organizations themselves have been constituted as responsible actors which must be responsive to how they are perceived.

Although reputational risk management is informed by discourses of opportunity and value, the heightened preoccupation with how organizations are seen, conceptualized, and instrumentalized in external metrics is a source of defensiveness. Reputational risk is a pure 'man-made' risk because it is the product of evaluative institutions which explicitly manufacture a new kind of uncertainty with a high degree of calculative rationalization. Organizations do not leave their reputations to chance in these environments and become focused on the legitimized performance indicators and formal structures which feature in worlds of ranking, audit, and evaluation. Organizations tend to spend more time and resource in making their reputation easily readable and auditable by outsiders who are conceptualized as sources of vulnerability and fear. It can be argued that corporate actors remain powerful in some objective sense (Gouldson and Bebbington, 2007) but greater demands for the visibility of operational matters by a variety of stakeholder bodies in the name of good governance, and as inscribed in metrics, also gives a highly defensive character to the management of reputation. While marketing specialists find a ready home in reputation management for brand-building practices, there is also a strong emphasis on what can be lost, rather than what might be gained. More significantly, reputational risk management is not simply a sub-area of risk management. It is the defining project of risk management itself, as we shall now see.

Notes

1. In more recent times it has suffered further adverse publicity for overstating its oil reserves.
2. Good corporate reputation has come to be recognized within human resource management as an imperative for attracting and retaining talent.
3. For example, CSR has not traditionally concerned itself with taxation issues. However, corporate citizenship can be thought of in terms of the propensity to pay tax. See Freedman (2004).
4. For a reply to the Shamir critique of CSR, see Parker (2007).
5. The 'normalization' of the CSR agenda was symbolized in the UK by the creation of the post of 'Minister for Corporate Responsibility' by the Labour government.
6. In the UK, the concept acquired political currency as a label for state-individual partnerships (Hutton, 1995).
7. For more on the rise of the stakeholder concept see Clarkson (1998); Ackerman and Alstott (1999); Friedman and Miles (2002; 2006). Indications of the late 1990s 'managerial arrival' of the 'stakeholder' are the special issues of *Critical Perspectives on Accounting*, 9(2) 1998 and *The Academy of Management Journal*, 42(5) 1999.
8. I owe this point to Jan Mouritsen.
9. The language of amplification and attenuation implies an 'objective' risk which may or may not be distorted by 'social' processes. This is a questionable assumption. The present argument only requires the observation that organizations increasingly operate *as if* social amplification is a new risk that they face and must manage.
10. B. Hunt, 'Corporate Social Responsibility as a new Self Regulation', Paper presented at the Centre for Analysis of Risk and Regulation, London School of Economics, April 2004. See also B. Hunt, 'Concerned Companies' *Spiked-Risk* www.spiked-online.com, April 2004.
11. I am grateful to Kerstin Sahlin-Andersson for this example.
12. For the political context of apology, see Cunningham (1999).
13. See Fombrun (1995); Larkin (2002); Rayner (2003); Alsop (2004); Morley (2002); Haywood (2002); Balmer and Greyser (2003); Dowling (2002); Nash (1999); Neef (1999).
14. See 'Barclays banks on a good name', *Financial Times*, 19 February 2004.
15. See, 'Trouble at home for overseas bribes', *Financial Times*, 2 February 2006.
16. In the context of CSR Roberts (2003) argues that much of this is the narcissistic management of appearance, a posture which contrasts with an organizational ethics based on making organizational identities and boundaries vulnerable via genuine dialogue with 'risky others'. Derived from the philosophy of Levinas, Roberts suggests that responsibility is a kind of constructed vulnerability in which reputations are actively risked in encounters with others. This view contrasts pointedly with conceptualizations of stakeholders and reputation within risk management.

6

Making Risk Auditable:
Legalization and Organization

In April 2005 the US Securities and Exchange Commission (SEC) held the first roundtable consultation exercise to assess the first year of implementation of the Sarbanes-Oxley legislation ('Sarbox'), and the effects of section 404 requirements for the certification of internal controls (Chapter 2). In the same month in the United Kingdom Phillip Hampton published his report on reducing the burdens of regulation (HM Treasury, 2005). In the North American case, response to the consultation has been predictable: even SEC registered companies well-disposed to Sarbox, and to the necessity of improving internal controls, have complained about the first year costs of compliance and bemoan the detailed documentation required for minor controls over financial reporting.[1] Many organizations demanded that the SEC adopt a more risk-based approach to the assessment of internal control effectiveness, and blamed the audit profession for amplifying bureaucratic requirements. Guidance to auditors has been revised as a consequence and in late 2006 there are signs that the legislation may be revised. Echoing these corporate criticisms of Sarbox, the UK Hampton report focuses explicitly on the administrative burden involved in the forms and documentation demanded by regulators. An implied belief is that risk-based regulation, as discussed in Chapter 3, will, among other things, reduce this administrative burden. In the arena of Basel 2, there has also been a strong undercurrent of criticism about the questionable benefits of document-intense processes, not least in the area of operational risk considered in Chapter 4. In 2005, many large financial institutions were required to find a way to integrate both Sarbox and Basel 2 requirements, not to mention the demands of international accounting standards conversion.

Common to these varied criticisms of regulatory burdens is a much cited enemy. All parties to discussion in the USA, UK, and elsewhere agree that something known as 'box-ticking' is to blame for an excessively rules-based approach to regulation and compliance. This popularized critique targets a rigid, mechanical practice involving the use of needlessly detailed 'standardized checklists' and pursued without regard to weighing costs against benefits. Yet, for all the stridency of these ubiquitous criticisms, and their near unanimous acceptance by both regulator and regulated, there is a striking and puzzling fact to explain: 'box-ticking' as finely grained process in some broad sense persists, with at best only incremental diminution. So, is the widespread critique so evident in April 2005 simply hypocritical rhetoric?

In this chapter we develop an explanation for this puzzle based on an analysis of deeply-held values of auditability and transparency. These values pervade the four cases of organizing uncertainty discussed in previous chapters. All these cases demonstrate a broad shift within risk management from risk analysis and calculation to risk governance. The organizational oversight and accountability dimensions of risk management have come to the fore. The arguments below suggest that a significant driver of this shift has little to do with risks in some inherent sense. It is part of deep-seated institutional pressures to make risk management practice auditable. In the process risk management is evolving into something it did not start as.

The chapter begins by addressing the 'managerialization' of risk management as a phenomenon which has its origins in a mixture of supply-side faddism and socially constructed fears, rather than being a self-evidently functional response to objective risks. We then consider the specific implications of the audit and accountability driven dimensions of risk management, conspicuous in the implementation of the Sarbanes-Oxley legislation. It is argued that the imperative of 'making risk management auditable' characterizes a distinctive path of managerialization which is informed by values of precision and evidence. This discussion leads naturally to a consideration of the theme of defensiveness in risk management and to the close parallels between auditability and the 'legalization' of organizations. The chapter concludes by suggesting how organizational culture has emerged as a new auditable object for governance purposes and how the prospects for a more intelligent risk management are constrained by 'tick-box' values which remain durable and rational at the world-level, despite intense criticism.

The Managerialization of Risk Management

Previous chapters have suggested that the rise of new frames for the management of risk management is a story of the metamorphosis of internal control and regulation. There are now designs for an all-embracing enterprise risk management process derived in machine-like fashion from the highest strategic objectives of the organization (Chapter 3). New categories of 'operational risk', 'legal risk', and 'reputational risk', have emerged to redescribe a wide range of disparate organizational practices under the banner of risk management (Chapters 4 and 5). These developments are partly driven by social demands for organizational resilience and the management of extreme events. Precautionary attention to potential disasters has always been a feature of organizations operating in fields where high reliability is demanded but extreme outcomes have become part of a widely diffused dramatology of rogue traders and corrupt senior management. The characterization of these events in the language of 'low probability, high impact' places them in new a space of expectation and rational risk management. All organizations are now expected to be 'reliability seeking' (Busby, 2006).

In his compelling analysis of the Mann Gulch disaster, Weick (1993) suggests that the spectre of low probability events should be understood less within the rubric of risk calculation and more as fundamental surprise, an analytic shift in focus from 'probabilities to feelings and social construction'. In the face of catastrophic events, loss of sense-making by organizational participants can lead quickly to a disintegration of role structure and of the organization itself. Weick's analysis normatively proposes the construction of resilience for organizations which involves the importance of 'bricolage', or creativity, under pressure, of capacities to substitute organizational orders when one collapses, and of an organizational role system which avoids hubris and which can sustain non-stop interaction to maintain coordination when formal structure fails. Only in this way, can sudden strangeness be negotiated in organizational groups, however small or large: 'When meaning becomes problematic and decreases, this is a sign for people to pay more attention to their formal and informal social ties and to reaffirm and/or reconstruct them.' At the very moment of crisis, when pressures exist to individualize, when it is 'everyman for himself' and organizational structures break down, Weick suggests that resilience can only be found in immediate and sustained investment in talk and interaction. He suggests that 'social sense-making may be most stable when it is simultaneously constitutive and destructive, when it is capable of increasing both ignorance and knowledge at the same time'. It follows normatively that excellent leadership in the face of possible crisis must consist in a capacity for a 'range of styles', a willingness to 'disavow perfection' and to offer less in the way of 'canned presentation' to staff.

Weick's analysis provides a stark and significant critical counterpoint to the developments in risk management and governance described in previous chapters. From his point of view, the standardized repertoires and blueprints visible in COSO and other projects are 'canned' and permeated by opportunistic cliché. Rather than prescribing capacities for a 'range of styles', as Weick advises, ERM and its variants promote the very opposite, namely decorative and *perfectionist* formulations of risk management which are unlikely to be a basis for resilience in organizations, and may even create paralysis when flexibility is needed. ERM emphasizes a process architecture which appeals to contemporary values of governance but which is likely to be unworkable and immediately abandoned in the very conditions of crisis which it has been designed for and motivated by. So why is there a revealed institutional preference for this rationalized representation of the risk management process?

It has been argued that risk management as a category has changed its meaning and expanded its scope well beyond its technical foundations in something called 'risk analysis'. It has become central to practical discourses of good governance and organizational design. Yet why have these models of a technocratic, non-calculative form of risk management become so dominant for so many different kinds of organization? For all the effort and cost, Weick's critique suggests that there is something deeply unconvincing about these prescriptions and little evidence that public trust in key risk management institutions, such as auditing or credit rating, is increasing. Critics of mega-regulations such as Basel 2 and Sarbanes–Oxley suggest, in a manner entirely consistent with Weick's analysis, that they do little to address the very problems for which they were created. Again the puzzle demands an answer. Why is there a massive investment in, and persistence of, practices whose operational functionality is widely disputed by both organizational sociologists and bankers?

The explanation concerns the manner in which risk management practice has itself become infused by ideas and values which represent *institutionally acceptable images of manageability*. This new mode of risk management is not simply an expansion of a well-defined practice with an agreed technical basis. Rather, it is the result of uneven and often very different forces giving rise to a common phenomenon, namely the extension of ideas of risk and risk-based descriptions to more and more areas of managerial and administrative activity, not to mention social life in general. In principle there is no limit to the kind of activity which may be thought of in terms of risk and as being 'at risk', a point which for some commentators renders the concept of risk vacuous. However, its apparent emptiness is important to its catalytic political and managerial role. The expansion of risk management involves the construction of more management and regulatory practices *in the name of risk*. Thus the shift from analysis to governance is not only a change in the accountability context of risk analysis techniques. It is also the extension of risk as an organizing category, with associated social expectations, to the management process itself.

As the basis for a new self-understanding of management practice, risk acts as a forensic category for responsibility allocation within and across organizations. Nowhere is this more evident than in the creation of new organizational roles—such as that of the chief risk officer. Risk management, governance, and accountability have become intertwined in a new *technical-moral project* in which organizational virtue and virtuosity are mutually constitutive (Boli, 2006). This means that the new mode of risk handling qua risk governance is only partly an instrumentalizing practice; it must also be understood as being fundamentally and inherently about the accountability of communities (Douglas, 1992). The formal infrastructures of categories, processes, and people, described in previous chapters provide a window on this new technical-moral discourse of risk management. This discourse, and the practices into which it seeks to breathe life and organizational form, can only be partially and exceptionally understood as an efficient response to an increasingly risky environment. Yet this explanation deserves serious attention before we move on.

Functional explanations for the rise of a distinctive style of risk management are often propagated by consultants and other carriers of management knowledge. They suggest that the emergence of systematic, generic, and broad approaches to risk management is a *rational* response to the fact that the environment of individuals and organizations, indeed the world, has become genuinely 'more risky'. So, financial markets have become more volatile, organizational activities have become more dangerous with ever greater negative externalities, new large scale threats exist from epidemics, from terrorism, and from climate change. Individual states are ever weaker to control their destinies in a system of global interconnectedness, while technology advances to create both new opportunities and threats (GM foods; nanotechnology). In the public sector, similar arguments can be made: universities and hospitals operate in more uncertain funding environments as governments struggle with budgetary processes. The image is of a 'runaway world' in need of new forms of risk governance (Giddens, 2003).

In such a world, the reconstruction of risk management and its repositioning as a model of virtuous organizational control is a natural and understandable response, reinforced and justified by each new dramatic headline event, from Barings to Enron and Parmalat, from Challenger to Columbia, from BSE to mobile phones, and from September 11th 2001 New York to 11th March 2004 Madrid. In specific organizations, new investments in risk management seem to be a rational response to local accidents, losses, and disasters. As noted from Chapter 3, the first dedicated risk management department in a financial services organization was a reaction to unexpected losses. In general, growing recognition that fundamental surprises must somehow be managed has been channelled into a probabilistic logic of appropriateness, and specifically into the category of low probability high impact risks. The aspiration is for a calculative 'organization of surprise' and the effectiveness of new management arrangements is affirmed by world-level constellations of expertise.

Functionalist rhetoric and myths for risk management have been identified at many junctures in previous chapters in terms of a pervasive 'logic of opportunity', namely widespread claims that risk management 'adds value' and 'makes business sense'. Thus, the spectre of self-produced, 'manufactured' risk becomes subsumed by the co-representation of risk and wealth creation. There are many examples where this extensive discourse of opportunity and reward is intuitive. For example, organizations have been able to reduce insurance premium costs with demonstrably enhanced risk management practices. Such practices are increasingly valued by regulators, resulting in reduced costs of regulatory attention. It also appears that governance and risk management league tables and rating systems will increasingly influence analysts of large corporations. In general, if institutional mechanisms exist to value risk management arrangements which conform to legitimate blueprints, then it is entirely rational to invest in such systems regardless of any internal benefits. Positive net economic consequences exist provided that benefits exceed the cost of creating the appearance of conformity.

Another reason why functional arguments are not always simply a rationalization of practice is that organizations usually work hard to construct functionality, even for practices which they have been forced to adopt. For example, it is clear that the Sarbanes–Oxley legislation has been costly for complying organizations, raising the spectre of de-listing, and of rising audit fees. However, Sarbox enthusiasts claim benefits for the new 'empirical mood' it has created within organizations, that is, a heightened concern with evidence and proof of managerial assumptions about the state of organizational control and risk management. And even those who believe that Sarbanes–Oxley may have gone too far, accept the need to find and construct its benefits, particularly as the period of fixed cost investment recedes into the past. It can be further hypothesized that organizations which believe that they largely conform with the shape of a regulation, either coincidentally or because they helped to write it in the first place, will tend to support the imposition of that regulation on competitors. In sum, the very scale of initial compliance costs which have been the object of public criticism also creates incentives to go beyond merely symbolic conformity.

Claims about the benefits and functionality of risk management are not just abstract arguments at the policy level; they have an internal organizational position. The 'logic of opportunity' requires the benefits of risk-based internal control to be affirmed. Agents, such as CROs or NEDs, work hard to cast control and risk activity as a value proposition and they draw on legitimated standards to do so. From this point of view, the functionality or effectiveness of risk management is something which is not static.[2] It is continually represented and re-constructed within elaborate constellations of interest which support myths of functionality. Such constellations can form around particular crises and disasters, and scandals have periodically raised risk management to the position of an almost untouchable internal principle. Indeed, rather like auditing in the 1980s, apparent failures of risk management result in reforms and ever more intensive affirmations of effectiveness.

Critics of these functionalist arguments suggest that there is no evidence that the world is more risky or dangerous than in previous ages in such a way that would necessarily explain the specific emergence and form of risk management in the last fifteen years. Even where it must be admitted that new 'modern' hazards have become evident (obesity replaces disease; longevity threatens pension funds) and it is widely accepted that climate change is a reality for the twenty-first century, it is still the case that the organizational form that risk management has taken in COSO and its variants, its specific expansion in scope and widespread diffusion, is far from being self-evidently functional in relation to these new dangers. It is the product of institutional ideas and prescriptions.

It is well known that some risks and dangers receive more attention at certain times than others, for example, organizational leaders' preoccupations with reputation. Such attention is the product of social and institutional practices, such as the media and the law, which construct and promote the salience of some issues and not others. This is a process, which some call amplification, and has little to do with any formal assessment of likelihood or impact as prescribed by risk analysis. The visibility or otherwise afforded to certain events by world media (September 11th 2001 as compared with the Toulouse factory explosion ten days later) and political attention systems are critical in determining the profile of issues. Not all events that might be are publicly registered as crises, accidents, or disasters. The same applies at the organizational level, namely that the processing of risk will be influenced by possibilities for making decisions and for allocating responsibility for historical and future outcomes. Accordingly, it is the contingent and conditioned way in which prospective critical events are processed by institutions, how actual and possible events are perceived, classified, dramatized, and mobilized, which will determine their relevance for risk management agendas, not some positivistic notion of real risk.

This institutional argument is developed by Hood et al. (2001) for whom the nature of any specific risk object itself is at best only one factor among many which explains the considerable variety in the shape of regulatory regimes for addressing risks. In the areas they analyse, such as radon and dangerous dogs, a better explanation of risk regulation is to be found by analysing the features of *institutional environments* which drive the construction of practices in specific ways. These environments are characterized by varied programmatic demands for control, accountability, and responsibility attribution which are as much cultural in form as they are instrumental. From this point of view, the primary question to be answered is not: 'has the world become riskier' but 'what are the collective institutional mechanisms by which some uncertainties and hazards become managerially and politically visible, and others do not?' This demands an analysis of the collectivities which shape the management of risk objects, whether we call them constellations, risk-regulation regimes, organizational fields, or socio-technical networks.

Closely related to this institutional style of explanation is the view that internal control, ERM, and operational risk are products of managerial, administrative, and governance *fashion*. In the UK of the late 1990s and early 2000s this can be characterized as the 'Turnbullization' of organizational life (Power, 2004c) as principles of risk-based internal control became very widely disseminated. This explosion of risk governance blueprints has all the characteristics of management fashion, namely scepticism about previous ways of doing things (expert risk analysis) because of perceived performance deficiencies (BSE; Derivatives scandals), and a new opportunistic rhetoric emphasizing both this performance problem and its solution in terms of new organizational scripts (Abrahamson, 1991). An active consulting and advisory industry plays a critical role in this process and is particularly evident in a risk management arena populated by conferences, flowering professional associations, an ever expanding web-based risk press, and business school risk programmes. As previous discussions of ERM and operational risk have shown, a multiplicity of website guides to better practice now exist, and values of integration have been promoted on the back of surveys of 'deficient' but improvable practice. New models of risk management get presented as a rational basis to deal with threats which are heightened by service providers. Future effectiveness is marketed and promised on the back of a defective past.

While this 'fashion-based' line of argument explanation should not be overstated, it is undoubtedly the case that supply-side professionals of varying kinds play an important role by reconstructing the conceptual architecture of risk management and responding to sensibilities about the need for change. They are also adept at making new designs readily portable and diffusible as models of best practice. Diffusability is maximized by abstracting from specific risk assessment practices and by framing risk management in process terms, terms which are aligned with broader values of corporate governance. A telling example within the emerging field of operational risk has been the re-framing of business continuity planning after September 11th 2001 with a new emphasis on organizational security and information infrastructure. Information security, as a discrete sub-set of ERM, has been reframed as a governance issue, has been promoted by associations like the IIA, and has come to be increasingly standardized.[3]

The selling of risk management frameworks based on a mixture of fashion and fear (Furedi, 2002) balances an emphasis on both the novelty and the obviousness of the solution. This trade-off is at the very heart of a new managerialization of risk management, which promises newly effective processes for dealing with surprise. Fashions succeed not just because they are able to appeal as new solutions to deep-seated fears, but also because they *conserve* deeper aspirations, values and world-views. In the case of risk management, the wave of managerialization embedded in the various standards and designs described in previous chapters conserves, and is continuous with, neoliberal logics of control, accountability, and audit (Power, 1994; 1997a).

Climates of Auditability

The extra-territorial character of the Sarbanes–Oxley legislation has been much discussed, but it has cast its shadow even more widely than this. Sarbox has challenged organizations via the drama of explicitly *responsibilizing* senior executives for financial statements and for the effectiveness of internal control systems. To lack internal controls, or for such controls to be judged as 'materially' weak, is to fail as a legitimate organization—something only mitigated by the early, voluntary disclosure of such weaknesses. Accordingly, internal control systems have been placed within a new moral logic of organizational self-awareness, which may lead to public confession and apology. Society, via its regulatory and legal representatives, will punish the failure to self-discover and confess weaknesses more than the weakness as such. The kind of knowledge produced by internal control and risk management is central to a characterization of organizational virtue, virtue which is manifested in audit, inspection, and evaluation *systems*.

As Chapter 2 showed, even prior to the Sarbanes–Oxley legislation, the growth of interest in internal control systems in the last ten years has accompanied an audit *implosion*, meaning that auditing and inspection are now part of what organizations do to themselves. In the name of good governance, auditing has been internalized and self-inspection marks the space of a new kind of organizational virtue which must be publicly certified. While external monitoring still exists, the auditable internal control and risk management system has become part of a new emphasis on self-inspection. If there is such a thing as an 'audit society' it is not necessarily an adversarial world of external inspectors, but a normalized world of increasing self-audit which produces organizational self-knowledge, a theme recognizable to followers of the Michel Foucault within management scholarship (e.g., McKinlay and Starkey, 1997). In this way internal control and ERM systems have become self-evident technologies of a newly constituted organizational self. Systems are now more significant than the forms of social internal controls identified by Weick and others because they encode world-level values.

Against official and stylized histories of internal control as a dry, technical, and progressive field, it was argued in Chapter 2 that it is being institutionalized as a foundational framework for organizing the management of risk, even as such frameworks are contested. Internal control systems have acquired significance because they are both moral and technical artefacts which give material expression to world-level ideas of virtue and virtuosity. Such systems promise to allocate responsibilities within organizations and prescribe specific procedures for the proper management of risk. Risk is not simply to be managed but also articulated within a system whose operations are auditable and inspectable.[4]

Auditability is *not* in the first instance a question about auditors, inspectors, evaluators, and their respective bodies of expertise. Such occupational concerns are important and relevant, as we saw in the case of financial auditors in Chapter 2 and risk officers in Chapter 3. However, auditability is concerned more fundamentally with the way in which organizations are made knowable as organizations both to themselves, as well as to external inspection agencies. While the concept of audit directs our attention to very specific practices of monitoring by distinctive bodies of experts, that of auditability suggests the close relationship between making things auditable and organizing in general (Meyer, 2002). A theory of auditability requires a much wider field of vision than audit alone because it delineates a distinctive *managerial* and *governmental* epistemology by which organizational practices can be publicly known both by their participants and by distant others. Auditability has become an important governance theme because 'preparedness for audit' has become a hallmark of organizational legitimacy. Risk auditability is at the very centre of a managerialization process in which the risk analytics which represent risk objects are subsumed within standardized elements of organizational control systems. Auditing and public control of risk is achieved indirectly via the inspection of management systems of control (Power, 2002). For example, the doubtful auditability of VaR calculations which makes them a problematic basis for reporting (Woods *et al.*, 2004) is overcome by placing them within a governance framework in which the management system is the primary audit object (Pillar 2 within Basel 2).

Auditability is not a static given and requires the construction of a material basis by which practices can be made 'legible' as a whole (Scott, 1998). This involves a process of *externalization* in which, as the case of operational risk shows, data traces of relevant phenomena are created, placed within an administrative infrastructure, and formalized in strings of procedure. Accounting systems seem to fit the paradigm case of an auditable process: they record economic transactions in accounts, which can then be examined and 'read' after the event by financial auditors. Auditability is at its most obvious and 'natural' when financial auditors want to check the existence of a physical asset—they simply inspect it, trust the testimony of their own eyes and cross-relate this to entries in books of account. However, this process is acceptable only because, over time, there is a community of accountants which is 'epistemic' in so far as it is defined by its agreement about the authority of this kind of evidence. In the case of intangible assets or contingent liabilities agreement is more fragile and auditability is often manufactured in difficult cases by placing trust in oral and written representations from internal and external experts (Power, 1996a). So, the nature of the traces which make auditability possible can be very varied and there is nothing necessarily 'natural' or obvious about them. The distinction between what is and is not auditable is manufactured at a particular point in space and time by practice communities which agree, often tacitly, about what constitutes an acceptable evidential base for something, such as the operation of a key risk control. Making objects auditable places them within a particular style or climate of proof and reasoning.

Collective ideas about auditability are founded on culturally constructed trade-offs between demands for evidence and trust. This trade-off is visible in the level of precision exhibited by evidence trails. Such values of precision may be taken for granted in the case of financial reporting and auditing, but become more problematic in other settings. Understanding the significance of the specific form of auditability demands a sociology of measurement precision and of demands for accuracy in constructing regulatory, managerial and even military objects (Mackenzie, 1993). The degree of legitimate granularity in systems which capture and record primary phenomena in quantitative terms for further processing and analysis (books of prime entry, timesheets, questionnaires, operational risk error books) constitutes an 'infrastructure of referentiality' (Lezaun, 2006), commonly known by practitioners as an audit trail. The precision of such a trail is not simply instrumental; it expresses values and virtues regarded as important in the institutional environment (Wise, 1995). A questionnaire may, even if widely recognized to be defective in design, be used because it exhibits a form and precision which gives it legitimacy.[5]

Audit trails ideally permit unique traceability between primary data and higher order representations of information. They are characterized not so much by a 'calculative' precision as by degrees of *precision of process*. This kind of administrative precision relates to the degree of elaboration and articulation which is designed into the formal specification of checkable stages in processes and sub-processes. It is a requirement for documentary evidence of the operation of that process component which is institutionally sufficient to make the operation visible, traceable, and provable at a later date. While standards for risk management systems and internal controls are articulated at a high level in order to maximize reach, they are also constructed within institutional contexts with varying demands for evidence of process precision capable of certification and audit.

Despite being widely and commonly criticized, box-ticking approaches persist because they correspond to a particular climate of auditability which pervades risk governance. For example, the Sarbanes–Oxley legislation was interpreted and operationalized by management and auditors operating under conditions of uncertainty as a demand for detailed trails of evidence and documentation. The trails had to be precise enough to be regarded as legitimate and capable of defending assertions about the effectiveness of internal controls over financial statements. In other settings, control systems for programmatic objects like teaching quality or patient care are also realized in specific climates of precision and auditability. Process precision, auditability, and trust co-constitute the 'organizational grain' according to which objects and ideas become managerialized, that is, literally become objects of management. The explosion of governance in the 1990s is also an explosion of demands for legitimized forms of proof of organizational virtue and virtuosity.

This theory of auditability takes its lead from elements of institutional theory, namely the idea that the function of any standardized management system is less its apparent contribution to efficient operations and more its role as a formal, legitimate, public, and auditable face of organizational activity. Risk can be audited on the basis of material traces in management systems. Metrics, scorecards, risk maps, and near miss data instrumentalize possible future risk in a governance space defined by values of auditability. This is a space of rationalized representations of risk management systems and processes whose design and functioning is to be made visible and checkable. In general, in areas where an object is complex, difficult to observe and measure, or contested, it is given auditable reality within a management process with observable characteristics. The risk management standards as discussed in Chapter 3 exist to make the management of risk, and hence the future, auditable.

As Chapter 4 has shown, the newly emerged field of 'operational risk' consists of a variety of different 'objects' such as business continuity, fraud, systems failure. Managerial attention to these objects tends to be path dependent, relying on how they come to be represented in legacy systems for medium impact, medium frequency events. Critical, high-impact operational risks, such as senior management malpractice, often fall outside, and are unrecognized by normal information systems, such as the knowledge of the riskiness of Leeson's trades which was well known outside Barings. Informal cultures of gossip often capture 'dirty' data which lie outside formal management systems. However, the capacity to encode and tame such issues in auditable management systems is constantly moving as efforts are made to bring such recalcitrant forms of intelligence within the reach of such systems. The emergence of operational risk represents an effort to create the relevant auditable traces for these risks in management systems. In this way, diverse resistant risk objects come to be auditable, knowable and actionable (Power, 2005a; 2005b). Uncertainty is organized in auditable form.

Auditability and management are closely intertwined; both reflect pressures for increasing rationalization of administration. Management and regulatory agendas increasingly permeate each other, and auditability is the mode of this interaction. Regulators demand evidence of this organizational self-knowledge capacity. Managers can only operate on, and intervene in, the organizations they manage on the basis of signals, measures, and representations within formal information systems. Without such systems, organizations are only amenable to a form of informal face-to-face manageability. As Weick argues, informal interaction is a valued style of control in crisis and may be highly valued as a dimension of good leadership and entrepreneurship. However, it is constantly challenged by demands to legitimize decisions and actions with auditable traces. The form of control is increasingly structured by the imagination of external demands for proof.

Recent decades have seen a growth of management knowledge and of the domains to which it is applied (Engwall and Sahlin-Andersson, 2002). This in turn is related to an expansion of organizing in which organizations have emerged as distinctive actors to which rational management practices must be applied (Meyer, 2002). More is demanded of organizations as units which are autonomous from states, and this generates demands for knowledge of *how* management performs its tasks. Values of auditability are a fundamental part of this general trend in organizing and the durability of the 'box-ticking' approach can be explained as a response to the need to know how decisions are made in great detail. Climates of auditability make possible a management process as a form of self-observation which is simultaneously a capacity to be observed externally. This is an essential and not a peripheral part of management knowledge. A theory of auditability is nothing other than a theory of the mode of organizational self-knowledge.

As suggested in Chapter 3, formal blueprints for internal control and risk management may appear to be fantasy policy documents, but they project a world-level moral order of a certain kind and define the limits of organizational virtue. As organizations, processes, and individual performances are made auditable in terms of acceptably precise risk control operations an implicit value system is reproduced. The capacity to display a high degree of precision in control processes, as the early experience of Sarbanes–Oxley suggests, may well be costly but it reproduces cultural values about science and proof in the field of management. At the same time, the production of auditable and certifiable process is an organizational virtue, and material weaknesses are sins which demand further efforts of self-discipline (Boli, 2006). That which is made auditable and formally and public visible is *de facto* validated as being significant and important. In 2006, a UK firm was fined by the FSA for failing to send a letter to its telesales clients outlining the nature of what they had bought. There was no complaint from any clients and no obvious victims. Many would have been informed about the product over the phone, but there was no institutionally acceptable proof about an exchange of information other than the letters. Such documents make an advisory process auditable in a manner considered legitimate by the regulator, yet the existence of such letters is hardly proof of good advice either. In general, activities and practices which are not made visible by legitimized documentary means are problematic and can lead to sanctions, as this example shows. Thus, the distinction between what is auditable and not-auditable at any particular time is not a technical or natural distinction. It simply reflects the climate and mode of proof-giving currently being demanded by society and its regulatory agencies.

As criticisms of the box-ticking and proof requirements of Sarbox, Basel and other regulatory initiatives demonstrate, practitioners are well -aware that the obsession with auditability and with seemingly spurious precision may reflect a risky preference for apparently precise, but less relevant, data. Comforting images of controlling the uncontrollable may be produced, such as the standardized letters described above, but are semi-publicly admitted to be of little use. So it should not be imagined that logics of auditability are not contested. On the contrary there is considerable street-level knowledge that internal control systems, so fundamental to the explosion of governance and organizing in the 1990s, may work poorly under stress, may be a source of organizational flexibility as Weick suggests, and may do little to enhance public confidence. But notwithstanding this level of pop-critique and official concessions which recognize that risk management systems are never perfect, there is a continuation of practices informed by dreams of perfect auditability and pure transparency which reproduce precisely documented audit trails for control processes.

It is as if there are two levels of critique which have little to do with each other; the operational level of ingenious practitioners trying to get things done and the world-level of rational designs for systems. Curiously, these two levels are not de-coupled but feed off each other. Practitioner critique of the effectiveness of risk management systems only serves to multiply the phenomenon. This is because state, regulatory, and professional circuits respond to, translate, and organize such critique in such a way as to reproduce such systems with even more elaboration in design and with numerous amendments and revisions. This means that the auditability of systems 'thickens rather than thins' in response to critique. Practitioner critique at the organizational level rarely becomes sufficiently organized at the global level, because this would necessarily be an attack on ideals of governance itself. Practitioner humour, irony, and stories of absurd side-effects are replaced at the world-level by earnest idealism, perfectionism, and design optimism—often by the very practitioners who would privately side with the critics. In this way resistance and acceptance trade off each other and amplify processes of managerialization which are constantly being revised to correct their own excesses. The defence of professional judgement and tacit knowledge lives side by side with logics of auditability in a constant ebb and flow. So the likely lack of functionality of risk management systems under extreme conditions identified by Weick is simply obvious to many practitioners. Box-ticking would be swept away if this kind of functionality was all that mattered. However, the mundane practice of ticking boxes in checklists is functional in a macro sense of expressing an administrative ideal, albeit in corrupted form, of scientific and rationalized risk management and internal control.

There is widespread diffusion of the risk-based internal control ideal. This ideal embodies a distinctive managerialization of risk management by which strings of control process must be elaborated, documented, and made routinely auditable. This phenomenon demands a new social epistemology of risk which draws less on psychology to understand the varied perceptions of *individuals* and more on organizational sociology to understand how risk is represented in management *systems*. The Sarbanes–Oxley Act section 404 has been criticized for the burden and cost of the precision of documentation. Supporters deny that such precision was ever specifically demanded by it. They are right because auditable precision is not a function of any particular rule, law or norm. It reflects an institutionalized belief system which defines a distinctive style of organizational self-representation. Such degrees of elaboration persist despite criticism because they are institutional in form and constitute the space in which public organizations define their virtue and defend themselves from the hostile world of stakeholders and organized criticism (Chapter 5). So-called 'tick-box' approaches to risk management and regulation are functional in this particular sense—they reflect the forms of self-presentation of practice which individuals and organizations believe will be successful for giving legitimate accounts. This suggests that making risk management auditable is only partly about signalling the virtues of self-discipline and control, it is also to do with signalling an absence of vice. Such a defensive aspect to risk management systems is closely related to another trend, namely the progressive legalization of organizational life.

Legalization and Auditability

Shifts in conceptualization from risk analysis to risk governance, a recurrent theme in this book, reflect intensifying concerns with accountability for the management of risk over and above operational knowledge. Many of the frameworks and standards discussed in previous chapters are explicitly linked to forms of organizational certification, either by private bodies or by regulators or both. More generally organizational preparedness for audit and evaluation has grown exponentially as a feature of organizing as such. The construction of trails of documents and processes which provide proof about operations reflects values in the institutional environment, not least conceptions of what would be regarded as reasonable practice in a court of law. So the managerialization of risk is not narrowly epistemological, in the sense of being only concerned with proof and evidence of 'objective' risks. It is indicative of legality as an institutionalized mode of self-presentation. This means that ideas of auditability and legalization are very similar; both refer to similar modes of organizational knowledge.

It has long been recognized that organizations in many national contexts are increasingly 'legalized', meaning subject to the 'the diffusion of legalistic reasoning, procedures and structures' (Sitkin and Bies, 1994b: 21). Law and law-like forms offer a normative source of organizational legitimacy and in this sense legalization involves the infusion of organizational governance with both the aspirations and constraints of a legal order. Scott (1994) argues that the legal environment of organizations is a source of governance systems and ideas, providing framing assumptions and constitutive rules for organizations. Indeed, legal culture and legal institutions themselves provide and diffuse legalistic norms and processes beyond the domain of formal law, particularly in the field of medical research (Heimer et al., 2005). So-called soft laws and voluntary standards often reflect, in their formal structure, law-like styles of reasoning and framing. Legalization in this sense shapes ways in which actors learn and construct problem and solution complexes (Argyris, 1994) and create spaces for strategic manouevre.

Legalization as an institutionalizing force does not imply that organizations are necessarily subject to any specific institutions of the law (although they often are), but rather that they increasingly operate, often collectively, as private governments, legislating internally by developing a focus on process controls and procedures. From this point of view, risk-based management control practices bear a closer resemblance to a legalistically constructed practice, in which rule-conformity is pre-eminent, than they do to one operating under the logic of economic calculation. This resemblance is likely to increase as frameworks for ERM are drawn into regulatory regimes. So the shift from risk analysis to risk governance is more than a story of the subordination of calculation. It is the creation of a form of organizational knowledge which is, despite appearances, defensive in intent and design.

Legalization blurs the distinction between enforced self-regulation and command and control as discussed in Chapter 2 because it does not focus on the sources of norms—only on their form and their organizational consequences. Self-created rules may be as legalistic, if not more so, than the law itself. So legalization refers not just to manifest changes in the specifically legal environment of organizations such as Basel 2 or Sarbanes–Oxley, changes which may require an explicit response. The concept primarily signifies a basis for *organizing* by the adoption of legal forms. According to Sitkin and Bies (1994a) the legalization of organizations is broader than a 'litigation mentality' and more fundamental than contemporary discussions about 'compensation culture' in the UK.[6] Legalization signifies the processes by which legal considerations are receiving more attention in organizational decisions as a long term trend of concern for what is defensible (Sitkin and Bies, 1994a: 20; Dobbin et al., 1988; Edelman, 1990). This process of legalization demands forms of defensibility which are legitimate—hence organizations must make themselves auditable and present their operations in specific ways which are aligned with legalized culture.

We should not confuse the phenomenon of legalization with what is popularly known as the problem of 'red tape', as discussed by the Hampton Report in the UK. The manifest concern here is explicitly with the costs and benefits of incremental regulatory initiatives, the disproportionate burden on small companies and impacts on enterprise more generally. The overriding critical agenda for more effective and proportionate regulation is framed by appeal to values of enterprise and innovation. However, processes of legalization and the construction of auditable trails have deeper roots and consequences than any specific regulatory burden or any direct possibility of litigation. They reflect rationalized values of legitimate organizational process which any specific reform is likely to leave untouched. 'Box-ticking' and red-tape endure because they embody a style of organizational knowing which has now become decoupled from specific regulatory and legal practices.

Legal initiatives in organizational environments get filtered in specific ways that are amenable to managerial agendas (Edelman *et al.*, 2001). Legal and other norms get embedded and 'hard-wired' into organizational routines not so much because the risks of litigation are precisely understood, but because they are institutionally legitimate and provide a basis for framing organizational knowledge. Records are maintained in a particular form both for possible legal consumption, but also for internal defensive purposes. From this point of view the traditional distinction between legal regulation, voluntary codes and organization-specific rules is not empirically useful, even if it matters for jurisprudence. All these modes of normativity are effectively experienced by organizational participants 'legalistically' and demand defensive compliance strategies. The much discussed distinction between principles and rules is a symptom of the phenomenon rather than its solution; principles will tend to be interpreted legalistically in organizations via in-house manuals, training courses, clarificatory memos, and spreadsheets. So, institutional pressures for legalization are decoupled from the law, just as auditability has become decoupled from audit because both are hybrid forms of organizational knowledge.

Chapter 4 discussed the problematic, conceptual, and practical position of legal risk management in relation to operational risk. At one level, it is an emerging and discrete sub-practice concerned with risks of non-compliance with regulatory requirements. To this can be added other specific 'legal' risks, such as product liability. But while these efforts to carve out distinct practices organized in terms of specific categories are interesting and important, 'legal risk' also operates, like reputation, as a more pervasive concept. This suggests that 'compliance' is less a specific functional area and increasingly constitutes a mode of managerial practice as such, in which the distinction between internal and external pressures for conformity, between so-called hard and soft law, are blurred and are experienced as equally pervasive sources of discipline. Compliance risk is much more than an agenda for a compliance committee. It defines a mode of organizational self-presentation about risk management.

Similarly, in Chapter 5 we saw how stakeholders have come to be conceptualized as a threat. One aspect of this threat is their ability to create specific legal risks for organizations by initiating formal actions. Organizations respond to this perceived threat with increased legalization of internal process. Indeed, the success of stakeholder groups in holding corporations to account, by generating increasing external participation and engagement in organizational governance, shifts such engagements from what Boli calls low to high rationalization, thereby increasing the legalization and formalization of the process by which they interact: 'Global critics have learned that hard data, comparative rankings, and other forms of expert generated knowledge carry greater weight than mere invocation of the global moral order, however eloquent and impassioned it may be' (Boli, 2006: 111). So legal risk is not only a specific threat to perceptions of organization virtue—legalization is becoming a significant mode of reputational risk management.

The forces of auditability and legalization may be culturally distributed. Auditability may be a peculiarly British phenomenon while legalization defines an agenda of concern in the USA. Whatever the truth of this, they are closely related as modes of knowledge. Preparedness for audit is simultaneously a defensive preparedness for possible blame. For example, in the case of Sarbanes–Oxley section 404, the primary risk is that material controls over the production of financial statements are weak or non-existent. The related secondary risk is the reputational and legal consequence of this being discovered. A rational reading of secondary risk suggests that it provides incentives to address the first order risk. This is what regulatory regimes intend as an outcome by using various enforcement mechanisms. However, for agents operating in institutional environments which are highly legalized, primary and secondary risks are blurred. The important normative and empirical question is whether this gives rise to the kind of 'normalized deviance' identified in the man-made disasters scholarship.

For example, as the energy of organizational participants is increasingly absorbed in the creation of legitimate appearances of due process, legalization processes can lead to what Frey and Jegen (2001) call a 'crowding-out' of good motives. Applied to the field of risk management, crowding theory suggest that monitoring mechanisms will positively incentivize organizational participants to manage first-order risk up to the point where the density of such mechanisms crowds out the focus on this task. At this point risk managers will have incentives to act self-interestedly, and even deviantly, to preserve reputation because of how they experience increasing efforts to control them While Frey and Jegen focus on the volume and frequency of monitoring, this may be less significant in crowding the management of risk than the density of legalized forms of knowledge. Motives to manage primary risk become crowded out and distorted by demands for reputation management and for displays of conformity to values of auditability. It is for precisely this reason that the distinction between primary and secondary risks, while intuitively plausible, is so difficult to draw.

Legalized organizational environments may be responsible for the perception of growing risk aversity in organizations which inhibits innovation and risk-taking (e.g., Hunt, 2003). In the United Kingdom for example, discussion about teachers becoming risk averse in the context of taking pupils on school trips, culminated in comment by the Prime Minister.[7] School trips have become risky for schools who need to demonstrate that they have taken all reasonable steps to ensure the safety of pupils. Yet, even if such trips are not curtailed (schools cannot costlessly 'exit' from this activity), the climate in which they are undertaken has created a risk management issue both to protect the pupils, the primary risk, but also to protect the school, the secondary risk. The two kinds of risk have become indistinguishable. Legalization means that auditors, insurers, state agencies, doctors, teachers, and any individual and organization exercising a judgement on behalf of others have become reflexively preoccupied with representing and accounting for *how* they do what they do, particularly in media and law-intense environments.[8]

The phenemona of legalization and auditability have a complex and variable empirical relationship to individual 'risk aversity'. The key question is how individual agents, such as doctors or teachers, change their working practices in response to these forms of knowledge (Pfeffer, 1994; de Waal, 2006). As with auditing, we might expect considerable variety of response ranging from decoupling ('business as usual) to the construction of new professional identities. Yet even individuals who might be characterized as having a high appetite for risk-taking will have costs imposed on them because they must accept and comply with institutionally demanded representations of what they do. The dynamics by which attitudes to risk are formed may be complex, but the significant point is that rationalized checklists have an institutional life of their own as a form of knowledge. This is likely to remain untouched, and most likely intensified, by successive state programmes of 'de-regulation'. Like the audit explosion before it, the new style of internal control focused risk management has created an intensified attention to process, and has defined the form in which management responsibility is expressed. Managers must constantly work hard to create appearances of process, via risk mapping and other techniques, in order to defend the rationality of their risk mitigation decisions. The 'risk game' and 'blame game' may be two sides of the same coin and blame shifting pays where secondary, reputational risk stakes are high (Hood, 2002). Yet, actual blame matters much less than its possibility. Blame shifting is exhibited as much in the articulation of due process as it is in explicit attempts to 'pass the buck' to other identifiable individuals and organizations.

Processes of legalization and of auditability are large coextensive. Both are implicated in risk management practices which embody the possibility of bureaucratic replication—a 'revisiting' of the basis of a risk control action. Both reinforce an intense concern with record keeping (Van Maanen and Pentland, 1994) as the Sarbanes–Oxley legislation dramatically demonstrates. The explosion of organizing as Meyer (2002) puts it, involves not just a growth in the number of formal organizations, but also the growth of highly articulated documentary trails within an organization, trails which give legalized form to trust (Shapiro, 1987). Legalistic attention to due process can result in an avalanche of information[9] but in other cases increased attention to documentation can result in more restricted information flows as potentially rich opinions on risk are replaced by truncated and standardized wordings (Chapter 2).[10] Such legalized forms of reporting are quickly devalued by individuals but form part of an industry of costly certifications and non-opinions. The paradox of increasing attention to documentation and process is that this often results in defensively tailored content with no sensitivity to the real likelihood of legal action.[11]

The legalization of organizations is also visible in the creation of new subunits, such as risk committees, and officerships, such as the CRO (Chapter 3). Both these elements of risk governance have become rapidly institutionalized in the last decade. As previously noted, these institutional forces are also self-amplifying and contribute to organizational climates in which managerial decisions come to be defensively framed in terms of steps taken to manage imagined threats. Legalistically constituted departments and units in organizations, which would include group risk functions in corporations, tend to gain in organizational power and tend to create further sub-units which match those of the regulatory environment.

Law has always been entangled in organizations and has always played a constitutive role in organizational practice. However, as regulation has grown in volume and become more complex for large and small organizations alike, the explicit management of legal and regulatory risk has emerged as a discrete professional service line as we saw in Chapter 4. In turn, more management time must be spent in the management of compliance, often adopting precautionary super-compliant modes of operation. But the question of legalization goes much deeper than this. Paradoxically perhaps, legalization is more managerial than legal (Edelman *et al.*, 2001). It is about the organizational internalization of legal form. All the hallmarks of legalization are to be found in the emergence of the formal designs for risk management systems described in Chapters 2 and 3, specifically their contribution to making risk management auditable and, by subtle translation, making risk manageable. This might well be compatible with the demands of efficiency if one can assume that the rules and procedures of risk management are the distillation of cumulative wisdom and experience. For institutional theorists this is always an open empirical question: conformity and efficiency are not necessarily mutually exclusive. Yet the rapidity of diffusion of the ideas about risk and its management which are derived from internal control and management system blueprints suggests otherwise.

Auditability and Risk Culture

Practitioner prescriptions regularly state that senior management commitment and culture, commonly called 'buy-in', is a necessary condition for the success of any kind of ERM programme. Accordingly, the 'risk culture' of an organization has become a new and paradoxical object of concern within risk management. 'Risk culture' is a label for a range of attributes of organizations which are not readily amenable to formalization in protocols, which operate as constraints on machine-like implementation and which shape, in almost unconscious ways, management decision-making. Risk culture has come specifically into view as an aspect of the retrospective reconstruction of disasters and crises. The investigation of the Challenger disaster concluded, just as the Barings enquiry did over ten years later, that there was a failure of organizational culture at NASA, of the tone at the top, rather than failure of technical knowledge or risk analysis. The 9/11 commission reached similar conclusions about the culture of security organizations in the USA. Risk culture, or lack of it, has become a specific post-disaster explanatory 'trope' (Jasanoff, 1994).

The scholarly literature on organizational culture is vast and is a conduit for anthropological, sociological, and psychological ideas in the management field. Simons (1999) suggests that 'risk culture' may be analysed in terms of three key variables: how rewards for entrepreneurial risk taking are balanced with demands for control; how organizations deal with executive resistance to bad news—the problem of 'upward' information flow; and the levels of internal competition which might prevent information sharing in critical situations.[12] Capacity to assemble information, a key feature of the man-made disasters literature, will be a function of how transaction velocity and complexity create gaps in diagnostic performance measures. But it is also a function of belief and boundary systems which determine what is and is not allowed. According to Simons internal controls are 'an essential foundation for controlling risk in all organizations' and his analysis suggests how discourses of culture and internal control have come to be co-extensive.

The significance attached to the factors deemed to constitute 'risk culture' is reflected in the highly inclusive concept of 'control environment' (COSO, 2004) which necessitates efforts to formalize, construct and make visible risk culture as an auditable object. The positioning of risk culture within risk management frameworks provides an illustration of the penetration of the logic of auditability into managerial practice. This demand overrides extensive critiques of 'box-ticking' and of the 'disfunctionality of transparency' (e.g., Strathern, 2000a; O'Neill, 2006). Checklists and indicators have been developed for the concept of risk culture which has become standardized, instrumentalized, and identified with the elements described in ERM standards. Formal arrangements such as codes of ethics, policies for whistleblowing, and staff training programmes, become the auditable manifestations of risk culture. Yet studies suggest that anthropological sensibilities about culture are antithetical to the logic of audit. The former tends to expand the complexity of context, while the latter, in its current form at least, is essentially reductive. Thus, efforts to render culture auditable, as an explicit object of management intervention, are very likely to interfere with collective patterns of operations and behaviour (Strathern, 2000a; 2000c). In essence, auditability as a value system constitutes 'risk culture' as a managerial object in its own image. By a process of administrative osmosis, indicators begin to lose their 'proxy' status and become regarded as the things they stand for.

It should not be imagined for an instant that practitioners are dupes and slaves to an 'iron cage' rationalization processes. Cultural features always escape efforts to control them via proxies, and risk management discourses are also replete with many critical prescriptions directed at the perceived excesses of managerialism, legalism, and auditability. It is often said by practitioners that risk management must be flexible, embody redundancy, have the capacity to support organized irritation, and challenge orthodoxies. There is also growing awareness that management overconfidence, biases, and deviant notional normalities identified in disaster analysis must be overcome if problems are not to 'incubate' over long periods. Some practitioners liken risk management to an organizational conversation sustained among key actors, a point which echoes Weick's (1993) emphasis on maintaining interaction and abandoning hierarchy during a crisis. All these critical prescriptions, in both practitioner and in academic papers, are demands for a risk management 'culture' which does not and cannot managerialize itself in the sense described above, that is, via auditable routines and legalized process.

Herein lies the essential dilemma of efforts to construct any 'intelligent' management information system which seeks to go beyond due process to create messy, ad hoc challenges to existing ways of doing things (e.g., Hedburg and Jönsson, 1978). In order to sustain legitimacy, travel, and become widely diffused, these approaches must of necessity adopt standardized protocols, questionnaires, checklists, and spreadsheets. An intelligent management practice would quickly come under pressure to represent itself as a process which is formal, replicable, portable and not owned by idiosyncratic groups of individuals. It would become scientized, represented in cybernetic form and subsumed within ERM standards. Complexity and local functionality would be lost, as Weick suggests, and the 'real' management of risk would migrate to other kinds of informal practice. Risk culture checklists and similar tools will therefore survive despite their simplifications because they are legitimate representations of the demand for making risk auditable.

Despite the motivational power of the many insights derived from post-disaster analysis, and their roots in soft organizational psychology, the managerial institutionalization of these insights has been problematic. It is not that practitioners of risk management are resistant to these ideas—quite the opposite is true; they are completely persuaded of the importance of 'risk culture' and constantly make judgements about it. But these judgements are difficult to represent within rationalized designs for risk governance and the climates of auditability within which they operate. Risk insights can only acquire formal managerial significance within the conceptual and operational space of auditing and internal control systems. This architecture, supported by an active advisory industry, has acquired considerable legitimacy because it is founded on deeply entrenched values which are immune to surface criticisms of bureaucracy, 'red-tape', or 'box-ticking'.

Conclusions

It should be clear by now that the transformations in the design of risk management described in this book are not at all identical with an ambition to measure everything. Indeed, the story is how the mathematical isolation of calculative idealists has come to be framed increasingly as a governance issue. Previous chapters suggest that the particular phase of risk management history since 1995 may have much less to do with the expansion of quantification than is commonly thought, despite the significance accorded to VaR and other techniques in this period. A cultural 'trust in numbers' has given way to an emphasis on systems and processes to define governance. These processes reveal deeply institutionalized values of auditability and legalization which have common roots as world-level forms of rationalization.

This story of rationalization parallels the related thesis of scientization, namely the claim that there has been a worldwide 'permeation of science-like logics and activities, with the underlying principles of universalism, scripts and proaction, to everyday activities' (Drori and Meyer, 2006: 44).

Like the concepts of auditability and legalization, scientization in this sense has little to do with efficiency or economic improvement, despite rhetorics to this effect. It is rather a defining feature of rationalization in the modern world. For example, parallels exist between cybernetic conceptions of risk management and quality discussed in Chapter 3 and the Taylorist principles of scientific management, which was also a world-level movement early in the twentieth century (Merkle, 1980).[13] And quality assurance paradigms in engineering can be traced to the emergence of the operational and decision sciences in the 1950s. These bodies of knowledge have been described as 'cyborg' sciences, because human behaviour is progressively embodied in machine-like control theory, which finds its way into business school education (Mirowksi, 2002: 316–17). The scientific ideal also found its way into early conceptualizations of audit, which were modelled on the hypothetico-deductive method (Mautz and Sharaf, 1961). It would require a robust historical analysis to do justice to the genealogy of scientific systems thinking in these different strands of management. The point is only to suggest how the modes of auditability and legalization might plausibly be regarded as traceable to more fundamental processes of scientization. Rationalized auditability as designed into risk management practices can be regarded as a particular aspect of the scientization of organizational life described by Drori and Meyer. Equally, legalization understood as the permeation of organizations by law-like governing logics can be traced to the very same processes of rationalization which they identify.

However, the shift from risk analysis to risk governance described in this book is much more than an epiphenomenon of world-level pressures for scientization. It represents a fundamental transformation and mutation of scientized thinking from the positivism of numbers and calculations of risk analysis to the administrative positivism of the accountant and auditor. This is a mode of rationalization which is misleadingly characterized in terms of the growth of science and scientific values. The rise of risk analysis and the development of VaR do fit a model of scientization which transforms 'mysteries into risk that must be managed' (Drori and Meyer, 2006: 31) but they have themselves been subsumed within world-level ideas of governance and the manifestation of these ideas in rational designs for risk management. From this point of view, the science of risk analysis is less significant than the 'organizational cultures' which govern that science. And this has given rise to intensified concerns with transforming the administrative mystery of 'risk culture' and 'tone at the top' into a governable and auditable object.

Risks do not exist in themselves, but this is not an anti-realist position at all. Many events occur with adverse consequences for many individuals and it would be better if they did not. Risks only have reality within social systems which have expectations of decision and action, expectations which increasingly crystallize as demands for management systems for risk. In this chapter, the managerial form of these representations of risk has been considered, a form which is visible in the stories of the rise of internal control, the emergence of ERM and operational risk, and the organizational significance of reputation. In all these cases, models of practice have been shaped by values of auditability and procedural defendability. Public reporting matters less to the theory of auditability than the construction of practice in light of a possibility that an account might one day need to be given. These values of auditability are deeply institutionalized principles of design which are anchored in world-level values of rational governance. Processes of auditability and legalization have intensified in the face of the spectre of low-probability, high-impact events as a category of event which demands the management of the unmanageable. The essence of the new risk management is to produce the governance and regulation of unknowable uncertainties via a distinctive kind of organizational proceduralization which prioritizes the auditability of process.

Risk management is no longer a private matter for experts, but is increasingly publicly certifiable and visible because of its role in defining organizational virtue and legitimacy. The 'taming of chance' and statistical classification has been essential to a public project of framing collectivities of individuals for intervention (Hacking, 1986). The managerialization of risk management described in this book has had similar effects—as a modality of organizational actorhood (Meyer, 2002) and as a 'mobilizer of moral community' (Ericson et al., 2003: 67). Fears of terrorism or rogue traders or wayward CEOs may or may not be exaggerated, but the significant driver of the managerialization of risk management is an institutional fear and anxiety, namely that which is associated with the demands of organizational and individual accountability. Distant dangers of low probability high impact events are invoked to solve institutional problems of control. The form of these efforts to organize uncertainty may have little to do with dangers themselves and more to do with the state of trust in organizational and political life. As Douglas (1992b: 77–9), puts it; 'accepting risks is part of accepting organizations'. If so, making risk management into an auditable and legalized practice tells us little about the state of the world and the dangers and opportunities it may contain, and much more about the role of risk in the construction and affirmation of organizations as actors and their respective accountabilities.

Notes

1. See 'A price worth paying?', *The Economist*, 21 May 2005, 81–3.
2. On the construction of the effectiveness of audit committees, see Gendron and Bedard (2006).
3. For example, ITGI (2006). I have greatly understated the significance of the emergence of risk governance in the domain of IT security. COBIT, control objectives for information technology, is one of several efforts to create security and integrity standards which parallel those of ERM more generally. Another chapter on this topic, with a very similar argument form to the treatment of operational risk, could have been written.
4. Formal practices of 'risk auditing' were evident in so-called hazard industries prior to 1995, where the International Safety Rating System prescribed internal control conditions as a basis for 'risk inspection' (Turner and Pidgeon, 1997: 185–6). However, this industry-specific manifestation of a systems-based style of risk audit did not acquire more general organizational and industrial significance until the rise of governance discourses in the 1990s.
5. See Diver (1983) on the optimality of precision in rules and trade-offs in design and related costs.
6. See, 'Watchdog to put a price on "claim culture" ', *The Financial Times*, 17 July 2003. The debate about whether 'compensation culture' is perceived or real also concedes that perceptions have real effects, and agents' actions in response to such perceptions may reinforce them e.g., individuals may make claims in the belief that insurers and courts are likely to pay; and an industry of claims lawyers is created which talks up their service on a no win, no fee basis. The legalization of organizational routines has little to do with how courts of law actually operate and settle cases, but it may affect beliefs about them.
7. 'Common sense culture not compensation culture'—a speech delivered at the Institute of Public Policy Research on 26 May 2005.
8. See de Waal (2006) for an excellent analysis of the impact on inspection regimes on secondary school teachers.
9. See, 'Money laundering tip-offs set to double', *The Financial Times*, 1 March 2004.
10. As freedom of information legislation has taken hold, employment references have become less informative in recent years, containing largely factual data. And as the information value of such references for information purposes go down, they are sought largely for formal reasons, i.e., to demonstrate due process and to defend a decision taken on other grounds.

11. There is a tendency for documents to be written in a style which anticipates their possible use in a court of law.

12. Similarly, Hood and Jones (1996: chapter 3) also suggest that a risk management system which embodies a blame-centred concept of responsibility, will inhibit vital information flows within the organization, flows which characterize the good intelligence and responsiveness needed for preventative action.

13. I am grateful to Howard Gospel for pointing this out.

7

Designing a World of Risk Management

In the 'Appendix to the Transcendental Dialectic' of the *Critique of Pure Reason*, Kant discusses the 'regulative employment of the ideas of pure reason' (Kant, 1978). Within his broad critical philosophy, Kant recognized that there were certain objects, transcendental objects, which are mistakenly regarded as referring to real things. This error of judgement, or transcendental illusion, characterizes rationalist philosophies which regard the idea of a teleology or purpose in nature as furnishing proof of the existence of a divine being. Yet, while Kant rebuts this inference and deconstructs the ontological status of the idea of teleology, he also argues that this idea, and others like it, have an indispensable 'regulative' use. This means that ideas which are 'unreal' and fictive can nevertheless guide reason in its investigation of reality. For Kant, 'regulative ideas' underwrite the systematization and purpose of the form of enquiry that interested him—natural science. They are not derived from nature but are the condition of possibility of our 'interrogation' of nature. Put very simply, regulative ideas in Kant's sense, though fictional, constitute practices and processes of enquiry—not reality itself. They are methodological.

Kant generated a fascination for the role of fictions for subsequent thinkers in the German idealist tradition. Vaihinger (1935) developed a comprehensive analytical inventory of fictional ideas and ideals. These are both impossible and necessary: 'the ideal is an ideational construct contradicting in itself and in contradiction with reality, but it has an irresistible power. The ideal is a practical fiction' (48). Vaihinger is also at pains to distinguish these fictions from hypotheses; they are rather presuppositions which make communication and ethics possible (176), an argument which anticipates Habermas' concept of the 'ideal speech situation'. The Kantian conception of 'regulative idea' also influenced many other thinkers, including Charles Peirce, whose pragmatism modelled truth as the product of an ideal, unlimited form of enquiry.

The role of ideas and fictional objects which constitute rationalities, and therefore regulate practices, has been an important underlying theme in this book, particularly the creation and institutionalization of design ideals. Kant wrestled with the metaphysical status of regulative ideas, but our analysis has been much simpler in principle with a focus on human institutions and the embodiment of fictions in standards, norms, guidelines, and descriptions. The fictions which constitute risk management practices are social rather than transcendental—but no less significant for that. Ideal designs and representations of practice are quick to diffuse and travel in varying degrees of rationalization and codification within laws and popular management texts. In this form they are unencumbered by science and academic knowledge, and unencumbered by specific risk objects and the sociotechnical frameworks which support them. They are 'unreal' fictions which are part of giving an immaculate account of how real practice can be. Through these fictions a reform process has reality and legitimacy in the present, whereas the substance of real change is always disappointing and efforts to regulate seem always to be doomed (Brunsson, 2000). Strategic ideas with abstracted content provide the necessary conditions of reform discourses in the face of 'permanently failing' organizations.

This book has analysed a number of distinctive fictional representations of risk management which have grown in significance since 1995. In Chapter 2 we traced the recent history of internal control and how it has become a distinctive practice design for regulatory systems, supporting a style of regulation which co-opts organizational resources and also delineating a world of new risk objects in the form of processes whose failure would trigger regulatory attention. The publications of the COSO report in 1992 and the Turnbull report in 1999 were critical events in the standardization and reconceptualization of internal control as risk management. The conceptual building blocks of internal control are also elements of a managerial process which must be made visible and auditable. These rationalized building blocks of internal control have been widely diffused and have become transnational norms of best practice.

Chapter 3 addressed the emergence of ideas of whole-of-entity risk management or ERM. In part this is a calculative project involving forms of analysis and measurement techniques aimed at a total risk profile or value for an organization. It was argued that ERM is an ideal abstracted from different sources—insurance, economic capital modelling, and internal control. It characterizes a new normative environment for organizations in the form of standards which prescribe the components of the risk management process. Both Chapters 2 and 3 suggest how managerial practice is increasingly suffused by risk-based descriptions, creating new sensibilities, values, and discourses of control and accountability. Like internal control, ERM ideas have acquired normative status, despite their obvious unreality, because they reproduce rational myths of controllability, not least of which is the fictional possibility of grasping an organization in its entirety (cf. Strathern, 2000a: 316).

Chapter 4 considered the specific case of operational risk and its emergence as a new risk category to organize a number of different risk objects within a common framework. The chapter showed how, under specific conditions, an idea in the form of a practice category has the power to organize new discourses of reform in organizations. Here it is the implementation of the idea, and the acceptance of the need for change across rival groups, which is the critical phase in the institutionalization of operational risk management. Chapter 5 considered the emergence of the category of reputation. Reputational risk does not exist outside the diverse discourses and instrumentalities which give it a governing role in organizational life. Reputation has come to play a central role in world-level conceptions of organizations as responsible actors with much to lose and which are being increasingly evaluated by external bodies. Organizational efforts to 'manage' reputation constantly encounter it as a disorderly, overflowing, and amplifying risk object. Reputation has come to be a modality of organizational governance but is not itself uniquely governed by any specific interest group or expertise.

These four studies depict key aspects of the emergence of rational designs for the management of risk management. These designs represent collective efforts to construct the governance of the risk management process and a new discourse of accountability. The language of organizational justification consists in being able to demonstrate conformity to standardized elements of a risk management system, such as objectives setting, risk identification, controls design, and risk appetite. These elements may be idealizations and grounded on poor organizational theory, but they delineate a conceptual framework for presenting and describing choice and decision. Chapter 6 provided a meta-argument in relation to these cases. While ideas of risk management have been mobilized in part by values of enterprise, opportunity, and governance, cultural ideals of precision and auditability also play a critical role in shaping the form of these designs. Building upon existing work on the legalization of organizations, it was suggested that a logic of auditability is more descriptive of the forces which are shaping risk management norms and standards and how they come to be experienced and realized by organizational agents.

Each chapter has analysed the contours of a recent process of institutionalization by which risk management standards, norms, and guidelines have been created and stabilized. The state is conspicuously absent as a producer of this abstract risk management knowledge, preferring indirect strategies of regulation which utilize and import it. This chapter revisits the themes outlined in Chapter 1 to suggest some broad conclusions and areas for further work and development. In the next section, we deal with the first two themes—the organizational construction and translation of uncertainty into risk, and the shift from analysis to risk governance. In particular, the social construction of risk *objects* is contrasted with the managerial construction of risk *processes*. This is followed by a synthesis of the scattered observations on the climate of normativity generated by risk governance design ideas. The discussion revisits the idea of a logic of opportunity and the constitutive role of ideas in practices. Finally, we consider the imperative of risk auditability inherent in norms of governance from the point of view of 'governmentality' scholarship. The chapter concludes with some thoughts on the policy issues raised by the entire analysis.

Organized Uncertainty: Constructing Risk Objects, Constructing Risk Management

To understand the organization of uncertainty as the emergence of new designs for risk management, it is necessary to attend to two key problematics and their interaction:

1. the construction of risk objects
2. the construction of risk management

Theme 1 has a long tradition in scholarship which exhibits the considerable variety of ways in which risks become part of political and institutional agendas. Some of this work has been discussed in Chapter 1 and focuses on the politics of institutional attention to risks (e.g. Douglas, Jasanoff, Hood, Wynne) and on the sociology of technology (e.g. Hilgartner, Mackenzie, Bijker, Pinch). Theme 2 has been the primary focus of the preceding chapters dealing with the emergence of designs for the management of risk management. This is a relatively underexplored theme in the risk management field, although more prominent within general management scholarship (e.g. Meyer, Brunsson, Engwall, Sahlin-Andersson). Whereas theme 1 typically leads to accounts of variety, context, and uniqueness, the focus of theme 2 is upon rationalized bodies of knowledge which are widely diffused. This book represents a preliminary attempt to sustain a dialogue across these two 'constructivisms' with regard to risk and risk management. On the one hand there is an ambition to build on the increasing recognition by sociologists of science and technology of the significance of managerial ideas. On the other hand, an attempt is made to build on scholarship within management focused on the conditions under which new management descriptions and prescriptions come into (and out of) being.

The Construction of Risk Objects Revisited

In Chapter 1 it was suggested that, while there has been considerable policy recognition of the significance of risk perceptions, the impact of this work on risk management practice has been variable and not particularly constructivist in its orientation. For this reason, Burgess (2006) argues that sociological analyses of risk have had relatively little impact on wider policy thinking, being at best co-opted under a more objectivist conception of risk (Vaughan's substantive engagements with the Columbia disaster enquiry are a notable exception). In Chapter 6, the durability of a certain kind of risk objectivism is analysed but it does not manifest itself as naïve scientific realism in risk policy—a traditional target for critique. It is rather the durability of an 'administrative' form of objectivity (Porter, 1992) embodying designs for the governance of risk and the auditability of risk management. Risk policy in both private and public sectors in the period since the mid-1990s has been increasingly informed by these rational constructions of a risk management process.

This thesis is entirely consistent with Hilgartner's (1992) plea for a sociology of the construction of risk objects which focuses on risk analysis experts and how they seek to enrol allies and expand sociotechnical networks for risk objects. The theory of sociotechnical networks is also consistent with the risk-regulation institutionalism of Hood *et al.* (2001). Risk objects can be of many different kinds and can change their character as networks of support mutate and create new possibilities for risk description. At any point in time such objects might include 'signals passed at speed (SPAD)'; 'defective O-rings', 'CO2 emissions', 'lack of segregation of duties', 'derivatives trading', 'solvency', 'value at risk', 'loss of aircraft separation'. Such objects may have the technical flavour of a particular analytical community, but equally they may have the status of popular explanatory tropes, or what Jasanoff (2005) calls 'civic epistemologies.' We might include here notions of 'rogue trader', 'corrupt management', 'casino capitalism', 'fat cat executives', 'tone at the top', 'risk culture', 'sustainability', 'terrorism', 'business resilience', and 'social responsibility'. This second class of risk object is more programmatic in nature, more fluid in form and significant as a class of potential boundary objects for communities of specialists, the public, political systems, and other centres of authority. Such risk objects also tend to be heavily mediatized.

Scientific risk analysis experts discussed in Chapter 1 are significant but not unique actors in this construction process. Many different kinds of specialist and agency work hard to construct and embed risk objects in systems for their management. The very idea of 'regulatory science', as paradoxical as it may sound, simply reflects the necessity for science-based risk analysts, or any risk expert, to adopt strategies to embed their risk objects in regulatory regimes. From this point of view the concept of 'regulatory science' characterizes the continual process of construction of sociotechnical networks for risks, assemblages in a constant state of movement (Bougen and Young, 2000). Such a perspective seeks to do analytical justice to the rich and crowded world of risk under many different descriptions, and to the regimes or networks in which such descriptions become temporarily stabilized. This book takes this picture of a variagated risk management world as its point of departure, and identifies the pressures for a unifying rationalization of it, a governance of risk management, in the form of normative management system designs.

The Construction of Risk Management Process

Sociotechnical network analysis suggests that technical experts' definitions of risk objects are vulnerable unless they can widen the basis of institutional support for them, not least by attaching them to broader norms, ideas, and categories. In Abbott's (1988) terms, risk objects originating in small technical communities can be dangerously concrete for the purpose of network building; abstraction is essential. The preceding chapters analyse a distinctive path of abstraction, namely the rapid genesis and diffusion of ideas of risk governance, understood as designs for the management of risk management. What we might call 'first-order' risk objects are increasing subsumed within a model of management process, which in turn constructs them as 'auditable' risk objects. Internal control systems, operational risk, and ERM create new risks in the form of 'material weaknesses', 'non-compliance', and various near miss 'flags', which may be a signal of increased first-order risk—'insolvency', 'train collision', 'reactor meltdown'. The growth of triggers built into management systems suggest that the risk society is mutating into a 'near-miss' society. These triggers reflect institutional habits of observability and risk acceptance, and create oversight and reporting responsibilities. However, the expectations space in which these second-order managerial risk objects have been generated has created yet a further risk, namely 'impaired reputation' and 'loss of legitimacy', resulting from the disappointment of those expectations. From this point of view the 'public perception of risk' has itself become a risk for regulatory agencies. It is a risk which technical specialists have worked hard to 'disemplace' and render irrelevant. Our preliminary distinction between first- and second-order risk objects begins to break down with the pervasive impact of reputation.

If the construction of sociotechnical networks requires strategies which emplace or disemplace risk objects, as Hilgartner (1992) suggests, such strategies must also draw such objects into (or exclude them from) management systems for their governance. These systems have tended to be regarded as one resource for network building among others. However, the role of design ideals for displaying risk management competence is more important than this, suggesting that such management systems are an increasingly obligatory feature of such networks. In addition, risk objects of different kinds may present problems of observability and monitoring for non-experts. Something close to scientific replication would be required in many cases. So management systems play the role, increasingly important since 1995, of making the process by which these objects are managed auditable and visible. The preceding chapters suggest that certain design standards for the risk management process provide the necessary resource not only for representing this meta-competence in the organization of risk objects, but also for organizational governance in general. However, an account of the construction of risk management must ask where these management blueprints have come from and who gains from them. The argument so far lacks a material theory of the production of these rationalized norms.

The 'managerial turn' in risk management is the product of newly powerful non-state global carriers of knowledge, consisting of an academic clergy, consultants, professional associations, and related meta-organizations. Indeed, just as scientists and risk analysts work hard to construct risk objects, consultants have done the same for governance and risk management ideas. This emergence and stabilization of ideas of risk management as a process is part, an important part, of the general growth of organizing and organizations (Meyer, 2002). A multiplicity of actors now occupies a transnational stage focused on governance and risk management. Technical risk specialists have created new roles, tasks, and occupational associations around the project of managing risk. Ideas of risk management have escaped the orbit of small groups and 'epistemic communities' to become a template for the management process as such. We have identified a number of significance actors already in this book: the Basel Committee, the Group of Thirty; large Banks and public corporations; influential stakeholder organizations; ISO, COSO, IFAC and many others. These bodies may constitute themselves as standard setters, as 'organizing organizations' which play a role in the production of norms. Many other large organizations contribute to norm production by exporting their own conceptions of best practice and transforming themselves into abstract management knowledge producers. Academics have also been powerful conduits for abstract representations of risk management practice (e.g., Hood *et al.*, 1992; Hood and Jones, 1996a). As Sahlin-Andersson and Engwall (2002a) argue, the boundaries between business schools in universities and the consulting fields are blurred; universities are good at following practice and formalizing, assembling, and organizing practitioner knowledge into syllabi, thus taking the practical domain onto to the level of abstract knowledge.

Conferences are significant platforms for the expansion of risk management knowledge, providing stages for risk gurus to transfer 'best practice' ideas: 'most commonly, ideas are circulated in the form of written presentations or oral communication. What is being transferred is not practice as such but accounts of this practice . . . ' (Sahlin-Andersson and Engwall, 2002a: 24). In conference presentations local concrete practices, or cases, are reconstructed and 'edited' to be presented as an account or application of best risk management. The process of knowledge transfer, both within a firm and across firms, involves the reduction of context in a process of self-reporting for specific audiences. Even at conferences where speakers gather to celebrate examples and stories of 'best practice', accounts are already edited into generalizable 'models with clear structure, procedures and intentions'. In this process of reformalization, certain aspects get erased and others are added: 'when carriers of management knowledge act globally, they also tend to construct the management knowledge they carry as global. In this way management knowledge that is circulated tends to be formulated in universal and general ways' (Sahlin-Andersson and Engwall, 2002a: 24). As we have seen, these formulations often attach their claims to broader cultural resources—most notably ideals of enterprise and value creation.

The role of states in authorizing and validating the production of knowledge has been significantly eroded by the rise of autonomous knowledge producing and standard setting bodies like COSO and IFAC. Such organizations and bodies, even if notionally or formally national, operate on the world-level. The first risk management standard published by Australia Standards and New Zealand Standards became a reference point far beyond those countries. Global consulting firms are also obvious carriers of management knowledge and promoters of risk objects which demand management. Sometimes they are sponsors of standards and blueprints in their own name (e.g. *Riskmetrics*), sometimes they work through larger associations to formalize, commodify, and standardize management knowledge. So the specific changes to risk management since the mid-1990s must be understood against the background of an increasingly generalized conception of management as an activity and the emergence of standardized models of that activity. The specificity in the application of this risk management knowledge is not the issue at the world-level. Surveys of practice, usually by the same knowledge carrying firms, always show patchy adoption and operationalization of the material elements of practice, but widespread adoption of the ideas. Regulatory organizations reinforce the status of these designs.

While the form of risk management knowledge is not radically new—the basic elements of ERM ideas have existed as long as control theory—its global rationalization and elevation as a model of good governance is more recent. ERM grew from ideas of internal control, which have a long history as a hybrid of systems, accounting, and organizational bodies of knowledge. ERM has become a conceptual umbrella, a view from above, for a mix of managerial risk objects which had been functionally separate: legal compliance, strategic clarity, market volatility, execution capability, information security, and many others can now be imagined together. Ideas for the rational organization of risk objects, diffused by consultants and others, have become central to conceptions of organizational accountability and governance. In the case of risk management, its emergence as an intimate feature of global corporate governance thinking is conditioned by abstraction and distance from technical first order risk objects. Local organization practices and actors are institutionally voiceless and invisible unless they publicly re-represent what they do in the rational form prescribed by global actors, even if they are critical of the rational forms.

The rise and influence of rational designs for risk management, for the management of risk management processes, cuts across the more traditional jurisdictions of, and distinctions between, different classes of risk. Health, finance, and environment all find themselves newly governed by similar risk management process standards and guidelines These standards and designs are moral technologies in so far as they express cultural values and beliefs about what it is to be a proper actor. However, these values are by no means unitary and this book has also shown that the institutional construction of risk management designs is profoundly schizophrenic.

Organizations and the Moral Economy of Risk Management

The managerial design of risk management signifies a general shift to a regulatory style which relies increasingly on the self-governing capacities of organizations. This capacity for self-observation depends critically on a system of observable objects. The elements of internal control and risk management systems provide just this; they are necessary conditions for an ideal of reflexive governance with its language and categories of self-observation. These elements also constitute the language of organizational accountability, and their normative power has its roots in discourses at the world-level which embody distinctive ideas of organizational actorhood. Ideas of risk governance have become a central part of the way that the decision capacity and responsibility of actors is defined. Meyer (2002) and Drori (2006) suggest that the emergence of these ideas of governance and responsibility is partly a response to the expansion of human rights principles which have swept the world.

In the new world of risk management, the distinction between regulating and managing has become blurred. There is a reasonably distinct and identifiable class of regulatory agencies, but they also fall under the influence of world-level norms about what it is to be an organization. This is a very different phenomenon from that of 'regulatory capture'. It is more that all organizations, including regulatory organizations, must constitute themselves as sovereign actors in a system where states have become weaker. Risk management standards and guidelines have grown in significance in part because they substitute for the guidance of the state and provide a different locus for authority, a managerial locus which is self-validating. So-called weak states, conscious of the growing sovereignty of organizations, must also become organized and must also adopt risk management principles. The practices of state organizations charged with the mission of risk management increasingly resemble those of the organizations they seek to regulate; ideals of risk-based regulation are a model for both regulator and regulated.

Corporate social responsibility (CSR) themes, which have their origins in critical social movements, have come to define new ideas and rhetorics of organizational identity. As we saw in Chapter 5, the conceptual ambiguity of 'sustainability' is critical to a project of harmonizing enterprise and responsibility, a reworking of older ideas of enlightened self-interest. Yet this abstract conception of sustainability is not only a resource for corporate claims that social responsibility is good business. It is also a conception which requires that social responsibility movements which hold other organizations to account must themselves become more business-like in their operations, adopting the very same risk management tropes as the organizations with which they seek to engage and criticize. So, the new processes, categories, and actors of a managerialized risk management have become a powerful source of normative isomorphism for all kinds of organizations, expressing a near irresistible model of rationality because it is anchored at the world-level. Organizations have been turned 'inside-out' and in the process a new kind of actor has been created which must self-consciously orchestrate its relationships with other organizations. Such 'proper' organizations must necessarily be run by 'proper' people, so the construction of risk governance evident in ERM designs necessitates senior management responsibilities and draws human resource management into the risk management field. 'Fit and proper' persons are co-extensive with fit and proper organizations.

This accent on the normative dimension of risk management as a language of organizational account-giving suggests much more than a shift in public reporting strategies. This may be happening, although corporate risk reporting remains underdeveloped (Woods *et al.*, 2004). The more profound effect, implicit in theories of 'self-validating' legal discourses at the world-level (Teubner, 1997), is that risk management has become its own authority. When organizations and key agents, such as risk officers, give an account of how they have organized the management of risk, they are accountable to an ideal model itself as much as to their own senior management, to a form rationality which is distinct from any of its particular institutional manifestations. Even the most cynical and instrumental motives for conformity with this rationality, reproduces the ideal, world-level, imaginary normativity of organizational actorhood.

How such juridified design fictions for risk management have transformative organizational consequences is the key empirical question, which deserves more attention than this book is able to give. However, for such empirical enquiries the issue is not only one of local implementation frictions, or of the coupling and decoupling of formal features of risk management with informal dimensions of organizational life. It is also that these formal designs define the contours of a style of organizational account-giving and support modes of external certification. In this way risk management ideas fill the normative vacuum created by weaker state-centred authority. Internal control systems are the state in miniature and are the embodiment of a managerialized political authority (Cooper and Lousada, 2005). From this point of view, the Turnbull report requirement for risk management to be 'embedded' is also a demand for risk management as a normative 'policy paradigm' of what it is to be a good organization. Not only does the construction of risk management involve the increasing recognition and influence of managerial 'factors' in risk management, for example, the quality of oversight by senior personnel is a recurrent theme. It also signifies something of greater significance, namely the role of risk in the reconstruction of ideals of management in its widest sense, meaning organization, governance and regulation. The rise of the chief risk officer is symptomatic of the creation of a new kind of organizational identity around risk. In reality, we know there is plenty of organizational sub-politics and conflict ahead of these people and their local status may be fragile. Yet, they also have the confidence of knowing that, as representatives of ERM, they represent world-level values.

The moral economy of risk governance should be understood for what it is; abstract ideas and values which inhere in risk management discourses and which are embodied and expressed in formal standards. While we should not overestimate the reach of these values in any particular organizational setting—this is a matter for empirical investigation—we should also not underestimate their role in defining modes of organizational self-presentation and therefore in defining an actor which is increasingly concerned about its reputation and about perceptions of its capacity to act responsibly. Herein lies the essential puzzle of the construction of risk management. It is relatively easy to find many critical commentators and there is evidence of resistance to the operationalization of world-level risk management constructs and their organizational effects—discourses of 'red tape' are widespread. Yet, what needs to be explained is the continuing *co-existence* of local critique and world-level conformity. For this issue, governmentality scholarship is suggestive.

Risk, Auditability, and Governmentality

It has been repeatedly observed that organizational discourses frame risk management and governance ideas in rhetorics of opportunity and in appeals to a neoliberal morality of enterprise. Yet these discourses are also constantly disturbed by counter images of organizations as 'timid' actors and by claims that it is really fear of blame, rather than enterprise, which motivates the rational designs for risk management which have developed since 1995. The Enterprise Risk Management language of risk 'appetite' sits uneasily with more populist discourses of precaution. Rogue executives, states, and organisms have become generic objects of fear, concern, and expectation. Whether or not aspects of these risk objects are exaggerated by the media or by interest groups with specific change agendas, organizations must increasingly be seen to respond. As noted above, these risk objects exist within dense sociotechnical networks populated by all manner of organizations which must represent and intervene in them: regulatory agencies, security services, banks, research centres, and think tanks—to name a few. For example, the risk of pandemic is certainly a subject for an expert community of epidemiologists, but it also enters the debate about operational risk management for large organizations. Countering the threat of terrorism is clearly the mandate for intelligence services, but this is also translated into business continuity concerns for a much wider range of organizations.

The intensity of these organizational translations and constructions of risk objects within management processes undoubtedly varies, but the pattern and form is the same: organizations have become accountable for how they deal with a growing inventory of risk objects. Uncertainties must be organized as risks to be managed and organizations must exhibit conformity to rational risk management principles. The demand for this conformity emanates from the same normative discourse of organizational actorhood identified by Meyer, Boli, and others. More is now expected of organizations; risks must be managed and must be seen to be managed. While a logic of enterprise, of responsible risk-taking, is manifest in various programmes for deregulation, it is also infused with consumerist ideals visible in the residual protections offered by states to individuals against organizations, namely rights. Both these forces combine to produce a juridification of risk management process design which is increasingly focused on a secondary or derived risk of failing to meet the expectations of being a good organization. In Chapter 6 it was argued that the defensive quality of risk management designs can be traced to world-level values of auditability and transparency (Hood and Heald, 2006).

Reputation and blame have emerged as distinctive kinds of meta-risk objects for all organizations. Whatever the first-order specific risk, whatever its content and scientific grounding, organizational attention must also focus on normative expectations and on the ability to be able to demonstrate rational management. There must be a trail of evidence to demonstrate this 'just in case'. This is a new mode of precaution which pervades risk management. It is not the precautionary principle to be found, for example, in debates about the carcinogenic and other health risks of GM foods. It is not about risk aversity as a feature of the acceptance or tolerance of particular risk thresholds. It is a precaution which pervades the design of an entire process, in which the possibility of blame and of being distrusted is built into the information architecture of risk management. It is the material organizational of precaution visible in the early years of the Sarbanes–Oxley legislation. Designed in a hurry to deal with a specific fear object—the rogue chief executive—its early realization suggests that all executives were to be 'prime suspects'.

A logic of auditability which ought to be a second order and derived feature of risk management design is in fact pervasive and constitutive. This logic is the antithesis of the spirit of free unbridled enterprise and unfettered judgement in the face of uncertainty. Risk as a mode of governmentality reveals itself, in the managerial form of standards and guidance, as a continuation of control via the indirect technology of self-audit. This mode of control relies on evidence and proof of conformity to due risk management process. The production of this proof in the form of auditable trails of process documentation is more significant than any external inspection. The organizational domain becomes juridified in *anticipation* of an inspection process which need not happen. The standardized forms of conformity which make audit possible are now more significant than audit itself. Neoliberal demands for enforced self-regulation or 'reflexive governance' require organizations to build an 'infrastructure of referentiality', an inventory of checkable facts about the self-management of risk. This is an internal 'tyranny of transparency' which increasingly institutionalizes second-order description (Strathern, 2000a: 313) and which reaches its most extreme and banal form in the realization of the Sarbox legislation. That US auditors have been blamed for amplifying the requirements of that legislation is no surprise. They did not do this entirely consciously, although they are certainly concerned about their own possibility of blame and liability. They did so because they are the institutionalized representatives and carriers of a logic of auditability which demands the gathering of proof according to ideals of precision. Standards and guidelines for enterprise risk management do not explicitly prescribe such precision but it is embedded in a wider legalistic construction of governance which does.

This is the essential tension in neoliberal modes of governance; two organizing logics of enterprise and auditability side by side engaged in a continuous dialectic. The logic of enterprise demands that control is indirect and exercised by autonomous value-creating selves. It must be self-governing and self-observing in character, constitutive of freedom and the capacity to innovate. However, the logic of auditability anticipates the realization of these values of enterprise with demands for accountability and transparency of due process, demands which build on cultural ideals of precision, proof, and calculability. This essential tension was already visible in the public sector management reforms known as the 'new public management'. In the present case of risk management as with the NPM, the auditable management system is a device with enormous governing significance because it is the place where these two logics are combined in a risk 'technology of performance' (Dean, 1999).

The emergence of rational designs for risk management constitutes a programme in Rose and Miller's (1992) sense. However, while ERM has developed without state leadership, it can be likened to a programme of 'seeing like a state' (Scott, 1998) in the sense of articulating an all-encompassing process, a view from the top, with the aim of intervention and improvement. Where society is made 'legible' in Scott's terms, we have shown how risk management makes organizations auditable; both processes project visions of administrative order onto society and nature. In recent times, the Sarbox legislation and Basel 2 regulations are almost perfect examples of efforts to 'see like a state' and compel organizations to adopt 'standardized formulas.' Indeed, the volume of regulation, commentary, and interpretations creates real and not just metaphorical issues of legibility.

This account of a new world of risk management amounts to the re-constitution of organizational governance by the idea of risk. There is no governance essence outside the instruments and designs which realize it. The preceding analysis of recent transformations in risk management is broadly consistent with the thesis that there has been a systemic shift in the location of security, from processes *external* to government to 'the security of governmental processes themselves' (Dean, 1999: 194). The rational designs for risk manage-ment discussed in previous chapters correspond to what Dean calls a 'govern-ment of governmental mechanisms' which demand the auditability and legibility of the mechanisms of governance. From the point of view of 'first-order' risk objects, management designs should change nothing. Yet instru-ments of accountability are not neutral and create new possibilities for risk description. The category of the 'low probability high impact event' has played an important role in the emergence of ERM. The normalization of this category as a risk map quadrant is simultaneously the construction of managerial responsibility in an area where organizations are traditionally insensitive (Douglas, 1992b: 66). The 'epistemological anxieties' created by these extreme events are to be assuaged by ERM.

In his critique of Beck, Dean (1999) favours a model of risk rationalities, calculation, and calculability which is more pluralistic than Beck's implicit insurance industry perspective. There is certainly a need for a richer inven-tory of risk tools and rationalities than social theory offers. However, citing Pearce and Tombs' (1996) study of the chemical industry, Dean also suggests that comprehensive risk management techniques based on systems, scenario analysis, training programmes and the like are just one risk rationality among others. This book challenges this assumption by suggesting that distinctive managerial designs for risk management have become a meta-rationality with wide reach. ERM instrumentalizes all the features men-tioned by Pearce and Tombs in an overarching framework for risk govern-ance. Indeed, their industry-specific analysis refers to a period when generic designs for risk management were not yet projected as standards onto the world-level. The idea of risk management systems, as prescribed by COSO, is as totalizing in aspiration as the quality movement was. Accepting the reality of local variety, of local scripts which translate generic models into operational practices, is not inconsistent with an observed isomorphism at the level of designs.

What are the consequences of these risk management fictions? There is no doubt that the institutionalization of risk management procedures has organizational effects—continued systemic decoupling over time seems unlikely—but links to risk aversity and motivation need to be proven. Risk assessment guidelines and questionnaires can be hastily designed, for example, lists of yes/no answers to 'risk' questions are problematic but organizational agents are not dupes and also realize that they may be participating in the costly construction of an illusion or fantasy of control: 'its silly but we have to do it'. Like all grand schemes of organizational reform and governance, the question of compliance costs always comes afterwards; critique is always after the event, despite ideals of better regulatory design intended to anticipate problems. Of particular interest are the possible consequences of defensive risk management record-keeping for the forms of professional judgement celebrated by the logic of opportunity and enterprise. Much depends on specific organizational environments, but there is suggestive evidence of a rise in legalistic disclaimers, small print, and judgement minimalism. Direct costs of compliance are a poor proxy for a phenomenon of 'normalized paranoia' in which organizational agents expend material amounts of time in creating defendable trails of process.

We need to know more about how these arrangements for the management of risk management contribute to the materialization of fear. Are teachers deterred from taking children on school trips simply because of the time taken to fill in the documents or because of the extra risk to which they feel exposed? Are they 'bureaucracy averse' rather than 'risk averse', or does the former create the latter in a process of 'crowding' by apparently neutral management demands for transparency (e.g., Prat, 2006). Critical research in accounting is suggestive for risk management; individuals may be constructed as 'governable persons' in organizations by risk as much as by notions of cost (Miller and O'Leary, 1987). This is not to say that agents are merely passive but that they think of themselves as responsible for risk and as being at risk. Are organizational agents more anxious as a consequence; are strategies for personal reputation management on the rise? ERM, which celebrates the entrepreneurial spirit of risk taking, may paradoxically lead to an exacerbation of control and account giving. Audit was the source of a distinctive kind of ethical renewal in public sector; and now risk management has become the latest mode of 'watchfulness in society' (Cooper and Lousada, 2005) which gives rise to new skills in 'controlled self-presentation' (Williams, 2000). Even if organizational agents are skilled and devious in games of compliance, the question still remains: what is the force and source of the imperative embodied in ERM designs?

From the perspective of governmentality theory, the public only exists by virtue of the instruments which represent it and its interests. So the empirical question is how and whether ERM ideals influence a range of consultative instruments and, in particular, the extent to which a threat-based view of the rights and claims of others is a further neoliberal episode in the 'decline of the public' (Marquand, 2004). ERM framed engagements with stakeholders may create a 'morally thin' atmosphere which overrides civic vitality and which seeps into the fabric of the organization and its participants. Despite the critical role attributed to public communication issues as being good for business, the dominant construction of the public within risk management is hostile. The civic or public sphere is simply one more variable to be accommodated in standardized structures and processes of internal risk control. In place of an actor constructed in accordance with world-level ideals of ethics and respon-sibility, reputational concerns may accentuate tendencies towards more indi-vidualistic, non-social, and potential psychotic behaviour (Bakan, 2005).

This book has suggested that risk management, like audit before it, has expanded rapidly from being a specific instrument of government to becoming an entire rationality of governing. More evidence for this shift is needed than is provided here, but enough has been said to suggest that the task for policy makers concerned with the side effects of risk governance are much harder than they may imagine. If this book has anything to tell them, it is that traditional forms of de-regulatory strategy will have no impact without a prior analysis of the hard-wiring of logics of auditability in organizational life. Demands for proof of a certain kind are now part of the common-sense of organizational routines, designed into a material infrastructure of juridified elements. ERM designs for risk management have been rapidly diffused pre-cisely because they service these demands in a way that organizationally and politically more realistic approaches, such as collibration discussed in Chapter 3 or 'heedful interrelating' (Weick and Roberts, 1993) do not. Caution and aversity cannot be re-engineered at the level of laws when they are, if anything, built into the information micro-structure of organizations. So in place of de-regulation, in the superficial sense of withdrawing or redrafting items of legislation, a much more difficult task is needed: the construction of an organizational counter-discourse or politics of uncertainty which (slowly) deconstructs perverse demands for proof and auditability. At the time of writing, there are indications in the USA that the Sarbanes–Oxley legislation will be reformed, particularly section 404, in the name of enterprise and competition, but we now know that values of auditability will be a significant constraint on this reform process.

A politics of uncertainty would need to connect two levels: the level of organizations and practice where critique resides and the world-level populated by fictions and regulative ideals. This would require the growth and legitimization of reflexive capacities to challenge the forms in which institutions process and construct risk objects, including standardized models of the process of their management. This would need to be a public politics in which world-level myths of rationalized manageability, and their material manifestations, are constantly challenged by the accumulated wisdom of the different 'sciences' of organization. It should not require disasters like Challenger or Columbia for organizational sociologists to become more relevant than accountants. For managers and practitioners, a new politics of uncertainty would demand and encourage organizational capacities to question the formal risk management system itself as a symptom rather than a cure, even at the expense of conflict with regulatory bodies. Internal control systems may 'imprison' risk management in a pretence of control, rather than enabling it to become a mechanism for encountering issues, including the problem of control itself (Weick, 1993; Holt, 2004: 261). The policy challenge is to attenuate and dampen the tendency for control systems to provide layers of pseudo-comfort about risk. There is a need to design soft control systems capable of addressing uncomfortable uncertainties at the limits of manageability which are not hostage to logics of auditability.

Risk imaginations (Pidgeon and O'Leary, 2000) would need to be decoupled from an industry of managerial and auditor certifications, and auditor certification of these certifications, which are the very antithesis of an intelligent, honest and experimental politics of uncertainty at the organizational level. These practices may constitute a risk in themselves, being both a palliative in the face of the essential disorder of organizational life and also a product of increasingly risk averse professional advisers. The CRO will have to become a chief 'ignorance' officer (Gray, 2003) and a greater degree of disorganization and ambiguity must become acceptable in accounting for risk management processes than current initiatives suggest. Risk management would be characterized more by learning and experiment, rather than by juridified processes.

To the extent that process represents the codification of accumulated wisdom, it should be sustained subject to the possibility of constant challenge. This would depend essentially on human capacities to imagine alternative futures to the present, rather than quantitative ambitions to predict *the* future. But all of these things are only possible in organizational and social environments which can be wholly or partly blame free, and which can create genuine spaces for enterprise rather than merely invoke neoliberal rhetoric.

Recognizing the inevitability of trade-offs is part of the rule of second best and it is not the purpose of this book to criticize risk management designs because they are not implemented. Uncertainty can never be perfectly organized and organizations and the individuals within them necessarily grapple with complex balances in the design and operation of procedures: routine processes contrast with non-routine interventions, formal mechanisms contrast with the necessity of expert judgement, autocratically designed accountabilities contrast with the claimed benefits of inclusion and democracy, central control ambitions contrast with the realities of decentralization. Whatever the merits of theoretical models of optima in these cases, in practice such trade-offs will be constrained and affected by mixtures of internal politics, resource availability and external institutional legacy. The puzzle for policy-makers and practitioners is to understand how and when a specific and common-sensical managerial instrument evolves from humble origins into a principle of rational organization and governance? In whose interests does this change take place and what are the side-effects? It is likely that we can know the answer to these questions; it is less likely that societies will find it easy to act on this knowledge.

Final Thoughts

Any form of organization is also a form of closure, restriction, and limitation, which is necessarily a source of risk itself. 'Organized uncertainty' is an inherently paradoxical idea which signifies that efforts to construct a knowledge of things as risks creates new forms of uncertainties. Technological systems will continue to be a source of 'man-made' risk, but man-made management systems also deserve attention. It has been said that the present age is more aware of what it does not know, but the rise of a broad risk management mandate since the mid-1990s suggests also a continuing ambition to control and managerialize the future. This ambition is reflected in the heightened accent on internal control systems in organizations, in the creation of new risk categories and definitions to focus managerial effort, in the creation of new agents and risk responsibility structures, and in the development of new procedures and routines which seek to align risk with a moral discourse of good governance. The reach of this ambition seems to be the 'risk management of everything' and reflects social demands for decidability and controllability, the appearance of which is created by a material abundance of standards, textbooks, and technical manuals. This extensive re-writing of organizational governance in the name of risk is no mere technical development. It also implicates a new moral economy of organizational life at all levels and defines general ideals of good governance for states, public regulators, professional associations, and private corporations.

The ubiquity of risk management blueprints is the result of a variety of factors: responses to specific scandals, opportunism by occupational communities for professional development, new modes of regulatory action, and the mutation and refashioning of instruments of accountability. However, a significant driver also lies in the rise of a distinctive individualism in which risk management designs both create and service a need for protection from blame. Individuals, organizations, and societies have no choice but to organize in the face of uncertainty, to act 'as if' they know the risks they face. Yet, the precise form of that organization is more cultural, a function of institutions, than it is determined by the nature of risk 'in itself'. Thus, the social construction of risk cannot be easily disentangled from the social construction of ideas about the organizational management of risk. This book suggests that, beneath the surface of rational risk management designs, and claims for value-enhancing practice, lurks a pervasive fear of the possible negative consequences of being responsible and answerable, of being required to produce decidability in the face of the undecidable. This is the essential schizophrenia of risk management discourse as it has developed since the mid-1990s and is constituted by opposed logics—of enterprise versus discipline, of freedom versus accountability, of democracy versus managerialism, and of opportunity versus auditability.

REFERENCES

Aalders, M. (1993), 'Regulation and In-Company Environmental Management in the Netherlands', *Law and Policy*, 15(2): 75–94.

Abbott, A. (1988), *The System of Professions*. Chicago: Chicago University Press.

ABI (2001), *Investing in Social Responsibility—Risks and Opportunities*. London: Association of British Insurers.

Abrahamson, E. (1991), 'Managerial Fads and Fashions: The Diffusion and Rejection of Innovations', *Academy of Management Review*, 16(3): 586–612.

AccountAbility (2002), *AA1000 Assurance Standard: Guiding Principles*. London: Institute for Social and Ethical Accountability.

Ackerman, B. and Alstott, A. (1999), *The Stakeholder Society*. New Haven: Yale University Press.

Adams, R. (1991). 'Audit Risk', in M. Sherer and S. Turley (eds.), *Current Issues in Auditing* (2nd edn.). London: Paul Chapman, 144–62.

Aerts, L. (2001). 'A Framework for Managing Operational Risk', *Internal Auditor*, (August), 53–9.

Ahrne, G. and Brunsson, N. (2006), 'Organizing the World', in Djelic and Sahlin-Andersson (eds.), Cambridge: Cambridge University Press, 74–94.

AICPA (1996), *Report of the AICPA Special Committee on Assurance Services (Elliott Committee)*. New York: American Institute of Certified Public Accountants.

AIRMIC (1999), *A Guide to Integrated Risk Management*. London: Association of Insurance and Risk Managers—Integrated Risk Management Special Interest Group.

AIRMIC/ALARM/IRM (2002), *A Risk Management Standard*. London: Association of Insurance and Risk Managers.

Alborn, T. (1996), 'A Calculating Profession: Victorian Actuaries among the Statisticians', in M. Power (ed.), *Accounting and Science*. Cambridge: Cambridge University Press, 81–119.

Alexander, C. (2003), 'Statistical Models for Operational Loss', in C. Alexander (ed.), *Operational Risk: Regulation, Analysis and Management*. London: Prentice Hall/Financial Times, 129–170.

Alsop, R. J. (2004), *The 18 Immutable Laws of Corporate Reputation: Creating, Protecting, and Repairing Your Most Valuable Asset*. London: Kogan Page.

Ambler, T., Barwise, P., and Higson. C. (2001), *Marketmetrics: What should we tell the Shareholders?* London: London Business School/Institute of Chartered Accountants in England and Wales.

APB (1994), *The Audit Agenda.* London: Auditing Practices Board.

—— (1995), *Internal Financial Control Effectiveness—A Discussion Paper.* London: Auditing Practices Board.

—— (1998), *Providing Assurance on Internal Control.* London: Auditing Practices Board.

Argyris, C. (1994), 'Litigation Mentality and Organizational Learning', in Sitkin and Bies (eds.), 347–58.

AS/NZS (1995) (1999), *Standard 4360: Risk Management.* Sydney: Australia Standards and New Zealand Standards.

ASB (2005), *Reporting Standard 1, Operating and Financial Review.* London: Accounting Standards Board.

Ashby, S. and Young, B. (2003), 'New Trends in Operational Risk Insurance for Banks', in Risk Books/SAS, *Advances in Operational Risk: Firm-Wide Issues for Financial Institutions.* London: Risk Books, 43–58.

Audit Commission (2003), *Strategic Regulation: Minimizing the Burden, Maximizing the Impact.* London: Audit Commission.

Ayres, I. and Braithwaite, J. (1992), *Responsive Regulation: Transcending the Deregulation Debate.* Oxford: Oxford University Press.

Bakan, J. (2005), *The Corporation: The Pathological Pursuit of Profit and Power.* London: Constable and Robinson.

Baker, T. and Simon, J. (eds.) (2002), *Embracing Risk: The Changing Culture of Insurance and Responsibility.* Chicago: Chicago University Press.

Baldwin, R. and Cave, M. (1999), *Understanding Regulation.* Oxford: Oxford University Press.

—— and Cane, P. (eds.) (1996), *Law and Uncertainty: Risks and Legal Processes.* Boston, MA: Kluwer Law International.

Balmer, J. and Greyser, S. (eds.) (2003), *Revealing the Corporation: Perspectives on Identity, Image, Reputation and Corporate Branding.* London: Routledge.

Banham, R. (1999), 'Kit and Caboodle: Understanding the Skepticism about Enterprise Risk Management', *CFO Magazine* (April).

Bank of England (1997a), *A Risk Based Approach to Supervision (The RATE Framework).* London: Bank of England.

—— (1997b), *Banks' Internal Controls and the Section 39 Process.* London: Bank of England.

Barton, T., Shenkir, W., and Walker, P. (2001), *Making Enterprise Risk Management Pay Off.* Morristown, NJ: Financial Executives Research Foundation.

Basel Committee on Banking Supervision (1994), *Risk Management Guidelines for Derivatives.* Basel: Bank for International Settlements.

—— (1998a), *Framework for the Evaluation of Internal Control.* Basel: Bank for International Settlements.

Basel Committee on Banking Supervision (1998b), *Operational Risk Management Survey*. Basel: Bank for International Settlements.

—— (2001a), *Working Paper on the Regulatory Treatment of Operational Risk*. Basel: Bank for International Settlements.

—— (2001b), *Sound Practices for the Management and Supervision of Operational Risk*. Basel: Bank for International Settlements.

—— (2001c), *Consultative Document—Pillar 2 (Supervisory Review Process)*. Basel: Bank for International Settlements.

—— (2003a), *The New Basel Capital Accord—Third Consultative Paper*. Basel: Bank for International Settlements.

—— (2003b), *Quantitative Impact Study 3—Overview of Global Results*. Basel: Bank for International Settlements.

—— (2003c), *Trends in Risk Integration and Aggregation*. Basel: Bank for International Settlements.

Beamish, T. (2002), *Silent Spill: The Organization of an Industrial Crisis*. Cambridge, MA: MIT Press.

Beaumont, P. B., Leopold, J. W., and Coyle, J. R. (1982), 'The Safety Officer: An Emerging Management Role?', *Personnel Review*, 11(2): 35–38.

Beck, U. (1992), *Risk Society—Towards a New Modernity*. London: Sage.

Bell, T., Marrs, F., Solomon, I., and Thomas, H. (1997), *Auditing Organizations through a Strategic Systems Lens*. New Jersey: KPMG LLP.

Berger, P. and Luckman, T. (1966), *The Social Construction of Knowledge*. London: Penguin.

Bernstein, P. (1996a), *Against the Gods: The Remarkable Story of Risk*. London: John Wiley and Sons.

—— (1996b), 'The New Religion of Risk Management', *Harvard Business Review*, March–April: 47–51.

Berry, A. and Phillips, J. (1998), 'Enterprise Risk Management—Pulling it All Together', *Risk Management*, 45 (September): 53–58.

Besley, T. and Ghatak, M. (2005), 'Incentives, Risk and Accountability,' in Hutter and Power (eds.), 149–66.

Bevan, G. and Hood, C. (2006), 'What's Measured is what Matters: Targets and Gaming in the English Public Health Care System', *Public Administration*, 84(3): 517–38.

Bezuyen, M. (1994), 'Product Risks and Reputation: Opportunities and Challenges', *Journal of Contingencies and Crisis Management*, 2(3): 179–83.

Bhansali, V. (2003) 'Stress Testing in Risk Management', in Field (ed), 159–67.

Bijker, W, Pinch, T., and Hughes, T. (eds.) (1989), *The Social Construction of Technological Systems: New Directions in the Sociology and History of Technology*. Cambridge, MA: MIT Press.

Black, J. (2001), 'Decentring Regulation: The Role of Regulation and Self-Regulation in a "Post-Regulatory" World'. *Current Legal Problems*, 54 (November): 103–146.

—— (2002), 'Mapping the Contours of Contemporary Financial Services Regulation', *Journal of Corporate Law Studies*, 2(2): 253–87.

—— (2003), 'Enrolling Actors in Regulatory Processes: Examples from UK Financial Services Regulation', *Public Law*, (Spring): 63–91.

—— (2005), 'The Emergence of Risk-Based Regulation and the New Public Risk Management in the United Kingdom', *Public Law*, (Autumn): 512–48.

Blattner, N. (1995), 'Capital Adequacy Rules as Instruments for the Regulation of Banks', *Swiss Journal of Economics and Statistics*, 131(2–4): 719–21.

Blyth, M. (1997), 'Any More Bright Ideas? The Ideational Turn of Comparative Political Economy', *Comparative Politics*, 29(2): 229–50.

Boli, J. (2006), 'The Rationalization of Virtue and Virtuosity in World Society', in Djelic and Sahlin-Andersson (eds.), 95–118.

—— and Thomas, G. (eds.) (1999), *Constructing World Culture: International Nongovernmental Organizations since 1875*. Stanford: Stanford University Press.

Bougen, P. and Young, J. (2000), 'Organizing and Regulating as Rhizomatic Lines: Bank Fraud and Auditing', *Organization*, 7(3): 403–26.

Bou-Raad, G. (2000), 'Internal Auditors and a Value-Added Approach: The New Business Regime', *Managerial Auditing Journal*, 15(4): 182–7.

Bowerman, M., Humphrey, C., and Raby, H. (2000), 'In Search of the Audit Society: Some Evidence from Health Care, Police and Schools in England and Wales', *International Journal of Auditing*, 4(1): 71–100.

Bowker, G. and Star, S. (2000), *Sorting Things Out: Classification and its Consequences*. Cambridge, MA: MIT Press.

Boyne, R. (2003) *Risk*. Milton Keynes: Open University Press.

Braithwaite, J. and Makkai, T. (1994), 'Trust and Compliance', *Policing and Society*, 4: 1–12.

Brewer, P. C. and Mills, T. Y. (1994), 'ISO 9000 Standards: An Emerging CPA Service Area', *Journal of Accountancy*, 177(2): 63–7.

Brilliant, D. (1998), 'Think Risk and Survive', *True and Fair*, (November), 3.

Briloff, A. J. (2001), 'Garbage In / Garbage Out: A Critique of Fraudulent Financial Reporting: 1987–1997 (the COSO Report) and The SEC Accounting Regulatory Process', *Critical Perspectives on Accounting*, 12(2): 125–48.

Browne, J. M. (2000a), 'Building an e-reputation', *European Business Forum*, 3: 13–15.

—— (2000b) 'Walking the Reputation Tightrope', *Accounting and Business*, 3(1): 12–13.

Brunsson, N. (2000). 'Standardization and Fashion Trends', in Brunsson and Jacobsson (eds.), 151–68.

—— and Jacobsson, B. (2000), 'The Contemporary Expansion of Standardization', in Brunsson and Jacobsson (eds.), 1–17.

—— Jacobsson, B., and Associates (eds.) (2000). *A World of Standards*. Oxford: Oxford University Press.

BSI (2000), *BSI 6079–3. Project Management—Part 3: Guide to the Management of Business Related Project Risk*. London: British Standards Institute.

Burchell, S., Clubb, C, and Hopwood, A. (1985), 'Accounting in its Social Context: Towards a History of Value Added in the UK', *Accounting, Organizations and Society*, 10 (4): 381–413.

Burchell, S., Clubb, C., Hopwood, A., Hughes, J., and Nahapiet, J. (1980), 'The Roles of Accounting in Organizations and Society', *Accounting, Organizations and Society*, 5 (1): 5– 27.

Burgess, A. (2006), 'The Making of the Risk-Centred Society and the Limits of Social Risk Research', *Health, Risk and Society*, 8(4): 329–42.

Busby, J. (2006), 'Failure to Mobilize in Reliability-Seeling Organizations: Two Cases from the UK Railway', *Journal of Management Studies*, 43(6): 1375–93.

Butterworth, M. (2000), 'The Emerging Role of the Risk Manager', in Pickford (ed.), 21–5.

Cabinet Office Strategy Unit (2002), *Risk: Improving Government's Capability to Handle Risk and Uncertainty*. London: Cabinet Office.

Cagan, P. (2001), 'Standard Operating Procedures', Online publishing, *Erisk.com*, March.

Callon, M. (1998), 'Introduction: The Embeddedness of Economic Markets in Economics', in M. Callon (ed.), *The Laws of the Markets*. Oxford: Blackwell, 1–57.

Calomiris, C. and Herring, R. (2002), 'The Regulation of Operational Risk in Investment Management Companies', *Perspective*, 8(2): 1–19.

Casper, S. and Hancke, R. (1999), 'Global Quality Norms within National Production Regimes: ISO 9000 Standards in the French and German Car Industries', *Organization Studies*, 20(6): 961–86.

CCAB (1975), *The Corporate Report*. London: Consultative Committee of Accountancy Bodies.

Cenker, W. and Nagy, A. (2004), 'Section 404 Implementation: Chief Audit Executives Navigate Uncharted Waters', *Managerial Auditing Journal*, 19(9): 1140–7.

Chambers, A. (1999), 'Reputational Risk—Control and Audit', London: The Moorgate Internal Audit Lecture Series, Chartered Accountants Hall, 6 July.

Chan, S., Leech, T., and Gupta, P. (2006), *Sarbanes-Oxley: A Practical Guide to Implementation Challenges and Global Response*. London: Risk Books.

Cheffins, B. (2000), 'Corporate Governance Reform: Britain as an Exporter', *Hume Papers on Public Policy*, 8(1): 10–28.

Choudhry, M. and Joannas, D. (2003), *Enterprise-Wide Risk Management: Integrating Market, Credit and Operational Risk*. London: Financial Times/Prentice Hall.

Ciborra, C. (2006), 'Imbrication of Representations: Risk and Digital Technologies', *Journal of Management Studies*, 43(6): 1339–56.

CIPFA (1994), *Auditing the Public Services: A Contribution to the Debate on the Future of Auditing*. London: Chartered Institute of Public Finance and Accountancy.

Clark, G. and Thrift, N. (2005), 'The Return of Bureaucracy: Managing Dispersed Knowledge in Global Finance', in Knorr-Cetina and Preda (eds.), 239–49.

Clarke, L. (1999), *Mission Improbable: Using Fantasy Documents to Tame Disaster*. Chicago: University of Chicago Press.

Clarkson, M. (ed.) (1998), *The Corporation and its Stakeholders*. Toronto: University of Toronto Press.

Coglianese, C. and Lazer, D. (2003), 'Management-Based Regulation; Prescribing Private Management to Achieve Public Goals', *Law and Society Review*, 37(4): 691–730.

Colbert, J. and Alderman, W. (1995), 'A Risk-driven Approach to Internal Audit', *Managerial Auditing Journal*, 10(2): 38–44.

Conference Board of Canada (2001), *A Composite Sketch of a Chief Risk Officer*. Ottawa: Conference Board of Canada.

Cooper, A. and Lousada, J. (2005). *Borderline Welfare*. London: Karnac Books, Tavistock Clinic Series.

Coopers and Lybrand International. (1996), *Generally Accepted Risk Principles*. London: Coopers and Lybrand.

COSO (1992) *Internal Control-Integrated Framework (2 Volumes)*. Committee of the Sponsoring Organizations of the Treadway Commission. www.coso.org

—— (2004). *Enterprise Risk Management*. Committee of the Sponsoring Organizations of the Treadway Commission. www.coso.org

Covaleski, M., Dirsmith, M., and Rittenberg, L. (2003), 'Jurisdictional Disputes over Professional Work: The Institutionalization of the Global Knowledge Expert', *Accounting, Organizations and Society*, 28: 323–55.

CSA (1997), *CAN/CSA–Q850–97, Risk Management Guideline for Decision Makers*. Mississauga, Ont.: Canadian Standards Association.

Cumming, C. and Hirtle, B. (2001), 'The Challenges of Risk Management in Diversified Financial Companies', *FRBNY Economic Policy Review*, March: 1–15.

Cunningham, M. (1999), 'Saying Sorry: The Politics of Apology', *The Political Quarterly*, 70(3); 285–93.

Curtis, E. and Turley, S. (2007), ' The Business Risk Audit—A Longitudinal Case Study of an Audit Engagement', *Accounting, Organizations and Society* 32(4/5): 439–61.

Czarniawska, B. and Joerges, B. (1996), 'Travels of Ideas', in B. Czarniawska and G. Sevon (eds.), *Translating Organizational Change*. Berlin: de Gruyter, 13–48.

Danielsson, J. (2001). 'VaR: A Castle Built on Sand', *Financial Regulator*, 5(2): 46–50.

—— and Shin, H. S. (2003), 'Endogenous Risk', in Field (ed.), 297–313.

Davies, G., Chun, R., Vinhas da Silva, R., and Roper, S. (2002), *Corporate Reputation and Competitiveness*. London: Routledge.

Davis, G. and Powell, W. (1992), 'Organization-Environment Relations', in M. Dinnette and L. Hough (eds.), *Handbook of Industrial and Organizational Psychology*. Palo Alto, CA: Consulting Psychologists Press, 315–75.

Day P. and Klein, R. (2004), *The NHS Improvers: A Study of the Commission for Health Improvement*. London: King's Fund.

de Waal, A. (2006), *Inspection, Inspection, Inspection*. London: Civitas.

Dean, M. (1999), *Governmentality: Power and Rule in Modern Society*, Thousand Oaks, CA: Sage.

Deephouse, D. (2002), 'The Term "Reputation Management": Users, Uses and the Trademark Tradeoff', *Corporate Reputation Review*, 5(1): 9–18.

Deloach, J. W. and Temple, N. (2000), *Enterprise-Wide Risk Management: Strategies for Linking Risk and Opportunity*. London: Financial Times/Prentice Hall.

Denney, D. (2005), *Risk and Society*. London: Sage.

Deragon, J. (2000), 'Old Knowledge with a New Name', Online publishing, *Erisk.com*, November.

Dewing, I. and Russell, P. (2005), *The Role of Auditors, Reporting Accountants and Skilled Persons in UK Financial Services Provision*. Edinburgh: The Institute of Chartered Accountants of Scotland.

Dibb, S. (2003), *Winning the Risk Game*. London: National Consumers Council, 2003.

Dickinson, G. M. (2001), 'Enterprise Risk Management: Its Origins and Conceptual Foundation', *Geneva Papers on Risk and Insurance—Issues and Practice*, 26(3): 360–6.

Diver, C. (1983), 'The Optimal Precision of Administrative Rules' *Yale Law Journal*, 93: 65–109.

Djelic, M-L. and Sahlin-Andersson, K. (eds.) (2006a), *Transnational Governance: Institutional Dynamics of Regulation*. Cambridge: Cambridge University Press.

—— (2006b), 'A World of Governance—The Rise of Transnational Regulation', in Djelic and Sahlin-Andersson (eds.), 1–28.

Dobbin, F., Dierkes, J., Kwok, M., and Zorn, D. (2001). 'The Rise and Stagnation of the COO: Fad and Fashion in Corporate Titles', Unpublished paper, Department of Sociology, Princeton University.

Dobbin, F. R., Edelman, L., Meyer, J. W., Scott, W. R., and Swidler, A. (1988), 'The Expansion of Due Process in Organizations', in L. G. Zucker (ed.), *Institutional Patterns and Organizations*. Cambridge, MA: Ballinger, 71–98.

Dobler, M. (2005), 'National and International Developments in Risk Reporting: May the German Accounting Standard 5 Lead the Way Internationally?', *German Law Journal*, 6(8): 1191–1200.

Doherty, N. A. (2000), *Integrated Risk Management: Techniques and Strategies for Managing Corporate Risk*. New York: McGraw-Hill.

Douglas, M. (1992a), 'Risk and Blame', in M. Douglas (ed.), *Risk and Blame: Essays in Cultural Theory*. London: Routledge, 3–21.

—— (1992b), 'Muffled Ears', in M. Douglas (ed.), *Risk and Blame: Essays in Cultural Theory*. London: Routledge, 55–82.

—— (1999), 'Les Risques du Fonctionnaire du Risque: La Diversité des Institutions et la Réparation des Risques' [The risks of the risk officer: diversity of institutions and the distribution of risks], *La Revue Alliage*, 40: 61–74.

Douglas, M. and Wildavsky A. (1982), *Risk and Culture: An Essay on the Selection of Technological and Environmental Dangers*. Berkeley: University of California Press.

Dowling, G. (2002), *Creating Corporate Reputations*. Oxford: Oxford University Press.

Drori, G. (2006), 'Governed by Governance: The New Prism for Organizational Change', in G. Drori, J. Meyer, and H. Hwang (eds.), *Globalization and Organization: World Society and Organizational Change*. Oxford: Oxford University Press, 91–118.

—— and Meyer, J. (2006), 'Scientization: Making a World Safe for Organizing', in Djelic and Sahlin-Andersson (eds.), 31–52.

Dukerich, J. and Carter, S. (2000), 'Distorted Images and Reputation Repair', in Schultz *et al.* (eds.), 97–112.

Dunsire, A. (1990), 'Holistic Governance', *Public Policy and Administration*, 5(1): 4–19.

—— (1993), 'Modes of Governance', in J. Kooiman (ed.), *Modern Governance: New Government-Society Interactions*. London: Sage, 21–34.

Edelman, L. (1990), 'Legal Environments and Organizational Governance: The Expansion of due Process in the American Workplace', *American Journal of Sociology*, 95: 1401–40.

—— Fuller, S. R., and Mara-Drita, I. (2001), 'Diversity Rhetoric and the Managerialization of Law', *American Journal of Sociology*, 106(6): 1589–641.

Eilifsen, A., Knechel, W. R., and Wallage, P. (2001), 'Application of the Business Risk Audit Model: A Field Study', *Accounting Horizons*, 15(3): 193–207.

EIU (1995), *Managing Business Risks—An Integrated Approach* (Written in cooperation with Arthur Andersen and Co.) London: Economist Intelligence Unit.

—— (2001), *Enterprise Risk Management—Implementing New Solutions* (In cooperation with MCC Enterprise Risk). London: Economist Intelligence Unit.

—— (2005), *Reputation: Risk of Risks*. London: Economist Intelligence Unit.

Elliot, R. K. (1995), 'The Future of Assurance Services: Implications for Academia', *Accounting Horizons*, 9(4): 118–27.

Ericson, R. (ed.) (2003), *Risk and Morality*. Toronto: Toronto University Press.

—— and Doyle, A. (2004), *Uncertain Business: Risk, Insurance and the Limits of Knowledge*. Toronto: Toronto University Press.

—— —— and Barry, D. (2003), *Insurance as Governance*. Toronto: University of Toronto Press.

Ermann, M. D. and Lundman, R. J. (eds.) (1996), *Corporate and Governmental Deviance: Problems of Organisational Behaviour in Contemporary Society*. Oxford: Oxford University Press.

Ernst and Young (2001). *Basel—A Better Use of Control* (Operational Risk Management Promotional Brochure). London: Ernst and Young.

Ewald, F. (1991), 'Insurance and Risk', in G. Burchell, C. Gordon, and P. Miller (eds.), *The Foucault Effect: Studies in Governmentality*. London: Harvester Wheatsheaf, 197–210.

Falkenstein, E. (2001), 'The Risk Manager of the Future: Scientist or Poet?', *RMA Journal,* (February), 18–22.

FEI Research Foundation (2002). *Risk Management: An Enterprise Perspective (Survey Results)* (Written in cooperation with Andersen). Washington DC: Financial Executives Institute.

Feldman, M. and March, J. (1981), 'Information in Organizations as Signal and Symbol', *Administrative Science Quarterly*, 26(2): 171–86.

Field, P. (2003), 'Introduction', in Field (ed.), xxv–xxxvii.

—— (ed.) (2003), *Modern Risk Management: A History*. London: Risk Books.

Fischoff, B., Watson, S., and Hope, C. (1984), 'Defining Risk', *Policy Sciences,* 17: 123–39.

Fishkin, C. A. (2001), 'Are You the Risk Manager of Tomorrow?' *RMA Journal,* (February): 23–7.

Fligstein, N. (1990), *The Transformation of Corporate Control*. Cambridge, MA: Harvard University Press.

Flyvbjerg, B., Bruzelius, N., and Rothengatter, W. (2003), *Megaprojects and Risk: An Anatomy of Ambition*. Cambridge: Cambridge University Press.

Fombrun, C. (1995), *Reputation: Realizing Value from the Corporate Image*. Boston: Harvard Business School.

—— (2005), 'Building Corporate Reputation through CSR Initiatives: Evolving Standards', *Corporate Reputation Review*, 8(1): 7–12.

—— and Foss, C. (2004), 'Business Ethics: Corporate Responses to Scandal', *Corporate Reputation Review*, 7(3): 284–8.

—— and Rindova, V. (2000), 'The Road to Transparency: Reputation Management at Royal Dutch/Shell 1977–96', in Schultz *et al.* (eds.), 77–96.

—— and Shanley., M. (1990), 'What's in a Name? Reputation Building and Corporate Strategy', *Academy of Management Journal*, 33(2): 233–58.

—— and Van Riel, C. (1997). 'The Reputational Landscape', *Corporate Reputation Review*, 1(1): 5–13 and 1(2): 5–13.

—— (2003), *Fame and Fortune: How Successful Companies Build Winning Reputations*. London: Prentice Hall/Financial Times.

Franklin, J. (ed.) (1997), *The Politics of Risk Society*. Cambridge: Polity Press.

Freedman, J. (1993). 'Accountants and Corporate Governance: Filling a Legal Vacuum?', *Political Quarterly*, 64(3): 285–97.

—— (2004), 'Defining Taxpayer Responsibility: In Support of a General Anti-Avoidance Principle', *British Tax Review*, 4: 332–57.

Freeman, R. E. (1984), *Strategic Management: A Stakeholder Approach*. Boston: Pitman.

Frey, B. and Jegen, R. (2001), 'Motivation Crowding Theory', *Journal of Economic Surveys.* 15(1): 589–611.

Friedman, A. and Miles, S. (2002), 'Developing Stakeholder Theory: A Social Realist Perspective', *Journal of Management Studies,* 39(1): 1–21.

—— (2006), *Stakeholders: Theory and Practice.* Oxford: Oxford University Press.

Froud, J. (2003), 'The Private Finance Initiative: Risk, Uncertainty and the State', *Accounting, Organizations and Society,* 28(6): 567–89.

FSA (2000), *A New Regulator for the New Millennium.* London: Financial Services Authority.

—— (2003), *The Combined Code on Corporate Governance.* London: Financial Services Authority.

—— (2005), *Operational Risk Management Practices: Feedback from a Thematic Review.* London: Financial Services Authority.

Furedi, F. (2002), *Culture of Fear: Risk Taking and the Morality of Low Expectations.* London: Continuum International.

Furusten, S. (2000), 'The Knowledge Base of Standards', in Brunsson *et al.* (2000), 71–84.

Gaines-Ross, L. (2002), *CEO Capital: A Guide to Building CEO Reputation and Company Success.* New Jersey: John Wiley and Sons.

GAO (2001), *Executive Guide: Maximizing the Success of Chief Information Officers.* Washington DC: General Accounting Office.

Garland, D. (2003), 'The Rise of Risk,' in Ericson (ed.), 48–86.

Gendron, Y. and Bedard, J. (2006), 'On the Constitution of Audit Committee Effectiveness', *Accounting, Organizations and Society,* 31(3): 211–39.

Giddens, A. (1990), *The Consequences of Modernity.* Cambridge: Polity.

—— (2003), *Runaway World: How Globalization is Reshaping Our Lives.* London: Routledge.

Gigerenzer, G. (2002), *Reckoning with Risk: Learning to Live with Uncertainty.* London: Penguin.

—— Swijtink, Z., Porter, T., Daston, L., Beatty, J., and Krueger, L. (1989), *The Empire of Chance.* Cambridge: Cambridge University Press.

Goble, J. (1997). 'Successfully Implementing CSA in a Multi-National Organisation: How IBM Assesses the Control Status of Global Processes and Businesses'. Paper presented at the Risk Self Assessment Summit, London, September.

Godman, R. (2006a), 'The Management of Tax Risk—Part 1', *Tax Adviser,* (April), 4–5.

—— (2006b), 'The Management of Tax Risk—Part 2', *Tax Adviser,* (May), 4–6.

Goodhart, C. (2001), *Operational Risk* (Special Paper no. 131). London: London School of Economics and Political Science, Financial Markets Group.

—— Hartmann, P., Llewellyn, D., Rojas-Suarez. L., and Weisbrod, S. (1998), *Financial Regulation: Why, How and Where Now?.* London: Routledge and Bank of England.

Goodwin, J. (2004), 'A Comparison of Internal Audit in the Private and Public Sectors', *Managerial Auditing Journal,* 19(5): 640–50.

Gotsi, M. and Wilson, A. (2001), 'Corporate Reputation: Seeking a Definition', *Corporate Communications—An International Journal*, 6(1): 24–30.

Gouldson, A. and Bebbington, J. (2007), 'Corporations and the Governance of Environmental Risk', *Environment and Planning C: Government and Policy*, 25(1): 4–20.

Gray, D. (2003), 'Wanted: Chief Ignorance Officer', *Harvard Business Review*, (November), 22–4.

Gray, J. and Hamilton, J. (2006), *Implementing Financial Regulation*. Chichester: John Wiley and Sons Ltd.

Gregory, C. and Nokes, S. (2002), *Minimizing Enterprise Risk: A Practical Guide to Risk and Continuity*. London: Financial Times/Prentice Hall.

GRI (2000), *Sustainability Reporting Guidelines*. Boston: Global Reporting Initiative.

Group of Thirty (1993), *Derivatives: Practices and Principles*. Washington, DC: Group of Thirty.

Gunningham, N. and Grabosky, P. (1998), *Smart Regulation: Designing Environmental Policy*. Oxford: Clarendon Press.

—— Kagan, R., and Thornton, D. (2003), *Shades of Green: Business, Regulation and Environment*. Stanford CA: Stanford University Press.

Hacking, I. (1986), 'Making up People', in T. Heller, N. Sosna, and D. Wellbery (eds.), *Reconstructing Individualism: Autonomy, Individuality, and the Self in Western Thought*. Stanford, CA: Stanford University Press, 222–36.

—— (1990), *The Taming of Chance*. Cambridge: Cambridge University Press.

—— (2003), 'Risk and Dirt', in Ericson (ed.), 22–47.

Haines, Y. (1992), 'Toward a Holistic Approach to Total Risk Management', *Geneva Papers on Risk and Insurance—Issues and Practice*, 17(64): 314–21.

Hajer, M. (1995), *The Politics of Environmental Discourse: Ecological Modernisation in the Policy Process*. Oxford: Oxford University Press.

Hall, P. (ed.) (1989), *The Political Power of Economic Ideas: Keynesianism across Nations*. Princeton: Princeton University Press.

Hamel G. and Valikangas, L. (2003), 'The Quest for Resilience', *Harvard Business Review*, 81(9): 52–63.

Hancher, L. and Moran, M. (eds.) (1989), *Capitalism, Culture and Economic Regulation*. Oxford: Clarendon Press.

Hanley, M. (1999), *Integrated Risk Management*. London: FT Books, 1999.

—— (2002), 'The Great Protector', *CFO Europe*, (February): 29–34.

Harrington, C. (2004), 'Internal Audit's New Role', *Journal of Accountancy*, (September), 65.

Hart, O. (1995), *Firms, Contracts and Financial Structure*. Oxford: Clarendon Press.

Hartman, W. (1994), 'Coming Soon: The Auditing of Control', *de Accountant*, (October), 123–6.

Hatherly, D. (1995), 'The Audit Research Agenda: The Drive for Quality and its Dependence on Professional Judgement', University of Edinburgh.

Hawkins, K. (2003), *Law as Last Resort: Prosecution Decision-Making in a Regulatory Agency*. Oxford: Oxford University Press.

Hay, B. (1993), 'Internal Control: How it Evolved in Four English Speaking Countries', *Accounting Historians Journal*, 20(1): 79–102.

Haywood, R. (2002), *Manage your Reputation*. London: Kogan Page.

Hedburg, B. and Jönsson, S. (1978), 'Designing Semi-Confusing Information Systems for Organizations in Changing Environments', *Accounting, Organizations and Society*, 3(1): 47–64.

Heimer, C. (1988), 'Social Structure, Psychology, and the Estimation of Risk', *American Review of Sociology*, 14: 491–519.

—— Coleman Petty, J., Culyba, R. (2005). 'Risk and Rules: The Legalization of Medicine', in Hutter and Power (eds.), 92–131.

Helbok, G. and Wagner, C. (2003), 'Corporate Financial Disclosure on Operational Risk in the Banking Industry', Operational Risk and Control Group, Bank Austria Credit Anstalt, Vienna.

Henning, R. (2000), 'Selling Standards', in Brunsson *et al.* (2000), 114–24.

Hermanson, H. (2000), 'An Analysis of the Demand for Reporting on Internal Control', *Accounting Horizons*, 14(3): 325–41.

Hilgartner, S. (1992). 'The Social Construction of Risk Objects: Or, How to Pry Open Networks of Risk', in Short and Clarke (eds.), 39–53.

HM Treasury (2005), *Reducing Administrative Burdens: Effective Inspection and Enforcement* (The Hampton Report). London: HM Treasury.

Hoffman, D. G. (2002), *Managing Operational Risk: 20 Firm-Wide Best Practice Strategies*. New York: John Wiley.

Hogan, W. (1997), 'Corporate Governance: Lessons from Barings', *Abacus*, 33(1): 26–48.

Holt, R. (2004), 'Risk Management: The Talking Cure', *Organization*, 11(2): 251–70.

Hood, C. (1996a), 'Control over Bureaucracy: Cultural Theory and Institutional Variety', *Journal of Public Policy*, 15(3): 207–30.

—— (1996b), 'Where Extremes Meet: "SPRAT" versus "SHARK" in Public Risk Management', in Hood and Jones (eds.), 208–27.

—— (2002), 'The Risk Game and the Blame Game', *Government and Opposition*, 37(1): 15–37.

—— and Heald, D. (eds.) (2006), *Transparency: The Key to Better Governance?*. Oxford: Oxford University Press.

—— and Jones, G. (1996a), 'Introduction', in Hood and Jones (eds.), 1–9.

—— —— (eds.) (1996b). *Accident and Design: Contemporary Debates in Risk Management*. London: UCL Press.

Hood, C., Jones, D., Pidgeon, N., Turner, B., Gibson, R., et al. (1992), 'Risk Management', in The Royal Society Risk: Analysis, Perception and Management. London: The Royal Society, 135–201.

—— Rothstein, H., and Baldwin, R. (2001), The Government of Risk: Understanding Risk Regulation Regimes. Oxford: Oxford University Press.

Hopkin, P. (2002), Holistic Risk Management in Practice. London: Witherby and Company Ltd.

HSE (2001), Reducing Risk, Protecting People: HSE's Decision Making Process. London: Health and Safety Executive.

Humphrey, C. and Moizer, P. (1990), 'From Techniques to Ideologies: An Alternative Perspective on the Audit Function', Critical Perspectives on Accounting, 1(3): 217–38.

Hunt, B. (2003), The Timid Corporation: Why Business is Terrified of Taking Risk. London: John Wiley.

Hutter, B. (1988), The Reasonable Arm of the Law? The Law Enforcement Procedures of Environmental Health Officers. Oxford: Clarendon Press.

—— (1997), Compliance: Regulation and Enforcement. Oxford: Clarendon Press.

—— (2000), Risk and Regulation. Oxford: Oxford University Press.

—— (2005), 'The Attractions of Risk-based Regulation: Accounting for the Emergence of Risk Ideas in Regulation', ESRC Centre for Analysis of Risk and Regulation, Discussion Paper 33, London School of Economics and Political Science.

—— and O'Mahony, J. (2004), 'Business Regulation: Reviewing the Regulatory Potential of Civil Society Organizations', ESRC Centre for Analysis of Risk and Regulation, Discussion Paper 26, London School of Economics and Political Science.

—— (2006), 'The Role of Non-state Actors in Regulation', ESRC Centre for Analysis of Risk and Regulation, Discussion Paper 37, London School of Economics and Political Science.

—— and Power, M. (2005a). 'Organizational Encounters with Risk: An Introduction,' in Hutter and Power (eds.), 1–32.

—— (eds.) (2005b), Organizational Encounters with Risk. Cambridge: Cambridge University Press.

Hutton, W. (1995), The State We're In. London: Jonathan Cape.

ICAEW (1994), Internal Control and Financial Reporting—Guidance for Directors of Listed Companies Registered in the UK. (The Rutteman Report). London: Institute of Chartered Accountants in England and Wales.

—— (1997a), Added Value Professionals: Chartered Accountants in 2005. London: Institute of Chartered Accountants in England and Wales.

—— (1997b), Financial Reporting of Risk: Proposals for a Statement of Business Risk. London: Institute of Chartered Accountants in England and Wales.

—— (1998b), Creating the Added-Value Business Advisor: The Detailed Proposals, London: Institute of Chartered Accountants in England and Wales.

—— (1999a), *Internal Control: Guidance for Directors of Listed Companies Incorporated in the United Kingdom*. London: Institute of Chartered Accountants in England and Wales.

—— (1999b), *No Surprises: the Case for Better Risk Reporting*. London: Institute of Chartered Accountants in England and Wales.

—— (2000a), *Risk Management and the Value Added by Internal Audit*. London: Institute of Chartered Accountants in England and Wales.

—— (2000b), *Human Capital and Corporate Reputation: Setting the Boardroom Agenda*. London: Institute of Chartered Accountants in England and Wales.

ICAS (1993), *Auditing into the Twenty First Century*. Edinburgh: Institute of Chartered Accountants in Scotland.

ICAS/ICAEW (1989), *Auditing and the Future*. Edinburgh and London: Institute of Chartered Accountants of Scotland/Institute of Chartered Accountants in England and Wales.

IFAC (2006), *Internal Controls—A Review of Current Developments*. New York: International Federation of Accountants.

IOSCO (1998), *Risk Management and Control Guidance for Securities Firms and their Supervisors*. Madrid: International Organization of Securities Commissions.

IPR (2003), *Reputation and the Bottom Line: A Communications Guide to Reporting on Corporate Reputation*. London: Institute of Public Relations, MORI, and Business in the Community.

Irwin, A. (1995), *Citizen Science: A Study of People, Expertise and Sustainable Development*. London: Routledge.

—— and Wynne, B. (1996), *Misunderstanding Science?: The Public Reconstruction of Science and Technology*. Cambridge: Cambridge University Press.

ISO/IEC (2002), *Guide 73: Risk Management—Vocabulary*. Geneva: International Standards Organization.

ITGI, (2006), *COBIT 4.0*. Rolling Meadows, Il.: IT Governance Institute.

Jackson, K. T. (2004), *Building Reputational Capital: Strategies for Integrity and Fair Play that Improve the Bottom Line*. Oxford: Oxford University Press.

Jacobsson, B. (2006), 'Regulated Regulators: Global Trends of State Formation', in Djelic and Sahlin-Andersson (eds.), 205–24.

Jameson, R. (1998), 'Operational Risk: Playing the Name Game', *Risk*, (October): 38–42.

—— (2001a). 'Between RAROC and A Hard Place'. Online publishing, *Erisk.com*, February.

—— (2001b). 'Operational Risk Charges: A Bad Case of Mission Creep?' Online publishing, *Erisk.com*, May.

Jasanoff, S. (1986), *Risk Management and Political Culture*. New York: Russell Sage Foundation.

—— (1990), 'America's Exceptionalism and the Political Acknowledgement of Risk', *Daedelus*, 119(4): 61–81.

Jasanoff, S. (1991), 'Acceptable Evidence in a Pluralistic Society', in Mayo and Hollander (eds.), 29–47.

—— (1994), 'Introduction: Learning from Disaster', in S. Jasanoff (ed.), *Learning from Disaster: Risk Management after Bhopal.* Philadelphia: University of Pennsylvania Press, 1–21.

—— (1999), 'The Songlines of Risk', *Environmental Values,* 8: 135–52.

—— (2005), *Designs on Nature: Science and Democracy in Europe and the United States.* Princeton: Princeton University Press.

Jennings, W. (2005), 'Running the Risk? London 2012 and the Risk Management of Everything Olympic', *Risk and Regulation,* 10, (Winter): 7–9.

Jeppessen, K. K. (1998). 'Reinventing Auditing, Redefining Consulting and Independence', *European Accounting Review,* 7(3): 517–39.

Jorion, P. (2001a), 'Value, Risk and Control: A Dynamic Process in Need of Integration', in Pickford (ed.), 119–24.

—— (2001b), *Value at Risk.* New York: McGraw Hill.

JSA (2001). *JIS Q 2001, Guidelines for the Development and Implementation of Risk Management System.* Tokyo: Japanese Standards Association—Japanese Industrial Standards.

Kahnemann, D. and A. Tversky (1979), 'Prospect Theory: An Analysis of Decision under Risk', *Econometrica,* 47: 263–91.

Kaltoff, H. (2005), 'Practices of Calculation: Economic Representations of Risk', *Theory Culture and Society,* 22(2): 69–97.

Kant, I. (1978) [1787] *Critique of Pure Reason,* translated by N. Kemp-Smith. London Macmillan.

Karapetrovic, S. and Wilborn, W. (2000), 'Generic Audit of Management Systems: Fundamentals', *Managerial Auditing Journal,* 15(6): 279–94.

Kavanagh, B. (2003), 'A Retrospective Look at Market Risk', in Field (ed.), 251–9.

Kinney, W. R. (1999), 'Auditor Independence: A Burdensome Constraint or Core Value?', *Accounting Horizons,* 13(1): 69–75.

—— (2000), 'Research Opportunities in Internal Control Quality and Quality Assurance', *Auditing: A Journal of Theory and Practice,* 19 (supplement): 83–90.

Klein, D. (1997), *Reputation: Studies in the Voluntary Elicitation of Good Conduct.* Ann Arbor: University of Michigan State.

Kloman, F. (1976). 'The Risk Management Revolution', *Fortune Magazine,* (July).

—— (1992), 'Rethinking Risk Management', *Geneva Papers on Risk and Insurance—Issues and Practice,* 17(64): 299–313.

—— (2005), *Mumpsimus Revisited: Essays on Risk Management.* Lyme, Ct.: Seawrack Press.

Knechel, W. R. (2007), 'The Business Risk Audit: Origins, Obstacles and Opportunities', *Accounting, Organizations and Society* 32(4/5): 383–408.

Knight, F. (1921) *Risk, Uncertainty and Profit.* Boston: Houghton Mifflin.

Knights, D. and Vurdubakis, T. (1993), 'Calculations of Risk: Towards an Under-standing of Insurance as a Moral and Political Technology', *Accounting, Organizations and Society*, 18(7/8): 729–64.

Knorr-Cetina, K. and Preda, A. (eds.) (2005), *The Sociology of Financial Markets*. Oxford: Oxford University Press.

Kunreuther, H. and Heal, G. (2005), 'Interdependencies within an Organization', in Hutter and Power (eds.), 190–208.

Kuritzkes, A. (2002), 'Operational Risk Capital: A Problem of Definition', *The Journal of Risk Finance*, 4(3): 47–56.

—— and Scott, H. (2005), 'Sizing Operational Risk and the Effect of Insurance: Implications for the Basel II Capital Accord', in H. Scott (ed.), *Capital Adequacy Beyond Basel: Banking, Securities and Insurance*. Oxford: Oxford University Press, 258–83.

Kurunmaki, L. (1999), 'Professional vs. Financial Capital in the Field of Health Care—Struggles for the Redistribution of Power and Control', *Accounting, Organizations and Society*, 24(2): 95–124.

Lam, J. (2000), 'Enterprise-wide Risk Management and the Role of the Chief Risk Officer', *Erisk Magazine*, 25 March.

—— (2003a), *Enterprise Risk Management—From Incentives to Controls*. Chichester: John Wiley.

—— (2003b). 'Enterprise-wide Risk Management', in Field (ed.), 287–96.

Larkin, J. (2002), *Strategic Reputation Risk Management*. London: Palgrave Macmillan.

Lee, C. R. (2000), 'Chief Risk Officer Stepping Up', *Risk Management*, (September): 23–27.

Leech, T. and McCuaig, B. (1999), 'CRSA: Current State of the Art, its Origins and Impacts', in Wade and Wynne (eds.), 37–52.

Lemon, W. M., Tatum, K. W. and Turley, S. (2000), *Developments in the Audit Methodologies of Large Accounting Firms*. London: Auditing Practices Board.

Levidow, L. (2001), 'Precautionary Uncertainty: Regulating GM Crops in Europe', *Social Studies of Science*, 31(6): 845–78.

Leyshon, A. (1994). 'Under Pressure: Finance, Geo-Economic Competition and the Rise and Fall of Japan's Postwar Growth Economy', in S. Corbridge, R. Martin, and N. Thrift (eds.), *Money, Power and Space*. Oxford: Blackwell, 116–45.

—— and Thrift, N. (1997), *Money/Space: Geographies of Monetary Transformation*. London: Routledge.

Lezaun, J. and Soneryd, L. (2006), 'Government by Elicitation: Engaging Stakeholders or Listening to the Idiots?', ESRC Centre for Analysis of Risk and Regulation, Discussion Paper 34, London School of Economics and Political Science.

—— (2006), 'Creating New Regulatory Objects: Making Transgenic Organisms Traceable', *Social Studies of Science*, 36: 499–531.

Lofstedt, R. and Renn, O. (1997), 'The Brent Spar Controversy: An Example of Risk Communication Gone Wrong', *Risk Analysis*, 17(2): 131–6.

Loya, T. and Boli, J. (1999), 'Standardization in the World Polity', in Boli and Thomas (eds.), 169–97.

Luhmann, N. (1988), 'Familiarity, Confidence, Trust: Problems and Alternatives', in D. Gambetta (ed.), *Trust: Making and Breaking Cooperative Relations*. Oxford: Blackwell, 94–107.

—— (1992), *Risk: A Sociological Theory*. Berlin: de Gruyter.

Mackenzie, D. (1993), *Inventing Accuracy: A Historical Sociology of Nuclear Missile Guidance*. Cambridge, MA: MIT Press.

—— (2005), 'Mathematizing Risk: Models, Arbitrage and Crises', in Hutter and Power (eds.), 167–89.

—— and Millo, Y. (2003), 'Constructing a Market, Performing Theory: The Historical Sociology of a Financial Derivatives Exchange', *American Journal of Sociology*, 109: 107–45.

Macrae, C. (2006), 'Harnessing Hindsight: Assessing Risk, Resilience and Operational Risk in Airlines', *Risk and Regulation*, (Summer), 10–11.

Maijoor, S. (2000), 'The Internal Control Explosion', *International Journal of Auditing*, 4: 101–9.

Makosz, P. (2005), 'Risk: Liability or Opportunity', *CA Magazine*, 2 September.

March, J. and Shapira, Z. (1987), 'Managerial Perspectives on Risk and Risk Taking', *Management Science*, 33(11): 1404–18.

March, J. G. and Simon, H. A. (1958), *Organizations*. New York: Wiley.

Marcussen, M. (2006), 'The Transnational Governance Network of Central Bankers', in Djelic and Sahlin-Andersson (eds.), 180–204.

Marquand, D. (2004), *The Decline of the Public*. Cambridge: Polity Press.

Mattli, W. (2001), 'The Politics and Economics of International Institutional Standards Setting: An Introduction', *Journal of European Public Policy*, 8(3): 328–44.

—— and Buethe, T. (2003), 'Setting International Standards: Technological Rationality or Primacy of Power?', *World Politics*, 56(1): 1–42.

Mautz, R. K. and Sharaf, H. A. (1961), *The Philosophy of Auditing*. Sarasota, FL: American Accounting Association.

Mayo, D. and Hollander, D. (eds.) (1991), *Acceptable Evidence: Science and Values in Risk Management*. Oxford: Oxford University Press.

McCormick, R. (2004a), 'The Management of Legal Risk by Financial Institutions in the Context of Basel II, Part 1', *The Journal of International Banking and Financial Law*, 9: 304–9.

—— (2004b), 'The Management of Legal Risk by Financial Institutions in the Context of Basel II, Part 1', *The Journal of International Banking and Financial Law*, 9: 354–6.

—— (2006), *Legal Risk in Financial Markets*. Oxford: Oxford University Press.

McKinlay, A. and Starkey, K. (1997), *Foucault, Management and Organization Theory: From Panopticon to Technologies of Self*. London: Sage.

McNamee, D. and McNamee, T. (1995), 'The Transformation of Internal Auditing', *Managerial Auditing Journal*, 10(2): 34–7.

Meidinger, E. (2003), 'Forest Certification As Environmental Law Making by Global Civil Society', in E. Meidinger, C. Elliott, and G. Oesten (eds.), *Social and Political Dimensions of Forest Certification*. Remagen-Oberwinter, Germany: Forstbuch, 293–329.

Mengle, D. (2003a), 'Risk Management as a Process', in Field (ed.), 3–10.

—— (2003b), 'Regulatory Origins of Risk Management', in Field (ed.), 417–25.

Mercer Oliver Wyman (2004), *Global Study of Operational Risk Management Practices*. London: Mercer Oliver Wyman.

Mercer, L. (1997), 'Friend or Foe: Determining how to Integrate CSA into the Internal Auditor's Tool Kit to help Enhance the Reputation of the Internal Audit Function rather than Undermine it', Paper presented at the Risk Self-Assessment Summit, London, September.

Merkle, J. (1980), *Management and Ideology: The International Scientific Management Movement*. Berkeley, CA: University of California Press.

Mestchian, P. (2003), 'Operational Risk Management: The Solution is the Problem', in Risk Books/SAS, *Advances in Operational Risk: Firm-Wide Issues for Financial Institutions*. London: Risk Books, 3–16.

—— Makarov, M., and Mirzai, B. (2005), 'In defence of COSO', *Operational Risk*, 6(3): 28–30.

Meulbroek, L. (2001), 'Total Strategies for Company-Wide Risk Control', in Pickford (ed.), 67–73.

—— (2002a), 'A Senior Manager's Guide to Integrated Risk Management', *Journal of Applied Corporate Finance*, 14(4): 56–70.

—— (2002b), 'The Promise and Challenge of Integrated Risk Management', *Risk Management and Insurance Review*, 5: 55–66.

Meyer, J. (2002), 'Globalization and the Expansion and Standardization of Management', in Sahlin-Andersson and Engwall (eds.), 33–44.

—— and Rowan, B. (1977), 'Institutionalized Organizations: Formal Structure as Myth and Ceremony', *American Journal of Sociology*, 83: 340–63.

—— Boli, J., Thomas, G., and Ramirez, F. (1997). 'World Society and the Nation State', *American Journal of Sociology*, 103: 144–81.

Miccolis, J., Hively, K., and Merkley, B. (2001), *Enterprise Risk Management: Trends and Emerging Practices*. Altamonte Springs, FL: The Institute of Internal Auditors Research Foundation, 2001.

Mikes, A. (2005), 'Enterprise Risk Management in Action', ESRC Centre for Analysis of Risk and Regulation, Discussion Paper 35, London School of Economics and Politics.

—— (2006), 'Enterprise Risk Management in Action'. Ph.D. Thesis. London: University of London.

Miller, P. (1991), 'Accounting Innovation Beyond the Enterprise: Problematizing Investment Decisions and Programming Economic Growth in the United Kingdom in the 1960s', *Accounting, Organizations and Society*, 16: 733–62.

Miller, P. (1994), 'Accounting as Social and Institutional Practice: An Introduction', in A. Hopwood and P. Miller (eds.), *Accounting as Social and Institutional Practice*. Cambridge: Cambridge University Press, 1–39.

—— and O'Leary, T. (1987), 'Accounting and the Construction of the Governable Person', *Accounting, Organizations and Society*, 12: 235–65.

—— (1993), 'Accounting Expertise and the Politics of the Product: Economic Citizenship and Modes of Corporate Governance', *Accounting, Organizations and Society*, 6: 1–40.

—— Kurunmaki, L., and O'Leary, T. (2006), 'Accounting, Hybrids and the Management of Risk', ESRC Centre for Analysis of Risk and Regulation, Discussion Paper 40. London School of Economics and Political Science.

Miller, R. and Young, M. (1997), 'Financial Reporting and Risk Management in the Twenty-First Century', *Fordham Law Review*, 5 (April), 1987–2064.

Millo, Y. and J. Lezaun (2006), 'Regulatory Experiments: Genetically Modified Crops and Financial Derivatives on Trial', *Science and Public Policy*, 33(3): 179–90.

Mills, R. W. (1997), 'Internal Control Practices within Large UK Companies', in K. Keasey and M. Wright (eds.), *Corporate Governance: Responsibilities, Risk and Remuneration*. London: John Wiley and Sons, 121–43.

Mirowski, P. (2002), *Machine Dreams: Economics Becomes a Cyborg Science*. Cambridge: Cambridge University Press.

Moody's Investor Service (2002), *Bank Operational Risk Management: More than an Exercise in Capital Allocation and Loss Data Gathering*. London: Moody's Investor Service, Global Credit Research.

Moran, M. (1986), *The Politics of Banking*. London: Macmillan.

—— (1989), *The Politics of the Financial Services Revolution: The USA, UK and Japan*. London: Macmillan.

—— (2003), *The British Regulatory State: High Modernism and Hyper-Innovation*. Oxford: Oxford University Press.

Morely, M. (2002), *How to Manage your Global Reputation*. London: Palgrave Macmillan.

Moss, D. (2004), *When All Else Fails: Government as the Ultimate Risk Manager*. Cambridge, MA: Harvard University Press.

Mouritsen, J. (2001), 'Intellectual Capital and the "Capable Firm": Narrating, Visualising and Numbering for Managing Knowledge', *Accounting, Organizations and Society*, 26: 735–62.

Muermann, A. and Oktem, U. (2002), 'The Near-Miss Management of Operational Risk', *The Journal of Risk Finance*, 4(1): 25–36.

Murray, K. and White, J. (2004), *CEO Views on Reputation Management: A Report on the Value of Public Relations, as Perceived by Organizational Leaders*. London: Chime PLC.

Nagy, A. and Cenker, W. (2002), 'An Assessment of the Newly Defined Internal Audit Function', *Managerial Auditing Journal*, 17(3): 130–7.

NAO (2000), *Supporting Innovation: Managing Risk in Government Departments*. London: National Audit Office.

Nash, M., Nakada, P., and Johnston, B. (2002), 'Start Today for Enterprise Wide Risk Management in 2006', *RMA Journal*, (November): 56–61.

Nash, T. (ed.) (1999), *Reputation Management: Strategies for Protecting Companies, their Brands and their Directors*. London: Kogan Page with the Institute of Directors.

National Research Council (1996), *Understanding Risk: Informing Decisions in a Democratic Society*. Washington, DC: National Academy Press.

Neef, D. (2003), *Managing Corporate Reputation and Risk: A Strategic Approach Using Knowledge Management*. London: Butterworth-Heinemann.

Nicholls, M. (2003a), 'Singapore Sting—Barings', in Field (ed.), 527–9.

—— (2003b), 'A Question of Authority—Hammersmith and Fulham', in Field (ed.), 531–6.

Nottingham, L. (1997), *A Conceptual Framework for Integrated Risk Management*. Toronto: Conference Board of Canada.

O'Malley, P. (2000). 'Uncertain Subjects: Risks, Liberalism and Contract', *Economy and Society*, 29(4): 460–84.

—— (2004), *Risk, Uncertainty and Government*. London: Glasshouse Press.

O'Neill, O. (2006), 'Transparency and the Ethics of Communication', in Hood and Heald (eds.), 75–90.

O'Regan, D. (2001), 'Genesis of a Profession: Towards Professional Status for Internal Auditors', *Managerial Auditing Journal*, 16(4): 215–27.

OECD (2001), *Improving Nuclear Regulatory Effectiveness*. Paris: OECD Nuclear Energy Agency.

Okrent, D. and Pidgeon, N. F. (eds.) (1998), 'Risk Assessment versus Risk Perception. Special volume of *Reliability Engineering and System Safety*, 59: 1–159.

Oliver Wyman and Company (2002), *The Evolving Roles of the Chief Financial Officer and the Chief Risk Officer: A Global Survey of Financial Institutions*. New York: Oliver Wyman and Company.

Parker, C. (2000), 'Reinventing Regulation within the Corporation: Compliance-Oriented Regulatory Innovation', *Administration and Society*, 32(5): 529–65.

—— (2002), *The Open Corporation: Effective Self-Regulation and Democracy*. Cambridge: Cambridge University Press.

—— (2007), 'Meta-Regulation: Legal Accountability for Corporate Social Responsibility', in D. McBarnet, A. Voiculescu, and T. Campbell (eds.) *The New Corporate Accountability: Corporate Social Responsibility and the Law*. Cambridge: Cambridge University Press, 207–237.

Paul-Choudhury, S. (2002), 'Converging Risk', Online Publishing, *Erisk.Com*, June.

Pausenberger, E. and Nassauer, F. (2000), 'Governing the Corporate Risk Management Function: Regulatory Issues', in M. Frenkel, U. Hommel, and M. Rudolf (eds.), *Risk Management: Challenge and Opportunity*. Heidelberg: Springer Verlag, 263–76.

Pearce, F. and Tombs, S. (1996), 'Hegemony, Risk and Governance: "Social Regula-tions" and the American Chemical Industry', *Economy and Society*, 25(3): 428–54.

Pearson, N. (2003), 'Markowitz Mean-Variance Portfolio Theory', in Field (ed.), 45–56.

Peecher, M. E., Schwartz, R., and Solomon, I. (2007), 'It's all about Audit Quality: Perspectives on Strategic-Systems Auditing', *Accounting, Organizations and Society*, 32 (4/5): 463–61.

Perrow, C. (1984), *Normal Accidents: Living with High Risk Technologies*. New York: Basic Books.

Peters, G. (2000), 'Reputational Capital: Where the New Economy is Heading', in ICAEW, *Human Capital and Corporate Reputation: Setting the Boardroom Agenda*. London: Institute of Chartered Accountants in England and Wales, 14–15.

Pfeffer, J. (1994), 'The Costs of Legalization: The Hidden Dangers of Increasingly Formalized Control', in S. B. Sitkin and R. J. Bies (eds.), *The Legalistic Organization*. Thousand Oaks, CA.: Sage, 329–46.

Phimster, J., Oktem, U., Kleindorfer, P., and Kunreuther, H. (2003), 'Near-Miss Management Systems in the Chemical Process Industry', *Risk Analysis*, 23(4): 445–59.

Pickford, J. (ed.) (2000), *Mastering Risk, Vol. 1: Concepts*. London: Pearson Education.

Pidgeon, N. and O'Leary, M. (2000), 'Man-Made Disasters: Why Technology and Organizations (sometimes) Fail', *Safety Science*, 34: 15–30.

Pidgeon, N. F., Kasperson, R. K., and Slovic, P. (eds.) (2003), *The Social Amplification of Risk*. Cambridge: Cambridge University Press.

Pildes, R. and Sunstein, C. (1995), 'Reinventing the Regulatory State', *University of Chicago Law Review*, 62: 1–129.

Pollack, R. (1995), 'Regulating Risks', *Journal of Economic Literature*, 23 (March): 179–91.

Porter, J. (2003), 'Evolution of the Global Weather Derivatives Market', in Field (ed.), 395–414.

Porter, T. (1992), 'Quantification and the Accounting Ideal in Science', *Social Studies of Science*, 22(4): 633–51.

—— (1995), *Trust in Numbers: The Pursuit of Objectivity in Science and Public Life*. Princeton: Princeton University Press.

Powell, W. (2003), 'The Capitalist Firm in the Twenty-First Century: Emerging Patterns in Western Enterprise', in P. DiMaggio (ed.), *The Twenty First Century Firm: Changing Economic Organization in International Perspective*. Princeton: Princeton University Press, 33–68.

—— and DiMaggio, P. (eds.) (1991), *The New Institutionalism in Organizational Analysis*. Chicago: University of Chicago Press.

Power, M. (1992), 'The Politics of Brand Accounting in the United Kingdom', *European Accounting Review*, 1(1): 39–68.

—— (1994), *The Audit Explosion*. London: Demos.

—— (1996a), 'Expertise and the Construction of Relevance: Accountants and Environmental Audit', *Accounting, Organizations and Society*, 22 (2): 123–46.

—— (1996b), 'Making Things Auditable', *Accounting, Organizations and Society*, 21(2/3): 289–315.

—— (1997a), *The Audit Society: Rituals of Verification*. Oxford: Oxford University Press.

—— (1997b), 'From Risk Society to Audit Society', *Soziale Systeme*, 3(1): 3–21.

—— (1999), *The Audit Implosion: Managing Risk from the Inside*. London: Institute of Chartered Accountants in England and Wales.

—— (2002), 'Standardization and the Regulation of Management Control Practices', *Soziale Systeme*, 8(2): 190–203.

—— (2003a), 'Auditing and the Production of Legitimacy', *Accounting, Organizations and Society*, 28(4): 379–94.

—— (2003b), 'Risk Management and the Responsible Organization', in Ericson (ed.), 145–64.

—— (2004a), 'Enterprise Risk Management and the Organization of Uncertainty in Financial Institutions', in K. Knorr-Cetina and A. Preda (eds.), *The Sociology of Financial Markets*. Oxford: Oxford University Press, 250–268.

—— (2004b), 'Counting, Control and Calculation: Reflections on Measuring and Managing', *Human Relations*, 56(6): 65–78.

—— (2004c), *The Risk Management of Everything*. London: Demos.

—— (2005a), 'The Invention of Operational Risk', *Review of International Political Economy*, 12(4): 577–599.

—— (2005b), 'The Theory of the Audit Explosion', in E. Ferlie, L., Lynn, and C. Pollitt (eds.), *The Oxford Handbook of Public Management*. Oxford: Oxford University Press, 326–44.

—— (2005c), 'Organizational Responses to Risk: The Rise of the Chief Risk Officer', in Hutter and Power (eds.), 132–48.

—— (2007), 'Corporate Governance, Reputation, and Environmental Risk', *Environment and Planning C: Government and Policy*, 25(1): 90–97.

Prat, A. (2006), 'The More Closely we are Watched, the Better we Behave?', in Hood and Heald (eds.), 91–103.

PwC/IFAC (1999), *Enhancing Shareholder Wealth by Better Managing Business Risk*. New York: PricewaterhouseCoopers/International Federation of Accountants.

Raban, C. and Turner, E. (2003), *Academic Risk: Quality Risk Management in Higher Education*. Higher Education Funding Council.

Rao, H. (1994), 'The Social Construction of Reputation: Certification Contests, Legitimation and the Survival of Organizations in the American Automobile Industry: 1895–1912', *Strategic Management Journal*, 15: 29–44.

Rayner, J. (2003), *Managing Reputational Risk*. London: John Wiley and Sons.

Rehbinder, E. (1991), 'Reflexive Law and Practice: The Corporate Officer for Environmental Protection as an Example', in A. Febbrajo and G. Teubner (eds.), *State,*

Law, Economy as Autopoietic Systems: Regulation and Autonomy in a New Perspective. Milan: Guiffre, 579–608.

Reiss, A. J. (1984). 'Selecting Strategies of Social Control over Organisational Life', in K. Hawkins and J. M. Thomas (eds.), *Enforcing Regulation*. Dordrecht: Kluwer-Nijhoff, 23–35.

Renn, O. (2004), 'The Challenge of Integrating Deliberation and Expertise: Participation and Discourse in Risk Management', in T. McDaniels and M. Small (eds.), *Risk Analysis and Society: An Interdisciplinary Characterization of the Field*. Cambridge University Press, 289–366.

—— (2008), *Risk Governance: Coping with Uncertainty in a Complex World*. London: Earthscan.

Rezaee, Z. (1995), 'What the COSO Report Means for Internal Auditors', *Managerial Auditing Journal*, 10(6): 5–9.

Richter, I., Berking, S., and Muller-Schmid, R. (eds.) (2006), *Risk Society and the Culture of Precaution*. London: Palgrave Macmillan.

Rijpma, J. (2003), 'From Deadlock to Dead End: The Normal Accidents-High Reliability Debate Revisited', *Journal of Contingencies and Crisis Management*, 11(1): 37–45.

Rittenberg, L. and Covaleski, M. (2001), 'Internalization versus Externalization of the Internal Audit Function: An Examination of Professional and Organizational Imperatives', *Accounting, Organizations and Society*, 26: 617–41.

RMA (1999), *Operational Risk: The Next Frontier*. Philadelphia, PA.: Risk Management Association.

Roberts, J. (2003), 'The Manufacture of Corporate Social Responsibility: Constructing Corporate Sensibility', *Organization*, 10(2): 249–65.

Robson, K., Humphrey, C., Khalifa, R. M., and Jones, J. (2007), 'Transforming Audit Technologies: Business Risk Audit Methodologies in the Audit Field', *Accounting, Organizations and Society*, 32(4/5): 409–38.

Rose, N. and Miller, P. (1992), 'Political Power beyond the State: Problematics of Government', *British Journal of Sociology*, 43(2): 173–205.

Rosen, D. (2003a), 'The Development of Risk Management Software', in Field (ed.), 135–48.

—— (2003b). 'Risk Management and Corporate Governance: The Case of Enron', *Connecticut Law Review*, 35(3): 1157–84.

Rothstein, H. (2003), 'Neglected Risk Regulation: The Institutional Attenuation Phenomenon', *Health, Risk and Society*, 5(1): 85–103.

—— (2004), 'Precautionary Bans or Sacrificial Lambs? Participative Regulation and the Reform of the UK Food Safety Regime', *Public Administration*, 82(4): 857–81.

—— Huber, M., and Gaskell, G. (2006a), 'A Theory of Risk Colonization: The Spiralling Regulatory Logics of Societal and Institutional Risk', *Economy and Society*, 35(1): 91–112.

—— Irving, P., Walden, T., and Yearsley, R. (2006b), 'The Risks of Risk-based Regulation: Insights from the Environmental Policy Domain', *Environment International*, 32(8): 1056–65.

Rouyer, S. (2002), 'Enterprise Risk Management for Financial Institutions', Online publishing, *Erisk.com.*, January.

Royal College of Anaesthetists (2000), *Raising the Standard: A Compendium of Audit Recipes*. London: Royal College of Anaesthetists.

Russell, P. (1996), 'Exercising Self-Control', *Accountancy*, (March): 126–7.

Sahlin-Andersson, K. and Engwall, L. (eds.) (2002), *The Expansion of Management Knowledge: Carriers, Flows and Sources*. Stanford: Stanford University Press.

Samad-Khan, A. (2005), 'Why COSO is Flawed?', *Operational Risk*, 6(1): 24–8.

Scaillet, O. (2003), 'The Origin and Development of Value at Risk', in Field (ed.), 151–8.

Schultz, M., Hatch, M. J., and Larsen, M. H. (eds.) (2000), *The Expressive Organization: Linking Identity, Reputation and the Corporate Brand*. Oxford: Oxford University Press.

Scott, J. (1998), *Seeing Like a State: How Certain Schemes to Improve the Human Condition Have Failed*. New Haven, CT.: Yale University Press.

Scott, S. V. and Walsham, G. (2005), 'Reconceptualizing and Managing Reputation Risk in the Knowledge Economy: Toward Reputable Action', *Organization Science*, 16(3): 308–22.

Scott, W. S. (1994), 'Law and Organizations', in Sitkin and Bies (eds.), 3–18.

Selim, G. and Mcnamee, D. (1999), 'The Risk Management and Internal Auditing Relationship: Developing and Validating a Model', *International Journal of Auditing*, 3: 159–74.

Shamir, R. (2004), 'Between Self-Regulation and the Alien Tort Claims Act: On the Contested Concept of Corporate Social Responsibility', *Law and Society Review*, 38(4): 635–64.

—— (2005), 'Mind the Gap: The Commodification of Corporate Social Responsibility', *Symbolic Interaction*, 28(2): 229–53.

Shapira, Z. (1995), *Risk Taking: A Managerial Perspective*. New York: Russell Sage Foundation.

Shapiro, A. (2003), 'Analysis of the Orange County Disaster', in Field (ed.), 497–509.

Shapiro, S. P. (1987), 'The Social Control of Impersonal Trust', *American Journal of Sociology*, 93(3): 623–58.

Sharman, R. (2006), 'Enterprise Risk Management in Industry—A Game of Two Halves', Paper presented at the Management Accounting Research Group (MARG) Conference, London School of Economics, May.

Sheedy, E. (1999), 'Applying an Agency Framework to Operational Risk Management', Working Paper 22, Macquarie Applied Finance Centre, Macquarie University.

Shiller, R. J. (2003), *The New Financial Order: Risk in the 21st Century*. Princeton: Princeton University Press.

Shimpi, P. A. (ed.) (2000), *Integrating Corporate Risk Management*. Thomson South Western—Texere Publishing.

Shin, H. (ed.) (2004), *Derivatives Accounting and Risk Management: The Impact of IAS 39*. London: Risk Books.

Short, J. (1992), 'Defining, Explaining and Managing Risks', in Short and Clarke (eds.), 3–23.

—— and Clarke, L. (eds.) (1992), *Organizations, Uncertainties and Risks*. Boulder, CO.: Westview Press.

Silbergeld, E. (1991), 'Risk Assessment and Risk Management: An Uneasy Divorce', in Mayo and Hollander (eds.), 99–114.

Simon, F. (2002), 'The De-Construction and Re-Construction of Authority and the Role of Management Consulting', *Soziale Systeme*, 8(2): 283–93.

Simon, J. (1988), 'The Ideological Effects of Actuarial Practices', *Law and Society Review*, 22(4): 771–800.

Simons, R. (1999), 'How Risky is your Company?', *Harvard Business Review*, 77 (May–June): 85–94.

Sinclair, T. (2005), *The New Masters of Capital: American Bond Rating Agencies and the Politics of Creditworthiness*. London: Cornell University Press, 2005.

Sison, A. J. (2000), 'Integrated Risk Management and Global Business Ethics', *Business Ethics*, 9: 288–95.

Sitkin, S. and Bies, R. (eds.) (1994a), *The Legalistic Organization*. Thousand Oaks, CA: Sage.

—— —— (1994b), 'The Legalization of Organizations: A Multi-Theoretical Perspective', in Sitkin and Bies (eds.), 19–49.

Skidmore, P., Miller, P., and Chapman, J. (2003), *The Long Game: How Regulators and Companies Can Both Win*. London: Demos.

Slovic, P. (1991), 'Beyond Numbers: A Broader Perspective on Risk Perception and Risk Communication,' in Mayo and Hollander (eds.), 48–65.

—— (2000), *The Perception of Risk*. London: Earthscan Ltd.

Smith, D. and Tombs, S. (2000), 'Of Course its Safe, Trust Me! Conceptualising Issues of Risk Management within the Risk Society', in E. Coles, D. Smith, and S. Tombs (eds.), *Risk Management and Society*. London: Kluwer, 1–30.

Spira, L. and Page, M. (2002), 'Risk Management: The Reinvention of Internal Control and the Changing Role of Internal Audit', *Accounting, Auditing, and Accountability Journal*, 16(4): 640–61.

Starr, C. (1969), 'Social Benefit versus Technological Risk', *Science*, 165: 1232–8.

—— Rudman, R., and Whipple, C. (1976), 'Philosophical Basis for Risk Analysis', *Annual Review of Energy*, 1: 629–62.

Stirling, A. (1998), 'Risk at a Turning Point?', *Journal of Risk Research*, 1: 97–109.

Strathern M. (ed.) (2000a), 'The Tyranny of Transparency', *British Educational Journal*, 26 (3): 309–21.

—— (2000b), *Audit Cultures: Anthropological Studies in Accountability, Ethics and the Academy*. London: Routledge.

—— (2000c), 'Introduction: New Accountabilities', in Strathern (ed.), 1–18.

Streeck, W. and Schmitter, P. (1985), 'Community, Market, State—and Associations? The Prospective Contribution of Interest Governance to Social Order', in W. Streeck and P. Schmitter (eds.), *Private Interest Government*. Thousand Oaks, CA.: Sage, 1–29.

Suddaby, R. and Greenwood, R. (2005), 'Rhetorical Strategies of Legitimacy: Vocabularies of Motive and New Organizational Forms', *Administrative Science Quarterly*, 1: 35–67.

Sullivan, L. (2001), 'Building a Risk Management Program from the Ground Up', *Risk Management*, (December): 25–9.

Sunder, S. (1997), *Theory of Accounting and Control*. Cincinnati, OH: South Western Publishing.

Sunstein, C. (2005), *The Laws of Fear: Beyond the Precautionary Principle*. Cambridge: Cambridge University Press.

Swinson, C. (2004), 'Limitations of Fail-Safe Systems', *Accountancy*, (May), 26.

Tackett, J. A., Wolf, F., and Claypool, G. (2006), 'Internal Control under Sarbanes-Oxley: A Critical Examination', *Managerial Auditing Journal*, 21(3): 317–23.

Tamm Hallstroem, K. (2004), *Organizing International Standardization: ISO and the IASC in Quest of Authority*. Cheltenham: Edward Elgar.

Tate, J. (2001), 'National Varieties of Standardization', in P. Hall and D. Soskice (eds.), *National Varieties of Capitalism*. Oxford: Oxford University Press.

Taylor-Gooby, P. (ed.) (2000), *Risk, Trust and Welfare*. London: Palgrave Macmillan.

Teubner, G. (1997), 'Global Bukowina: Legal Pluralism in World Society', in G. Teubner (ed.), *Global Law without a State*. Aldershot: Dartmouth Publishing, 3–28.

Thrift, N. (1994). 'On the Social and Cultural Determinants of International Financial Centres: The Case of the City of London', in S. Corbridge, R. Martin, and N. Thrift (eds.), *Money, Power and Space*. Oxford: Blackwell, 327–55.

Tickell, A. (1996), 'Making a Melodrama out of a Crisis: Reinterpreting the Collapse of Barings Bank', *Environment and Planning D: Society and Space*, 14: 5–33.

Tillinghast-Towers Perrin (2001), *Creating Value Through Enterprise Risk Management—A Practical Approach for the Insurance Industry*. New York: Tillinghast-Towers Perrin.

—— (2002), *Enterprise Risk Management in the Insurance Industry: 2002 Benchmarking Survey Report*. New York: Tillinghast-Towers Perrin.

Tolbert, P. S. and Zucker, L. G. (1983), 'Institutional Sources of Change in the Formal Structure of Organizations: The Diffusion of Civil Service Reform, 1880–1935', *Administrative Science Quarterly*, 28: 22–39.

Tribe, K. (1978). *Land, Labour and Economic Discourse*. London: Routledge.

Tschoegl, A. (2000), 'The Key to Risk Management: Management', in M. Frenkel, U. Hommel, and M. Rudolf (eds.) *Risk Management: Challenge and Opportunity*. Berlin: Springer, 103–20.

Tsingou, E. (2003), 'Transnational Policy Communities and Financial Governance: The Role of Private Actors in Derivatives Regulation' (Working Paper 111/03). Warwick: University of Warwick. ESRC Centre for the Study of Globalization and Regionalization.

—— (2007), 'The Role of Policy Communities in Global Financial Governance: A Critical Examination of the Group of Thirty', in T. Strulik and H. Willke (eds.), *Towards a Cognitive Mode in Global Finance.* Chicago: The University of Chicago Press, 213–8.

Tucker, L. and Melewar, T. C. (2005), 'Corporate Reputation and Crisis Management: The Threat and Manageability of Anti-corporatism', *Corporate Reputation Review*, 7(4): 377–87.

Turner, B. and N. Pidgeon (1997), *Man-Made Disasters* (second edition). London: Butterworth-Heinemann.

Turner, M. (2004). *Reputation, Risk and Governance.* London: Housing Corporation.

Underhill, G. (1991). 'Markets beyond Politics? The State and the Internationalisation of Financial Markets', *European Journal of Political Research*, 19: 197–225.

Vaihinger, H. (1935) [1911], *The Philosophy of the 'as if': A System of Theoretical, Practical and Religious Fictions of Mankind*, translated by C. K. Ogden. London: Kegan and Paul.

Van Maanen, J. and Pentland, B. T. (1994), 'Cops and Auditors: The Rhetoric of Records', in Sitkin and Bies (eds.), 53–90.

Vasarhelyi, M. and Halper, F. (1991), 'The Continuous Audit of Online Systems', *Auditing: A Journal of Practice and Theory*, (Spring), 110–25.

Vaughan, D. (1996), *The Challenger Launch Decision.* Chicago: University of Chicago Press.

—— (2005), 'Organizational Rituals of Risk and Error', in Hutter and Power (eds.), 33–66.

Vieten, H. (1996), 'Banking Regulation in Britain and Germany Compared: Capital Ratios, External Audit and Internal Control'. Ph.D. thesis. University of London, London School of Economics and Political Science.

Vinten, G. (1998), 'Corporate Governance: An International State of the Art', *Managerial Auditing Journal*, 13(7): 419–31.

Vogel, D. (1986), *National Styles of Regulation: Environmental Policy in Great Britain and the United States.* Ithaca, NY: Cornell University Press.

Wade, K. (1999), 'The Rise and Rise of Control Self Assessment', in Wade and Wynne (eds.), 3–36.

—— and Wynne, A. (eds.) (1999), *Control Self-assessment: For Risk Management and Other Practical Applications.* London: John Wiley and Sons.

Walker, P., Shenkir, W., and Barton, T. (2002), *Enterprise Risk Management: Pulling it All Together.* Altamonte Springs, FL.: Institute of Internal Auditors Research Foundation.

Walshe, K. and Sheldon, T. (1998), 'Dealing with Clinical Risk: Implications of the Rise of Evidence-Based Health Care', *Public Money and Management*, (October–December): 15–20.

Ward, S. (2001), 'Exploring the Role of the Corporate Risk Manager', *Risk Management*, 3(1): 7–25.

Wartick, S. L. and Heugens, P. (2003), 'Future Directions for Issues Management', *Corporate Reputation Review*, 6(1): 7–18.

Watson, M. and Emery, R. (2004), 'Environmental Management and Auditing Systems: The Reality of Environmental Self-Regulation', *Managerial Auditing Journal*, 19(7): 916–28.

Weait, M. (1993), 'Icing on the Cake? The Contribution of the Compliance Function to Effective Financial Regulation', *Journal of Asset Protection and Financial Crime*, 1(1): 83–90.

Weber, J. and Liekweg, A. (2000), 'Statutory Regulation of the Risk Management Function in Germany: Implementation Issues for the Non-Financial Sector', in M. Frenkel, U. Hommel, and M. Rudolf (eds.), *Risk Management: Challenge and Opportunity*. Heidelberg: Springer Verlag, 277–94.

Wedlin, L. (2006), *Ranking Business Schools: Forming Fields, Identities and Boundaries in International Management Education*. Cheltenham: Edward Elgar.

Weick, K. E. (1993), 'The Collapse of Sensemaking in Organizations: The Mann Gulch Disaster', *Administrative Science Quarterly*, 38: 628–52.

Weick, K. and Roberts, K. (1993), 'Collective Mind in Organizations: Heedful Interrelating on Flight Decks', *Administrative Science Quarterly*, 38: 357–81.

Whitley, R. (1986), 'The Transformation of Business Finance into Financial Economics: The Roles of Academic Expansion and Changes in US Capital Markets', *Accounting, Organizations and Society*, 11: 171–92.

Wilkinson, A. and Willmott, H. (1995) (eds.), *Making Quality Critical: New Perspectives on Organizational Change*. London: Routledge.

Wilkinson, I. (2001), *Anxiety in a Risk Society*. London: Routledge.

Williams, R. (2000), *Lost Icons: Reflections on Cultural Bereavement*. London: Continuum.

Willman, P., Fenton-O'Creevy, M., Nicholson, N., and Soane, E. (2002), 'Traders, Managers and Loss Aversion in Investment Banking: A Field Study', *Accounting, Organizations and Society*, 27(1–2): 85–98.

Wilson, D. (1995), 'VaR in Operation', *Risk*, 8: 24–5.

—— (2001), 'Operational Risk', in L. Borodovsky and M. Lore (eds.), *The Professional's Handbook of Financial Risk Management*. Oxford: Butterworth-Heinemann, 377–413.

Wise, N. M. (1995). 'Introduction', in N. M. Wise (ed.), *The Values of Precision*. Princeton: Princeton University Press, 3–13.

Wood, D. (2002a), 'From Cop to CRO', Online publishing, *Erisk.com*, March.

—— (2002b), 'Profiting from a Zero Based Policy', Online publishing, *Erisk.com*, June.

—— (2003), 'Counting the Cost of Legal Risk', Online Publishing, *Erisk.com*, January.

Woods, M., Dowd, K., and Humphrey, C. (2004), 'Credibility at Risk? The Accounting Profession, Risk Reporting and the Rise of VaR', Discussion Paper 2004.III. ESRC Centre for Risk and Insurance Studies, University of Nottingham, UK.

Wynne, A. (1999), 'CSA Risk Management and Internal Audit: The Future', in Wade, and Wynne (eds.), 387–97.

Wynne, B. (1982), *Rationality and Ritual: The Windscale Inquiry and Nuclear Decisions in Britain.* London: British Society for the History of Science Ltd.

—— (1995), 'Public Understanding of Science', in S. Jasanoff, G. Markle, J. Peterson, and T. Pinch, (eds.), *Handbook of Science and Technology Studies.* Sage, 361–88.

—— (2003), 'Is Environmental Risk a Cinderella Issue?', Paper presented at the NIESR/ESRC joint workshop, 16 January, London.

Zech, J. (2001), 'Rethinking Risk Management: The Combination of Financial and Industrial Risk', *Geneva Papers on Risk and Insurance—Issues and Practice,* 26(1): 71–82.

INDEX

Aalders, M. 39
Abbott, A. 13, 57, 83, 84, 85, 110, 131, 189
ABI 134, 137, 139
Abrahamson, E. 160
AccountAbility 146
accountability 4, 23, 31, 42, 180
  demands for 17, 88
  and ERM 89, 92, 98
  and internal control 87
  standards for 110
accountants 36, 45
accounting
  and auditability 163
  intangibles 132, 133
  socially sensitive 133
Accounting Standards Board 53
Adams, R. 44
administrative burden 152–3
advanced measurement approach
      (AMA) 108
advisory services 45, 46, 49, 54, 160, 178
  governance 47
  reputation management 129, 131, 145
  section 44, 55
Aerts, L. 122
agency relationships 39
agents
  roles under ERM 78
  see also risk officers
Ahrne, G. 105
AICPA 45, 46
AIRMIC 67, 83, 92
ALARP 14
Alborn, T. 69
Alderman, W. 57
Alexander, C. 120
Ambler, T. 133
amplification 142–3, 159
and ERM 78

anti-capitalism movements 136, 144
architecture of risk management 178
  and auditability 180
  reconstruction 160
  regulation 87
  and senior management 113
  standardization of 93
  see also designs; Enterprise
Argyris, C. 170
ARROW framework 89
Arthur Andersen 38, 145
Ashby, S. 118
assurance services 46, 60
attitudes to risk 174
audit 96
  of control systems 46
  explosion 4, 42
  implosion 42–7, 162
  as value adding 43
  see also internal auditor
Audit Commission 39
Audit Practices Board (UK) 54
audit risk model 44
audit society 30, 162
audit trails 164, 167, 196–7
auditability 11, 20, 23, 31, 78, 178
  climates of 161–9
  COSO framework 80
  documentary evidence 167
  and ERM 91
  externalization 163
  and legalization 169–75
  logic 197
  and management 166
  and organizational
        legitimacy 163
  pressures for 153
  and risk culture 175–8
  theory of 162–3, 166

auditing 152–81
  business measurement process 44–5
  contemporaneous 46
  growth of 42–3
  internalization of 162
  and operational risk debate 122
  risk-based 47
  self-audit 162
Australia 52, 67, 191
Ayres, I. 37

Bakan, J. 200
Baker, T. 22
Baldwin, R. 7, 36, 37
Banham, R. 99
Bank of England 38, 89
  regulatory supervision 38
Bank for International Settlements 105
Banking Act 1987 (UK) 107
banking regulation 106–7
  in-house models 106, 107
  and operational risk 104–10
banks/banking 103, 104
  capital cushion 74
  CROs 84
  RAROC 74
Barclays Bank reputation 147
Barings Bank 10, 103, 107, 108, 113, 115, 119,
    157, 165
  enquiry 176
Basel Committee on Banking
    Supervision 103–4, 109, 114, 190
  and capital adequacy 105–6
  and internal controls 107
  on operational risk measurement 115
  Pillar 1 107, 116, 120, 122, 123
  Pillar 2 107, 108, 110, 116, 122, 123
Basel II 74, 96–7, 108, 109–10, 124
  and corporate governance 125
  criticism of documentation 152–3
  defining operational risk 111, 113
  effects of 109–10
  and insurance 118
  seeing like a state 198
Beamish, T. 10
Beaumont, P.B. 85
Bebbington, J. 16, 134, 150
Beck, U. 2, 6, 110, 198
  risk society thesis 1, 21–2

Bell, T. 44
Berger, P. 92
Bernstein, P. 5, 12, 76
best practice 29
  diffusion 190–1
Bevan, G. 142
Bezuyen, M. 146
Bhansali, V. 72
Bhopal disaster 10, 134
Bies, R. 85, 99, 169, 170
Bijker, W. 25, 26, 187
Black, J. 18, 37, 38, 87, 88, 89, 90
blame 31, 174, 196, 197
  avoidance 54
  culture 86
  and operational risk definitions 113
  as reputational risk 89
  as risk object 196
  shifting 174
Blattner, N. 105
Blyth, M. 26
Boli, J. 66, 95, 96, 133, 135, 144, 156, 167, 172
  on conformity 196
Bou-Raad, G. 59
Bougen, P. 188
boundary object 27
  operational risk as 104
Bowerman, M. 39
Bowker, G. 27
box-ticking 153, 164, 166, 167, 168, 171, 176,
    178
Boyne, R. 13
BP Amoco 70
Braithwaite, J. 37, 39
brand equity 129, 132
branding and reputation 129, 131, 132
Brent Spar 128–9, 137, 141, 145
Brewer, P.C. 51
bricolage 154
Brilliant, D. 59
Brilloff, A.J. 52
Browne, J.M. 139
Brunsson, N. 24, 66, 92, 93, 99, 105, 110, 184,
    187
BS5750 (BSI) 50–1
BSE crisis 17, 62, 157, 160
Buethe, T. 92
Burchell, S. 14, 123, 124, 133, 141
bureaucracy aversion 199

bureaucratization 76, 174
Burgess, A. 11, 18, 187
Busby, J. 9, 154
business measurement process 44–5
business risk management 44–5, 67, 87, 97
    auditing 90
Butterworth, M. 82
buy-ins 175

Cadbury Code 34–5, 36, 50, 52, 54, 56
Cagan, P. 115, 121
calculation of capital 119–23
    differing ideologies 120–2, 123, 126
    performative nature of 122–3
calculative approach to risk 13–14, 68
    and ERM 69–75
calculative idealists 120, 121–2, 123, 139, 178
calculative pragmatists 120–2, 123
Callon, M. 74
Calomiris, C. 118
Canada 54, 67
Cane, P. 7
capital
    adequacy
        monitoring 48–9
        regulation 71, 105
        self-management 107
    allocations 72–3
    calculating 71, 82, 105–6, 119–23
    calculative idealists 120, 121–2, 123
    calculative pragmatists 120–2, 123
    measuring OR capital 108–9
    quantitative impact studies 109
    RAROC 73, 74, 75
Carter, S. 142
Casper, S. 51
catastrophic events 114, 154
categorizing risk 110, 111–12
Cave, M. 36, 37
CCAB 136
Cenker, W. 57, 59
Challenger space shuttle 10, 27–8, 157, 176
Chambers, A. 149
Chan, S. 55
Chase Manhattan Corporation 72, 96
checklists 168, 176, 177, 178
Chernobyl 10
Chief Ethics Officer 148
Chief Finance Officer (CFO) 84, 99

chief information officers 111
chief risk officer 29, 59, 68–9, 97, 99, 156, 174,
        194, 201
    functional explanations 86
    institutionalization of 84, 86
    operational conflicts 69
    oversight role 82–3
    professionalization of 85
    representations of risk activity 158
    rise of 82–6
    role of 83–4, 92–3
    and value proposition 83–4
Ciborra, C. 72
civic epistemologies 188
Clark, G. 76
Clarke, L. 76, 97, 125
Clarkson, M. 136
CLASS audit system 43
climate change 157, 159
clinical risk management 63
CoCo framework 50, 66
Coglianese, C. 51
Colbert, J. 57
Columbia space shuttle 10–11, 157
    enquiry 187
command and control model 36, 93–4
communication and ERM 78
compensation culture 86, 170
compliance 114
    costs 152, 158, 199
    culture 42
    incentives for 37
    management 175
    neoliberal 41
    performance standards for 38
    and reputation 147–8
    self-enforced 38
    variable nature of 36
    violation alerts 62
compliance officer 83
concept of risk 3, 5
    in COSO framework 80
    managerial 27–8
consultancy services 22–3, 45, 47, 160
consumer activism 136
continuous data assurance 46
contracts and risk-sharing 7
control activities 78
control environment 40, 49, 176

Control Self Assessment (CSA) 57–8, 59
Cooper, A. 194, 199
Coopers and Lybrand audit system 43
corporate governance 5, 34, 41, 42, 95
    principles 49
    voluntary principles 34–5
    see also governance; internal control
corporate social responsibility 30, 40, 133–4,
        193
    and reputation 146, 149, 150
    and stakeholders 136, 139
corruption and reputation 148, 154
COSO framework 51, 52, 54, 61, 76–80, 81,
        96, 176, 184, 191
    and architecture of regulation 87
    and banking regulation 107
    calculative idealists 120
    calculative pragmatists 122
    concept of risk 80
    criticisms of 155
    and derivatives 76
    diffusion of 94
    ERM standard 67, 68, 88, 92
    guidance document 49–50
    head of risk role 69
    limitations 79
    and operational risk 111, 112, 113
    and proper organizations 95
    sequence of process 77–8
Covaleski, M. 56, 57
credit rating organizations 140
crises
    and reputation 146
    resilience in 154–5
    visibility of 159
    see also failures
crowding-out 173
Cumming, C. 73
Curtis, E. 45
Czarniawska, B. 27

Daiwa 10, 108, 113
Danielsson, J. 9
data
    availability 115, 117, 118
    dirty 165
    loss 114, 115
    operational risk 115, 116, 117–19, 126
databases 46

Davies, G. 130
Davis, G. 8
de Waal, A. 173
de-regulation 200
Dean, M. 4, 197, 198
decentred regulation 37, 66
Deephouse, D. 146
definitions of risk 3, 13
    creating boundary objects 113–14
    operational risk 103–4, 110–14, 126
    and risk objects 26
Deloitte and Touche
        audit system 43
democracy in risk analysis 20
democratization of risk policy 16
Deragon, J. 94, 99
derivatives control framework 76
derivatives scandals 160
designs for risk management
    climate of normativity 186
    defensive quality 196
    diffusion of 200
    meta-rationality 198
    as moral technologies 192
    rational 185, 197
    values shaping 186
    see also architecture
deterrence model of regulation 37–8
Dickinson, G.M. 82
Dimaggio, P. 8
Directors' responsibility 54
disasters 17, 134
discourses 1, 2
    categories 1
    CSR 134–5
    ease of diffusion 93
    managerial logic 4, 23
    neoliberal enterprise logic 6
    operational risk 122, 123, 124
    reputation management 130
disruptive intelligence 11
Djelic, M.-L. 66, 135
Dobbin, F. 85, 86, 170
Dobler, M. 53
documentation trails 164, 167, 174, 196–7
Doherty, N.A. 67, 72
Douglas, M. 5, 15, 83, 94, 113, 156, 181, 187,
        198
Doyle, A. 13, 69, 118

Drori, G. 7, 19, 40, 60, 67, 69, 131, 135, 178, 179, 192
Dukerich, J. 142
Dunsire, A. 99
dynamic nominalism 25, 26, 48, 61
  and CROs 85
  operational risk 104
  and regulators 125

early warning signals 10
Edelman, L. 148, 170, 171, 175
effectiveness concept 56
Eilifsen, A. 45
EIU 150
Elliott, R. 45
EMAS 40
endogenous risk 9
enforced self-regulation 37, 106, 122
Engwall, L. 131, 146, 166, 187, 190–1
Enron 43, 55, 60, 145, 157
enterprise 22, 23, 36, 52
  risk as opportunity 22
Enterprise Risk Management (ERM) 22, 67–8
  buy-in 175
  and chief risk officer 82–6
  criticisms of 95
  definition 76–7
  as fiction 185
  as good governance 191–2
  as illusion of control 95, 98
  implementation 99
  integration of control and strategy 68
  as model of regulatory process 87–8
  normalization of 98
  organizational barriers to 99
  as organizational process 76–81
  re-internalization of 92, 97
  rise of 180
  as risk calculation 69–75
  seeing like a state 197–8
  stages of process 77–8
  stakeholder identification 138
  and standardization of regulators 86–92
  subsuming internal controls 78
  unreality of principles 95
  as world model 94, 98, 100, 194
enterprising liberalism 23
environmental management systems 51

Equitable Life 90
Ericson, R. 13, 69, 118, 180
Ermann, M. D. 10
ethics 95
ethics officers 148
evaluation systems 161
events
  crises 146, 154–5, 159
  differing perceptions 159
  identification 77
  visibility of 159, 160
Ewald, F. 4
expectations
  of management 6
  public 91
  societal 5, 134
  stakeholders 145
expected loss 114, 116
external auditing 45, 46, 48, 60
external auditors 40
  guidance for 49
external inspection agencies 162
external supervision 38
Exxon Valdez 134

failures 5
  accountability for 83
  consequences of 55
  and early warning signals 10
  institutional causes 9–10
  no-blame 90
  public acceptance of 90
  and risk-based regulation 89
Falkenstein, E. 82
fear 77, 161, 199
  institutional 180
  objects of 195
fictional ideas 183–4, 201
  embodied in norms 184, 185
Field, P. 70
finance and operational risk debate 122
financial auditing 42, 43
  re-conceptualization 44–5
  risk-based approaches 43–4
  see also audit
financial risk
  management 13
  measurement 70–1
  models 9

financial scandals
  and CRO role 86
  misdiagnosed 108
  see also scandals
Financial Services Act 1986 (UK) 83
Financial Services Authority (UK) 37, 38,
    59, 148
  mission 89, 90
  and risk categorization 113
financial statements 39, 43, 45
first order risk 189, 192
  risk objects 198
Fischoff, B. 3
Fishkin, C.A. 82
Fligstein, N. 84
Flyvbjerg, B. 14, 15
focus groups 77
Fombrun, C. 128, 131, 137, 140, 145, 148
Foss, C. 148
Foucault, M. 162
fraud 165
  losses 117
Freedman, J. 34, 52
Freeman, R.E. 136, 138
Frey, B. 173
Friedman, A. 136, 137, 138, 145
Froud, J. 7
functionality of risk management 158–9
Furedi, F. 161
Furusten, S. 51, 79, 80

Gaines-Ross, L. 130
game theory and regulatory model 37
Garland, D. 4
GE Capital 82
German Accounting Standards Board 53
German banks 105
Giddens, A. 39, 157
Gigerenzer, G. 3
Global Reporting Initiative 137
GM foods 16, 63, 157, 196
Goble, J. 58
Goodhart, C. 39, 111, 117, 118
goodwill 132
Gotsi, M. 146
Gouldson, A. 16, 134, 150
governance 7, 18–19
  advisory services 47
  and auditability 165

democratic and managerial control 135
  discourses 87
  and ERM 78, 89
  financialization of 75
  global 66
  institutionalization of 174–5
  as organizational process 19–20
  and organizational virtue 95
  and responsibilities 192, 193
  and risk management 2, 125
  shift to 153, 156, 170, 200
  world level values 179, 180
governmentality 4, 195–202
Grabosky, P. 37, 39
Gray, D. 201
Gray, J. 38, 39, 113
Greenpeace 128, 133, 137
GRI (Global Reporting Initiative) 134, 137
Group of Thirty 76, 103, 113, 190
guidance 2, 28
  COSO framework 49
  for government departments 17–18
Gunningham, N. 37, 39, 40

Habermas, J. 184
Hacking, I. 12, 24–5, 70, 82, 85, 180
Haines, Y. 97
Hall, P. 60
Halper, F. 46
Hamilton, J. 38, 39, 113
Hampton, P./Report 88, 152, 171
Hancher, L. 41
Hancke, R. 51
Hanley, M. 82
hard law 172
Harrington, C. 59
Hart, O. 7
Hawkins, K. 36
Hay, B. 48
Heal, G. 9
Heald, D. 196
health care control systems 63
Health and Safety Executive (UK) 88, 90
Hedburg, B. 177
Heimer, C. 170
Henning, R. 95
Hermanson, H. 54
Herring, R. 118
Heugens, P. 146

Hilgartner, S. 25, 26–7, 28, 187, 189
Hirtle, B. 73
Hoffman, D.G. 111, 122
Hogan, W. 10
holistic risk management 67
Hollander, D. 15
Hood, C. 2, 13, 30, 51, 88, 93, 187, 188, 190
    on blame shifting 174
    on conflict 79, 99
    on defensive design 196
    on ranking 142
    reporting incentives 117
    on risk objects 25, 159
    stakeholder management 138
Hopkin, P. 67
human rights principles 192
Humphrey, C. 44
Hunt, B. 173
Hutter, B. 16, 36, 38, 85, 88, 89, 137

IBM 58
ICAEW 2, 34, 36, 44, 50, 53, 54, 57, 132, 146
    Audit Faculty 44
ICAS 2, 44, 50, 53, 56
ideas
    implementation of 24–5
    performative 28
    role of 6
    see also neoliberalism
IFAC 61, 191
implementation 73–4
    deficits 95
    difficulties 99
    of ideas 24
incentives 56
    to hide errors 117
incubation of risks 10, 114, 115, 177
indicators 176
    losing proxy status 177
information
    and ERM 78
    security 161
    systems 2, 46
innovation, inhibited 173
inspection 161
    external agencies 162
    intensity of 39
Institute of Chartered Accountants see
    ICAEW

Institute of Internal Auditors 56, 57, 58,
    92, 97
Institute of Operational Risk (UK) 107
institutional risk 18
institutionalization
    of operational risk 107, 109, 123, 124
    of reputation management 147
    of risk management 9, 29, 92, 96, 186
insurance 70
    and operational risk 118
    premium reductions 158
    as risk management 22
    Turnbull report on 50
intangible assets, auditability 163
intelligence failures 10, 17
internal assurance 82
internal audit 59
    risk-based approach 57
internal auditors 29, 59
    and ERM 78
    as experts 57
    new platform for 47
    organizational position 58
    and risk knowledge 36
    as risk managers 56–60
    surveying function 58–9
internal control 27, 29, 39–40, 180
    accountability 20
    auditability 168
    and banking regulation 107
    as boundary object 61
    as carrier of values 52
    central to regulatory state 40–1
    definition 61
    and ERM process 78
    explosion 47
    as management responsibility 52
    as moral technologies 38, 40
    as object of public disclosure 54–5
    observability 48
    as organizational virtue 63
    as pretence of control 201
    as public policy object 42, 47
    public role 62
    quality assurance approach 38, 51
    real-time assurance 46
    and reporting 55
    rise of 34–63
    as risk management 48–53, 56, 61

internal control (*cont.*)
  risk-based approach 50, 61
  society and organizations 41–2
  standardization 184
  systems 162
  transformation of 48
  within governance 38
  see also section 404
internal environment 77
International Accounting Standards
      Board 105
IOSCO 88, 91
IPR 146
Irwin, A. 15
ISO 67, 92
ISO 9000 51, 79
ISO 14000 51
isomorphism as strategy 8
issue management 146
IT systems 111

Jackson, K. T. 130, 134
Jacobson, B. 66, 91
Jameson, R. 73, 111
Japan 67, 105
Jasanoff, S. 14, 15, 19, 96, 176, 187, 188
Jegen, R. 173
Jeppesen, K. K. 44
Joerges, B. 27
Johnson and Johnson 146
Jones, G. 13, 30, 190
Jönsson, S. 177
Jorion, P. 72, 73
J. P. Morgan 71, 72, 96
just-in-time audits 46

Kahnemann, D. 15
Kaltoff, H. 123
Kant, I. 183, 184
Karapetrovic, S. 51
Kavanagh, B. 71
Kinney, W. R. 50, 52
Klein, D. 131
Kloman, F. 76, 97, 98
Knechel, W.R. 45
Knight, F. 5, 13
Knights, D. 4, 12
knowledge transfer 190–1
KPMG audit approach 43, 44–5

Kunreuther, H. 9
Kuritzkes, A. 111, 115, 118, 121
Kurunmaki, L. 84

Lam, J. 82, 86
language 3
  of reputation 131
Larkin, J. 129, 133, 134, 136, 139, 145, 147
Lazer, D. 51
Leech, T. 57, 58
Leeson, N. 107, 165
legal risk 111–12, 117, 154, 171–2
legalization 178, 179, 181
  and auditability 169–75
  and defensibility 170
  institutional pressures for 171
  as institutionalizing 170
  as managerial 175
legitimacy 8
Lemon, W. M. 44
Levidow, L. 16
Leyshon, A. 124
Lezaun, J. 16, 109, 164
Liekweg, A. 53
listing rules (UK companies) 41
litigation mentality 170
Lofstedt, R. 128
Lousada, J. 194, 200
low probability events 154, 157, 180, 198
Loya, T. 96
Luckman, T. 92
Luhmann, N. 5
Lundman, R. J. 10

McCormick, R. 112
McCuaig, B. 57
Mackenzie, D. 13, 14, 123, 164, 187
McKinlay, A. 162
McNamee, D. 57, 59
McNamee, T. 57
Macrae, C. 114
Maijoor, S. 47, 52
Makkai, T. 39
Makosz, P. 57, 58
man-made disasters 9, 172, 176
man-made risk 202
manageability of risk 6, 123–6
management
  activity 28

control system 3
and ERM process 77–8
information system 177
overconfidence 177
responsibilization of 39, 93, 161
standards for 50–1
systems for risk 4
see also responsibility
managerial
categories 28
concept of risk management 3
frameworks for risk management 29
logic 23
turn in regulation 36, 42, 99, 190
managerialization of risk 153, 154–61, 169, 180
and neoliberal ideas 161
Mann Gulch disaster 154
mapping risk *see* risk maps
March, J. 14, 98, 138
Marcussen, M. 87, 105
market risk models 112
Marquand, D. 200
Mattli, W. 92
Mautz, R. K. 179
Maxwell, R. 34, 107
Mayo, D. 15
measurement of risk 70
acceptability of 73–4
and experts 74
RAROC 73, 74, 75
VAR 68–9, 71–3, 74–5
whole of enterprise 70
media amplification 159
Meidinger, E. 51
Melewar, T. C. 137
Mengle, D. 76
Mercer, L. 58
Mercer Oliver Wyman 124
Merkle, J. 179
Merrill Lynch 71
Mestchian, P. 118, 121
meta-regulation 40, 42, 48, 85, 87
meta-risk analysis 90
metrics 75, 76, 92, 165
and CROs 84
reputation 140–1, 144, 149, 150
RiskMetrics 71, 119, 191
see also measurement

Meulbroek, L. 70, 75
Meyer, J. 135, 174, 187, 190, 192, 196
on auditability 162, 179
on ERM 94, 95, 96
on organizations 23, 66, 106, 133, 166, 180
on scientization 131, 178, 179
Mikes, A. 73, 74, 82
Miles, S. 136, 137, 138, 145
Miller, P. 13, 24, 68, 74, 93, 197, 199
on Basel 2 108, 124
on CRO 84
on neoliberal regimes 23, 41, 60
Miller, R. 46
Millo, Y. 13, 109, 123
Mills, R. W. 48
Mills, T.Y. 51
mimicry as strategy 8
Mirowski, P. 179
misdiagnosis 115
mission 91
mission-based regulation 88–9
mistrust, institutional 21
Moizer, P. 44
monitoring 4, 78
Moody's Investor Service 116
moral economy
of organizational life 69, 98, 203
of risk management 92–7, 192–5
moral hazard and banking regulation 106
Moran, M. 41, 42, 104
Moss, D. 23
Mouritsen, J. 132
Muermann, A. 114
Murray, K. 146
mutual regulation 37

Nagy, A. 57, 59
NASA 10–11, 27–8, 84
investigation 176
Nash, M. 73
Nassauer, F. 53
National Health Service (UK) 52
near misses 62, 114, 115
data 165
disincentives to report 117
neoliberalism 22, 23, 29, 87, 201
contracting principles 7
decline of the public 200

neoliberalism (*cont.*)
  enterprise logic 6, 195
  governance logic 63
  managerial logic 60, 96
  moral economy 95
  and officerships 85
  opportunity society 69
  regulatory strategies 41, 60
  self-regulation 197
new institutionalism 8
new public management 87, 96, 197
New Zealand 52, 67, 191
NGOs 136, 139
Nicholls, M. 76, 108
Nigerian Shell operations 129, 145
normal accident 9
normalized deviance 77, 172
normalized paranoia 199
normativity 5, 92, 98, 186
norms
  ERM 92
  of governance 186
  legal 171
  for management systems 51
  production of 66–7, 97, 190
    and enforcement 37
  of proper organizations 94
  world level 193
Nottingham, L. 67
Nuclear Energy Agency 88–9

objective setting 77
objectivication of risk 18
OECD 61, 88, 97
officerships 84–5, 174
  ethics 148
  see also chief risk officer
Oktem, U. 114
O'Leary, M. 201
O'Leary, T. 23, 199
O'Mahoney, J. 137
O'Malley, P. 4, 12, 13, 22, 23, 44, 54
O'Neill, O. 176
operational risk 10, 30, 103–26, 154, 165, 171
  and banking regulation 104–10
  and construction of
    manageability 123–6
  data availability 115, 116
  data collection 117–19

  defining 103–4, 110–14
  emergence of 104, 111, 125, 180
  as governance concept 113
  institutionalization of 107, 109, 123,
    124, 185
  managerialization of 119
  managing as operational risk 118
  as new discipline 109
  organizing practice 114–19
  and political demands 125–6
  risk as routines 115, 116–19, 124
  as world level category 109
operational risk manager 107
opportunity 44
  and banking regulation 106
  logic of 23, 58, 157, 158
  and reputation management 133
  risk as 22–3, 27
opportunity society 69
option pricing models 13
O'Regan, D. 56
organizational culture 40, 176
  as auditable 153–4
organizational virtue 95, 161, 165, 166
organizations
  environment relationship 7–8
  new moral economy 98
  responsibility allocation 5
  self-observation 41
  see also corporate; management;
    responsibility
outsourced internal auditing 45, 56–7
oversight, quality of 194

Page, M. 35, 50, 54, 57, 58
Parker, C. 38, 40, 85
Pausenberger, E. 53
Pearce, F. 198
Pearson, N. 13
Peecher, M. E. 45
Peirce, Charles 184
Pentland, B. T. 174
perception
  of control and manageability 5
  public 15, 16, 17, 21, 137, 189
  of reputation 144
  of risk 16, 17, 187
  variations 15
perfect place arrogance 11

performance measurement systems 43
  and reputation 141
Perrow, C. 9
Peters, G. 133
Pfeffer, J. 173
Phimster, J. 114
Pidgeon, N. 9, 114, 142, 201
Pildes, R. 60
Piper Alpha disaster 10
politics of uncertainty 15, 89
Pollack, R. 14, 19
Porter, J. 75
Porter, T. 13, 96, 120, 187
portfolio theory 13
Powell, W. 8, 92
practitioners 110
  best practice representatives 29
  legal risk 112
  new identities for 104
  redefining remits 112
Prat, A. 199
precision of process 164, 165
preference aggregation 16
pressure groups 16, 128–9, 133, 136–7
PricewaterhouseCoopers 67, 76, 96
primary risk: crowding-out 173
principal-agent theory 60, 62
  models 7, 41
principles and rules 171
private sector 20
product liability 171
product recall 146
public management reforms 140
Public Oversight Board 54
public perceptions 15, 16, 17
  as source of risk 21
public reporting function 53
public sector
  and ERM ideas 87
  governance principles 42
  risk as opportunity 22
public understanding of science (PUS) 18

quality assurance approaches 51–2
  and internal control 51

ranking 150, 158
  internalized systems 144
  multiplying effect of 142–3

reputation 139–44
Rao, H. 131, 140
RAROC 73, 74, 75, 120, 121
RATE system 89
rational actors 14
rationalization 166, 172, 179, 184
  and scientization 178–9
re-internalization of ERM 92, 97
red-tape 171, 178, 195
reflexive governance 85, 197
regulation 2
  administrative burden 152–3
  deterrence model 37–8
  from inside 36–42
  growth of 2, 175
  management control as
      resource 40
  managerial turn 36, 42, 99, 190
  and proportionate intervention 88
  resource-based 91
  self 37, 39, 40
regulative ideas 183, 184
regulatory agencies 18, 19, 91
  amplifying risk aversion 21
  enforcement process 37
  number of 88
  secondary risks 143
  standardization of 86–92
  transparency demand 17
regulatory regimes
  design 36, 38–9
  variance in 159–60
  see also Enterprise Risk Management
      (ERM)
regulatory science 188
regulatory state 2, 40–1, 42
Rehbinder, E. 85
Reiss, A. J. 38
reliability seeking 154
Renn, O. 15, 16, 128
reporting 53, 90–1
  disincentives 117
reputation 128–51
  as asset 132, 133
  assurance 145
  as boundary object 149
  individuals 130, 148
  intangibles 132, 133
  and legal compliance 144

reputation (*cont.*)
  man-made risk 150
  as measure of success 129
  metrics 140–1, 149, 150
  quotient 140
  as risk object 130
  socially constructed 129
reputation management 30, 96, 128, 142
  construction of 145–9
  and CSR 133–4
  defensive dimension 144, 150–1
  institutionalization 147
  personal 199
  power of stakeholders 136–7
  and public evaluation 135
  services 129, 131
  and social concerns 134
reputational risk 18, 89, 154
  emergence of 185
  see also reputation management
residual risk 7
resilience and crisis 154–5
responsibility 83
  management structures 93
  officerships 85
  operational risk definitions 113
  senior management 113
responsibility allocation 156, 162
  COSO framework 80, 81
  and operational risk 112–13
responsibilization 93, 150
  of management 39, 93, 161
Rezaee, Z. 57
Rindova, V. 128, 145
risk
  acceptance 14, 16
  appetite 77–8, 195
  assessment and ERM 77
  avoidance 77
  committees 2
  defined 13
  distinct from uncertainty 5–6, 13
  increasing threats 157
  knowledge and auditors 36
  and organizational governance 5
  as organizing category 22
  policy 16–17
  reflexivity 4
  response 77–8

responsibilization 5
sharing 7, 77
social construction of 20, 203
risk adjusted return on capital
  (RAROC) 73, 74, 75, 120, 121
risk analysis 155
  development of 13, 20
  as discipline 12
  and risk management 14–15
  subsumed within governance 12–21,
    27–8, 35
risk assurance services 58
risk aversity 21, 173, 199
risk capital *see* capital
risk communication 15, 16, 17, 18, 20–1
risk culture 180
  and auditability 175–8
  and demands for control 176
  standardization of 176–7
risk governance 4, 18–19
  cultural variations 19
  shift to 12–21, 27–8, 29, 35, 62
  and worst-case scenarios 11
risk improvement managers (RIMs) 18
risk management
  concept of 6
  construction of process 186–7, 188–92
  defensiveness 153, 199
  defined 53
  expansion of 3, 7
  as governing framework 6
  history of 12
  internal control as 48–53, 56, 61
  moral economy of 92–7, 192–5
  normative dimension of 193–4
  as pillar of governance 2
  public 89
  representation of 84
  and risk analysis 14–15
  risk scares as 11
  as uncertainty management 26
risk management systems 56
  critiques of 167–8
  lack of functionality 168
  as risk governance 4
risk maps 77, 80–1, 121, 165
  actionability of 81
risk metrics *see* measurement; metrics
risk objects 8–9, 25–6

auditability 165, 189
  conceptualization of 28
  construction of 26, 186–8, 195
  creation of new 26, 30
  definition of 4
  first-order 189
  as harms 26–7
  management of 28
  reputation as 130
  second-order 189
  social construction 31
  technical experts' definitions 188–9
  types of 188
  within management 27–8
risk officers 78
  types of 82–3
  see also chief risk officer
risk reporting 53–6, 78, 193–4
  risk objects 54
risk silo managers 82
risk society 1, 6, 21–3, 27
  managerial instruments 4
risk visualization 80
  see also risk maps
risk-based auditing 47
risk-based internal control 61
risk-based regulation 38, 89–90, 91–2, 93,
    143, 152
  as mission-based regulation 88–9
RiskMetrics 71, 119, 191
Rittenberg, L. 56
Roberts, K. 200
Robson, K. 43, 44, 45, 46, 47, 57, 74
rogue traders 116, 119, 154, 180, 188
roles and responsibilities under ERM 78
Rose, N. 24, 41, 60, 68, 108, 124, 197
Rosen, D. 70, 72
Rosen, R. 55
Rothstein, H. 16, 18, 88, 89, 142, 143
Rouyer, S. 70
Rowan, B. 106, 133, 135
Royal Society report (UK) 13, 16
rules and principles 171
Russell, P. 58
Rutteman report 54

Sahlin-Andersson, K. 66, 131, 135, 146, 166,
    190–1
Samad-Khan, A. 81, 120

Sarbanes–Oxley legislation 43, 125, 161, 162,
    166, 170, 174, 196, 198
  audit trails 164
  benefits of 158
  criticisms of 152, 153, 155–6, 168
  effect on internal auditor 59
  future reform 201
  and markets for assurance 47, 60
  public certification requirements 55
  section 404 55, 152, 172, 201
  tyranny of transparency 197
Scaillet, O. 71
scandals 5, 10, 17, 43, 134
  and Cadbury Code 34
  and regulatory concern 48–9
  regulatory consequences 52
  use of derivatives 76
scenario analysis 106
Schmitter, P. 36
school trips 173, 199
Schultz, M. 131
science
  accountability of public 18
  displaced by management 96
  public trust in 19
science-based risk analysis 188
scientific expertise 14, 15
scientificity 14, 15
scientization and rationalization 178–9
Scott, H. 118, 121
Scott, J. 163, 197
Scott, S. V. 132
Scott, W. S. 169
Sears 58
secondary risk 172, 173, 196
  institutionalized 197
  management 139–44
  regulatory agencies 143
section 404 55, 152, 172, 201
  see also Sarbanes–Oxley legislation
Securities and Exchange Commission
    (US) 87, 152
security services 2, 17, 176
self-assessment 58
self-assessment return (RMAR) 90
self-inspection 162
self-observation 41, 46, 60, 192
  and ERM 78, 79
self-regulation 37, 38, 39, 40, 170, 197

self-regulation (*cont.*)
  enforced 106
  and measurement techniques 74
Selim, G. 57, 59
senior management responsibility 42, 113,
    161, 193
September 11th attacks 10, 111, 157, 159
  effects of 161
  enquiry results 10, 176
Shamir, R. 134
Shanley, M. 131
Shapira, Z. 14, 81
Shapiro, A. 76
Shapiro, S. P. 39, 174
Sharaf, H. A. 179
shareholder value 75, 132, 134
shareholder value-added (SVA) 71–3
Sharman, R. 81
Sheldon, T. 63
Shell Group 128–9, 131, 136, 137
  reputation recovery 145
Shiller, R. J. 72
Shin, H. 9, 105
Short, J. 14, 28
Silbergeld, E. 14
Simon, F. 100
Simon, H. A. 98, 138
Simon, J. 22
Simons, R. 176
Sinclair, T. 140
Sison, A. J. 134
Sitkin, S. 85, 99, 169, 170
Slovic, P. 15
smart regulation 37
Smith, D. 11, 16
social amplification of
    risk (SAR) 142
social expectations 5
social responsibility 193
social responsiveness 141
social risk 96
socially responsible investment 134
Society for Risk Analysis 12
sociotechnical networks 25, 26, 160, 187–8,
    189, 195
soft law 37, 66, 137, 170, 172
soft norms 133, 145
soft risk management 121
Soneryd, I. 17

sovereignty of organizations 193
Spira, L. 35, 50, 54, 57, 58
stakeholder analysis 96, 99,
    138, 145
stakeholder management 137, 138–9
stakeholder organizations 138–9, 190
stakeholders 135–9, 142
  engagement 137, 138, 200
  expectations 145
  participation 20
  and reputation management 130
  as source of risk 137
  as threat 172
standardization
  of regulators 86–92
  stages of ERM 92
  and transnational
      organizations 66
standards 66, 92
  embodiment of fictions 184
  for management systems 50–1
  production of 97
  VAR 71–3, 74–5
  voluntary 170
Star, S. 27
Starkey, K. 162
Starr, C. 12, 16
state, regulatory 2
Stirling, A. 26
strategy of organizations 8
Strathern, M. 24, 176,
    177, 185, 197
Streeck, W. 36
Sullivan, L. 73
Sumitomo 10
Sunstein, C. 16, 60
supervision 38
  limited capacity of 40
sustainability 193
system performance 51
systems failure 111, 165

tail events 115
Tate, J. 51
technical risk analysis 15, 35
  Turnbull report 50
technical risk specialists 190
technical-moral discourse 156
technology

and information systems 2
and new threats 157
terrorism threat 157, 195
Teubner, G. 194
Thomas, G. 66, 133
threats, increasing 157
Thrift, N. 76, 124
Tickell, A. 108
Tillinghast-Towers Perrin 95
Tombs, S. 11, 16, 198
tone at the top 40, 176, 180, 188
tools for risk analysis 2
top-down approach 79, 90
Touche Ross, 76
Toulouse factory explosion 159
trail of evidence 174, 196
    audit 164, 167, 196–7
transaction costs theory 7
transparency 16–17, 42
    demands for 88
    disfunctionality of 176
    and ERM 91
    tyranny 197
Transparency International 140
Treating Customers Fairly programme 148
Tribe, K. 25
triple bottom line accounts 132, 134
trust
    breaking of 40
    in organizations 49
    relationships 39
Tschoegl, A. 10, 108
Tsingou, E. 124
Tucker, L. 137
Turkish earthquake 10
Turley, S. 45
Turnbull Report 2, 50, 57, 59, 61, 69, 87, 184,
    194
Turner, B. 9, 11, 114
Turner, M. 134
Tversky, A. 15
Tylenol recall 146

unanticipated correlations 70
uncertainty
    distinct from risk 5–6, 13
    as feature of organizations 6
    organization of 6
    transformation to risk 6

uncertainty management 7, 26
    unintended consequences 9
United Kingdom
    auditability 19
    civil service risk programme 22
    creation of guidelines 17–18
    public change programme 87
    public management reforms 140
    regulatory bodies 88
    standards 67
United States 56
    legalism 19
    Public Oversight Board 54
    risk analysis 19
    risk disclosure 53–4
    see also Sarbanes-Oxley legislation

Vaihinger, H. 183–4
value adding 157, 158
    audits as 43
value at risk (VaR) 68, 71–3, 95, 106,
    178, 179
    auditability 163
    emergence of 97
    event identification 77
    as ideal form 94, 120
    institutionalization of 75
    motivation for 72
    and operational risk 121
value creation 6, 23
value reporting 132
value-added statements 133
Van Maanen, J. 174
Van Riel, C. 131, 140
Vasarhelyi, M. 46
Vaughan, D. 10, 84, 114, 115,
    118, 187
Vieten, H. 106
Vogel, D. 15
voluntary standards 170
Vurdubakis, T. 4, 12

Wade, K. 57
Walsham, G. 132
Walshe, K. 63
Ward, S. 83
Wartick, S. L. 146
Weait, M. 83, 84, 85
wealth creation and risk 157

weather bonds 75
Weber, J. 53
Wedlin, L. 140
Weick, K. 11, 154–6, 162, 166, 167, 168, 177, 200, 201
White, J. 146
Whitley, R. 13, 70
whole of entity risk management 29, 86, 94, 185
  metrics 70, 97
  see also Enterprise
Wilborn, W. 51
Wildavsky, A. 5, 15, 94
Wilkinson, A. 52
Wilkinson, I. 11

Williams, R. 200
Willmott, H. 52
Wilson, A. 146
Wilson, D. 71, 112, 121
Wise, N.M. 14, 164
Wittgenstein, L. 24
Wood, D. 71, 82, 86, 117
Woods, M. 71, 95, 163, 194
World Bank 61, 97
Wynne, A. 58
Wynne, B. 15, 18, 116, 187

Young, B. 118
Young, J. 188
Young, M. 46